Hockey Plays and Strategies

Second Edition

Mike Johnston
Ryan Walter

HUMAN KINETICS

Library of Congress Cataloging-in-Publication Data

Names: Johnston, Mike, 1957- author. | Walter, Ryan, 1958- author.
Title: Hockey plays and strategies / Mike Johnston, Ryan Walter.
Description: Second Edition. | Champaign, Illinois : Human Kinetics, [2019] |
Ryan Walter is the principal author printed on published title page of
previous 2010 edition. | Includes index.
Identifiers: LCCN 2018009002 (print) | LCCN 2018009527 (ebook) | ISBN
9781492562542 (ebook) | ISBN 9781492562535 (print)
Subjects: LCSH: Hockey--Offense. | Hockey--Coaching.
Classification: LCC GV848.7 (ebook) | LCC GV848.7 .W35 2018 (print) | DDC
796.962--dc23
LC record available at https://lccn.loc.gov/2018009002

ISBN: 978-1-4925-6253-5 (print)

The web addresses cited in this text were current as of June 2018, unless otherwise noted.

Acquisitions Editor: Diana Vincer; **Managing Editor:** Ann C. Gindes; **Copyeditor:** Bob Replinger; **Proofreader:** Anne Rumery; **Indexer:** Dan Connolly; **Permissions Manager:** Martha Gullo; **Graphic Designer:** Dawn Sills; **Cover Designer:** Keri Evans; **Cover Design Associate:** Susan Rothermel Allen; **Photograph (cover):** Marissa Baecker/CHL Images, 2018, Mastercard Memorial Cup; **Senior Art Manager:** Kelly Hendren; **Printer:** McNaughton & Gunn

Human Kinetics books are available at special discounts for bulk purchase. Special editions or book excerpts can also be created to specification. For details, contact the Special Sales Manager at Human Kinetics.

Printed in the United States of America   10 9 8 7 6 5 4 3 2 1

The paper in this book is certified under a sustainable forestry program.

Human Kinetics
P.O. Box 5076
Champaign, IL 61825-5076
Website: www.HumanKinetics.com

In the United States, email info@hkusa.com or call 800-747-4457.
In Canada, email info@hkcanada.com.
In the United Kingdom/Europe, email hk@hkeurope.com.

For information about Human Kinetics' coverage in other areas of the world,
please visit our website: **www.HumanKinetics.com**   E7251

I would like to dedicate this book to the many youth coaches who spend countless hours helping our youngsters enjoy the best game in the world. As parents, we really appreciate when our kids can be part of a team that plays together on one page and learns life lessons while competing.

Mike Johnston

I dedicate this book to Viona and Bill Walter, my Mom and Dad, the perfect hockey parents. They were always involved (with Dad coaching me throughout Minor Hockey), but never pushed. They always praised the team's effort, but never put down other players. Mom and Dad, you fanned the flame of my Hungry Hockey Spirit as a player, president, and coach. I thank you and I love you.

Ryan Walter

Contents

Foreword

The spray paint was black, which likely added to the point. It was also in stark contrast to the ice at Rutherford Arena, where it was used by our coach to draw a massive happy face. In the slot. During the second intermission of a CIAU league game. In front of a crowd of supportive, but likely befuddled, University of Saskatchewan fans. It was shocking, hilarious, and, without question, completely effective. After all, Dave King does nothing without a plan.

Let me backtrack a bit. Dave had been coaching the University of Saskatchewan hockey program for a couple of years. We had a history with the University of Alberta, and not much of it was all that great. But for the past week, he'd had our team working on a new system that had one of us stay in the slot. To demonstrate, he'd drawn a happy face on our practice ice the day before the game and demanded one of us stay inside it while we were in the offensive zone. Fast forward to the actual game, where we found ourselves losing 3-2. Clearly, Dave decided we needed a little visual reminder. Thus the ice art. It worked, and we quickly scored three goals. We also won the game, which, at the end of the day, justifies a good old-fashioned happy face. Probably.

A strategy is kind of like a good recipe: It's only deemed worthy if somebody else is willing to repeat it. I'm not sure how many coaches are packing paint in their hockey bags these days, but that story proves that if you have a solid idea and players willing to carry it out, good things happen.

I firmly believe that the key to having a successful team and a successful season is getting everyone on the same page. *Hockey Plays and Strategies* really does a masterful job of breaking down a complex game into a simple and easy-to-execute system. So what makes strategies so important? First and foremost, they allow a group of individuals to play as a complete team. A team with good structure and great habits can often overachieve and defeat superior talent. But you can't develop proper habits without structure. That is often the difference between an average coach and a winning one. Good structure can cover up weaknesses on the individual level. For example, it can allow slow skaters to get to their positions a step quicker, simply because they know where to go. And if a skater can get to his position, his chances of succeeding rise dramatically. Structure can give an average player a great career. At the very least, it provides confidence, and confidence is critical for success.

However, there has to be a buy-in on both ends, meaning that coaches and players have to be on the same page. I once ran a video session in which I pointed out the errors one particular player was making.

Me: So, that's not where you're supposed to be.

Number 14: That's not me.

Me: That's not you? But you're number 14, right?

Number 14: Definitely.

Me: Rewind. But you can clearly see on the video number 14 making the mistake?

Number 14: Uh huh.

Me: But that's not you?

Number 14: Nope.

Me: Then who is it?

Number 14: Good question.

This is where this book comes in handy. It breaks each system down, including what roles individual players are responsible for. And more importantly for number 14, it demonstrates the proper feedback for these players. That will lead to a much better understanding of the overall goal and, ultimately, the game.

I talked a little bit about what I think makes a good coach, but one of the biggest skills is the ability to make adjustments. Years ago when I was just starting out, I coached against the great Clare Drake. His University of Alberta teams were almost unbeatable—almost—and that included his power play. He ran a power-play breakout I had never seen, and, for the life of me, I couldn't figure out a way to stop it. So the next time our teams met, I ran the exact same power play against him. If I couldn't stop it, maybe he could. He did, of course, and, in so doing, taught me how. This book is a much less confrontational way of achieving the same ends, but in a more sophisticated way. In fact, many of the strategies (and their counters) used by Team Canada and our opposition during the Olympics are carefully explained here.

It almost goes without saying (but apparently not, since I'm about to say it): Great hockey really comes down to decisions made by the players. Those on-ice reads absolutely come from the basic structure they've learned at practice or from the bench. Sometimes it's cause and effect. Growing up in a small town in Saskatchewan, we cobbled together teams made up of players of all ages. One guy who was about 20 years older than me absolutely hated backchecking, and he devised a simple strategy: Richie would simply lie on the ice behind the opposition net and wait for the puck to show up. No skating, no hitting, no problem. There was some logic involved (except for the offside), because there's no arguing that it was an energy conserver. This book has some better ideas. I'm not sure they'll convince Richie, but you can't win them all.

One thing all great players (including Richie) possess is their unending quest to get better. From veterans like the Sedins to established talents like Jamie Benn or up-and-comers like Bo Horvat, they simply cannot abide being average. This book will give players of all abilities an improved understanding of how to get better. It also gives incredibly valuable insight into what other players on the ice think and how that knowledge can lead to championships. It's really all about instilling confidence. For coaches, these pages contain a road map. For players, the tips and explanations will enable them to play their best games and show off their skills.

Speaking of skills, I've been fortunate to know both authors for a very long time, and both possess enough skill in their chosen professions to last multiple lifetimes. They're both pretty good at spotting it too. In fact, the very first time I met Mike at the University of Calgary, he invited me to join him in an adult rec league volleyball game. For fun. I was pretty sure he emphasized "fun." I quickly agreed. He then asked how long I'd played. I said, "Well, not since about grade 5." He said he'd call with the details about when and where. I'm still waiting.

Enjoy the book!

—Will Desjardins

Preface

We are thrilled with how well the first edition of *Hockey Plays and Strategies* was received throughout the hockey coaching community worldwide. One USA Hockey level 4 instructor recently said about the book, "This is the best book that you can purchase to help you coach hockey at any level." Our goal in writing this technical look at our great game was to give coaches more options as they decided what strategies best suited their team's skill set. Instead of telling coaches which breakouts we preferred, we laid out several options so that coaches could better understand the concepts and then decide which structure would give their team the advantage.

Since the NHL Stanley Cup Final went to the best-of-seven format in 1939, the team that has won game 1 has gone on to capture the Stanley Cup 78 percent of the time (60 of 77 series), including each of the past five years. Coaching is about preparing your team to compete at its highest level, every game. Teams prepared to win game 1 at the NHL level increase their chances of achieving success.

As we participate in coaching conferences across the world, we love asking coaches at every level, "What is your pillow pain? What keeps you up at night as a coach?" Obviously, coaches have different pieces of our game that they want to do a better job at, but the overwhelming answer from coaches is that they wonder whether they did a good enough job preparing their teams for the games ahead. Great teams focus on process, not outcome. Great coaches prepare their teams to implement the processes that give them their best chance to win—and that is what this book is about.

We have some good news for you coaches: This second edition of *Hockey Plays and Strategies* gives you more! The game of hockey is ever evolving, and we are excited to add to our previous body of knowledge. A large chunk of the foundational structure in this book will obviously remain the same, but many of the following chapters have been added to and upgraded. We have also added two new sections—one on how to pre-scout your opponent and a second on how to get these processes, this structure, into your practices. Many of you coaches asked us for drills that would practice certain breakouts or forechecks, and now you have them.

Hockey Plays and Strategies is still broken down into three primary sections dealing with offensive play, defensive play, and special situations. Does great defensive play win championships, as the saying goes? Not necessarily. If you look at the results of the major professional leagues in baseball, football, basketball, and hockey, an equal number of dynasties were built by teams remembered for their offensive prowess. We believe that a good balance is best, although as a coach your natural tendency will be to lean slightly toward the offensive or defensive side depending on your style and comfort level.

The sequence for the offensive and defensive chapters works from the net out and from the opposition's net back. Offensive chapters cover the breakout, neutral zone attack and regroups, offensive zone entry (including odd-man rushes), the attack zone, and power plays. Defensive chapters cover the forecheck, neutral zone forecheck, backcheck, defensive zone entry (including odd-man defensive play), defensive zone coverage, and penalty kill.

We have attempted to explain in detail the key teaching points involved in executing the systems discussed. As mentioned in the book, it is not the system you choose that will make you successful; rather, it is how effectively your players execute your team structure that gives you the advantage. When breakdowns occur, you need to know where to look to make corrections. Understanding the key teaching points will help in this area as well as allow the players to grasp the concepts easier. Our goal in writing this book is to give both coaches and players the information they need to play their best game. Enjoy!

Acknowledgments

I would like to thank my family, especially my wife Myrna, for sacrificing some of our free time and allowing me to complete this exciting 2nd edition.

—Mike Johnston

I also would like to thank my best friend and wife Jenni, who encourages me to write and is my favorite TEAM-Mate!

—Ryan Walter

Introduction: Preamble on Coaching

Coaching is a complex job. We have found through experience and in our previous book, *Simply the Best—Insights and Strategies From Great Coaches* (ryanwalter.com), that coaching is both an art and a science. The "art" refers to instincts and feel, and the "science" refers to technical and physiological elements. This book deals primarily with the technical side of the game, but we would be remiss if we didn't highlight a few more key details on the art of coaching that are directly linked to the systems and strategies in the book. Developing your team identity, understanding teaching and learning, and conducting good practices all fit into being a well-rounded coach.

The game of hockey is constantly changing. Rules change. Tactics change. Players are becoming faster and stronger. Coaches talk about taking away their opponent's time and space. This area of our game has experienced huge change. Because overall player speed has increased in today's game, the puck carrier is under increased pressure to make a next-move decision. Over these past five seasons, coaches have also done a great job of teaching the stick-on-puck concept. Players in today's game take away passing options better than we did when we were playing. Both of these changes have generated more puck turnovers, and turning the puck over creates much more offense.

Over the past five years, the core parts of the game have remained constant, but the edges of the game (the way we teach the game) have changed. That is one of the reasons we wanted to update and add to the book that you are reading.

All great organizations and great teams have a clear identity. Teams are recognized as being hard working, dynamic offensively, gritty and tough, fast and young, or sound defensively. You know what the identity of a team is simply by observing how they operate. The saying that a team is a reflection of their coach is true. The coach and management impart an identity on the team through which players they select, what system they play, how they practice, and generally, how they behave on and off the ice. Unfortunately, many coaches miss this step in preparing for the season, so the team does not really have any identity. They look different from game to game. They have no foundation that defines who they are to fall back on in tough times, and the coach will constantly be reacting to situations with quick-fix solutions but never really getting anywhere. Remember, if your team doesn't know your identity, you are in trouble. A team is much like a corporation or business—those with a clear identity and purpose that everyone buys into tend to flourish, and those without tend to struggle. Therefore, establishing an identity is one of the most important things you can do in preparing for a successful season. Is it difficult? No. Basically, you need to follow just three steps to identify what type of team you want to be.

1. Picture yourself watching your team in late January; see them on the ice for practice, in game action, training off the ice, at a restaurant for a team meal, and possibly even in the classroom.

2. Now write down everything you want to be observing five months from now. What personal and physical qualities do you want to see? How does the team behave? How do they train? How do they treat each other? How do they handle pressure? How does your team play? We all want a big, fast, skilled, and sound defensive team, but we all know that having everything is not realistic. What is most important to you? Discuss this with your staff. What values do you want to impart to your team?

3. After you have thoroughly developed your identity with your staff, you need to share it with the team as well as other parties who are close to your team (e.g., parents, manager, support staff, and media). Constantly reinforce the identity throughout the season by repeating it over and over. This is how we practice, this is how we play, and this is how we act. Your players will get it over time and eventually take on this identity. More important, they will take ownership of it. Challenge your staff and team to come up with a slogan, logo, or song that exemplifies your identity.

Teaching and Learning

As a coach, you may find yourself asking, Why aren't my players learning? Why does he always do that? Doesn't he get it? The first place to look for answers is your coaching strategy, because if no learning is occurring, no coaching is taking place. This book is all about teaching. At times you will get frustrated with your players' progress, but you need to recognize that coaching has many challenges. Don't get caught in the cycle of looking at reasons why you can't win. Instead, challenge yourself and your staff to find a way to win.

No matter what level you are coaching, you must never make assumptions. If you believe that players should know certain things because of their age, you may be eager to start at a higher level, but you should always start with the basics. When using this book, choose a system or strategy and then review the key teaching points. Teach the system or strategy to your team by using basic drills and then progressing to more complicated or involved drills. Be careful to resist the urge to change when your process is not working well. Progress at a pace appropriate for the team and age level. We suggest you use a checklist so that you can monitor the progression of the team and of specific positions. A checklist involves all aspects of your team play written down one side of the page. Then as you practice each item, you note the date beside it. This checklist will keep your coaching staff focused on what has to be done. Additionally, it will keep you from moving too fast. You can even note the date by which you would like to have taught that particular system or strategy to the team. For instance, with the power play, early in the year the priority will be on breaking out and zone setup for a five-on-four power play. As the year moves along and team competency progresses, you will start to focus more on the five-on-three and four-on-three power-play options. Accept that with only so much practice time, you can't do everything at once, so you'll need to develop priorities.

The basic skills or teaching points within a system are often what separate the top players and teams from the others. Most players are motivated and willing to learn or develop in any area that will help elevate their play or create longevity in their careers. Show them a plan to be successful, work on developing it, and stay strong when your plan is challenged. The particular system that you use is not what wins championships; winning is all about quality of execution.

Practices

Although many players would much rather play the games, remember that you develop through practice. Statistically, the average player in a game takes one or two shots on goal, makes 15 to 20 passes, and is on the ice for 20 out of the 60 minutes. According to one of the more revealing statistics from the 2002 Olympic Games in Salt Lake City, elite players had the puck on their sticks for less than 90 seconds for the whole game. Most players were under a minute. During a well-run practice, a player should be able to take 30 or more shots, make 50 passes, receive the puck 50 times, and have the puck on his stick at least 25 percent of the time. Therefore, approximately 15 games would be needed to simulate the amount of skill repetition that takes place in an effectively run 60-minute practice.

Listed here are eight keys to maximizing your practice time. Ice sessions are expensive and difficult to obtain, so you need to get the most out of each one.

1. Prepare yourself and your coaching staff.
   - Use a set practice form that has room to explain the execution of the drill, teaching points, and length of time. Keep your practice forms in a book or file them away.
   - All coaches on the ice should know the drill sequence and teaching points. The head coach should outline who is responsible for teaching the drill to the team and where the coaches will be positioned when the drill begins.
   - Come to the rink with energy and energize your staff. Players look forward to these sessions all week and will feed off your enthusiasm.

2. Provide practice rules.
   - To manage the practice properly, especially because of the poor acoustics in most rinks, you need to communicate practice rules

before the team is on the ice. Inform the team that for everyone to benefit, players need to adhere to the rules. One rule that can often speed up practice is this: "Every time the whistle blows, all players come in quickly to the coach. Then after the next drill is described, you go to your specific area and get ready to go." Depending on how much help the head coach has, try to get the players to collect the pucks and set them up in the appropriate area.

3. Create a positive learning environment.
   ○ Use positive talk and positive gestures.
   ○ Talk to every player every practice. Even if you talk about the movie that the player saw last night, your staff should never leave the arena without having touched base with every player.
   ○ Provide feedback throughout practice. Try to do it constructively and do not stop the drill. Get to the players while they are waiting in line. Bring the group together only for key points or messages.

4. Balance individual skill with small-group and team-play work.
   ○ Vary the drill formations and alignments to work on team play and individual skills.
   ○ Use stations for small-group skill work. This approach is effective for concentrated effort and high repetition.

5. Repeat, repeat, and repeat again.
   ○ Players develop through the "agony of repetition"—that is the fact.
   ○ Keep the players moving throughout practice; activity is key. This approach will develop endurance and ensure that they're making the best use of practice time by always working on skills.
   ○ Have a set bank of practice drills to teach your system's plays.
   ○ Repeat drills often but change the focus or teaching points.
   ○ Constantly push the team for better execution.

6. Incorporate challenges and fun games.
   ○ Open and close practice with a bang.
   ○ Challenge yourself to come up with drills that are fun but that also work on key skills.
   ○ Incorporate competitive challenges. Keep score during drills.

7. Have teaching aids available.
   ○ Use ropes, tires, balls, spray paint, chairs, and pylons to add to the practice environment.
   ○ Make sure that a rink board is also available so that players can visualize what you're explaining. Practice drawing the drills clearly.

8. Conduct your warm-up and conditioning off the ice.
   ○ Ice time is valuable, so as much as possible, stretch and warm up off the ice as a group.
   ○ Try to get a conditioning effect by the way you keep the practice moving and by the demands you make on effort throughout prac-

tice. Stopping practice and forcing the players to do a conditioning skate is necessary at times, but working on conditioning and skill at the same time is much better.

The key to developing players is to catch them doing something right, and the practice environment provides many opportunities for you to do this. Strive to achieve practice perfection and good habits. Coach the players to "think the game"; they will enjoy the game more and get more out of it.

Key to Diagrams

C	Center
F	Forward
D	Defensive player
LD	Left defensive player
RD	Right defensive player
O	Offensive player
RW	Right wing
LW	Left wing
G	Goalie
EX	Extra forward

Note: an (L) or (R) subscript indicates the direction a player will shoot.

⟶	Player skating without the puck
∿∿∿⟶	Player skating with the puck
- - - - ⟶	Pass
⟹	Shot
⟶⊣	Screen, pick, or block
⌒⌣⌒⌣	Skating backward
⏐⏐⏐⏐⏐⏐	Lateral movement crossover steps

Part I

Offensive Play for Forwards and Defensemen

Chapter 1
Breakouts

A breakout is initiated when the puck is in a team's defensive zone. All five skaters and even the goaltender need to be involved to exit the zone successfully. Players react to the position of the puck to initiate or support the breakout. Breakouts can take place in four situations: (1) after a dump-in by the opposition, (2) on a rebound from a shot, (3) after intercepting a pass, or (4) when a player takes the puck away from the opposition. The most difficult part in executing a successful breakout is handling pressure from the opposition and completing a good first pass. The first step is to realize where the pressure is coming from so that you can execute the appropriate option to escape your defensive zone.

Reading Pressure and Options

When a defenseman picks up the puck to initiate a breakout, he could face three different situations. In the first, there is no forechecking pressure; in the second, the forechecker is 6 feet (1.8 m) or more away; and in the third, the forechecker is right on the defenseman's back.

In most situations the defenseman has mere seconds to make a play, so buying time is often important. To do this effectively, you have to fake one way by looking at that option with your eyes while putting the puck in a passing position. The forechecker will often bite on this fake pass, or look-away, and turn his feet in that direction, which will give you more time to make a play. The art of deception is a skill that must be practiced; once they master it, defensemen gain extra time in a critical area and reduce the chance of being hit.

The following four examples for defensemen all deal with varying fore-checking pressure that occurs after a dump-in by the other team, after a rebound, after an intercepted pass, or when a player takes the puck away from the opposition.

1. **No forechecking pressure.** In this situation the defenseman is concerned about getting back quickly, collecting the puck, and turning up ice. Check your shoulder as you go back for the puck to read your options. Goaltenders should communicate options to the defenseman retrieving the puck. Simply using a verbal cue such as "time" is enough to let the player know he has an opportunity to look up and turn the puck up ice without having to protect it from pressure. Specific communication calls are critical to successful breakouts because the player retrieving the puck is focused on getting the puck and has limited opportunity to read the other team. His teammates, while moving to support the breakout, have a chance to read the opponent's forechecking pressure. When turning the puck up ice, get your feet moving right away while at the same time keeping the puck at your side (hip pocket) in a position to pass. If you have no options, then put the puck out in front of you and jump up ice.

2. **Close forechecking pressure.** When the forechecker is 6 feet (1.8 m) or more away, the defenseman should go back for the puck under control while checking both shoulders to read the forecheck and the passing options available. Performing this routine is important regardless of the checking pressure. As you get close to the puck, square your feet, glide, and then fake one way and go the other. This action will shake the forechecker and give you time to escape or make a quick play. The fake doesn't have to be complicated; just a slight movement one way with your stick or shoulder while tight turning to the other side will do. Take three quick strides to separate from the forechecker and then make a pass or continue skating.

3. **Quick, hard forechecking pressure.** In this situation, the forechecker is right on the defenseman and it looks as if the defenseman will get hit. When going back for the puck, check both shoulders and then slow down as you approach the puck. Your first priority is to protect the puck while at the same time leaning back against the forechecker to gain control over that player. Absorb the forechecker's momentum and either spin away with the puck or rebound off the boards in a position to make a play. Never expose the puck; stay on the defensive side and protect it until you can make a play.

4. **Reversing off the hit.** In some situations the defensemen can't avoid the hit. If this occurs, your team should have a rule that the defensemen being hit will always reverse the puck to the space where he came from, against the flow. If this happens, then the low center or other defenseman must be ready to get the reverse. The defenseman being hit should reverse the puck, absorb the hit, and then quickly get back into the play.

Triangle Breakout Alignment

The basis of all good breakouts starts with three players getting back to the puck quickly. Usually these players are the two defensemen and the center or low forward (figure 1.1). One player goes to the puck, one player goes to the net or backside corner, and one player stays in the slot (mid-ice). If every breakout starts this way, you will have the ability to spread the breakout and handle any type of forecheck. In addition, with a player always in mid-ice you are set defensively in case of a breakdown.

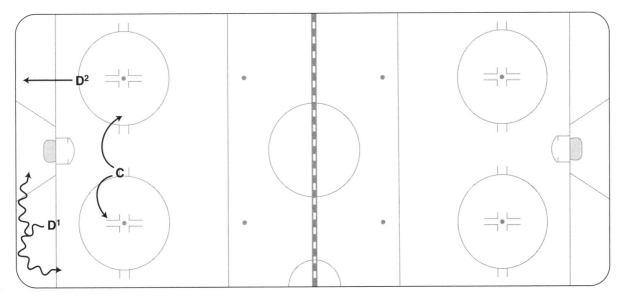

Figure 1.1 Triangle breakout alignment.

Reacting to Support the Breakout

All three forwards have key positional responsibilities on the breakout. Breakouts are initiated by the defense, and most of the time the primary role of the forwards is to provide support options. The option of having forwards leave the zone early may be a team philosophy or a coaching philosophy, but allowing your wingers to leave the zone early on certain breakout plays is worth considering—especially because the red line was removed from the game at all levels. The key read for wingers is puck possession and checking pressure; after you see your defenseman or center get the puck under control with minimal forechecking pressure, move out into the neutral zone and look for the stretch pass (figure 1.2). The pass does not have to be a direct pass; it could be an indirect pass off the boards where the winger can skate into it or a high flip pass where the winger can skate under it. This type of strategy is intimidating for the opposition because they will generally move at least one of their Ds back and often they

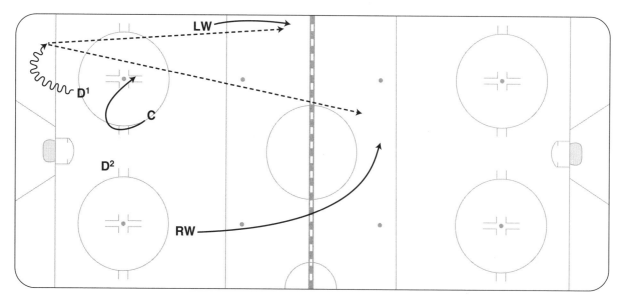

Figure 1.2   Leaving the zone early on the breakout.

get caught with a soft or loose gap in the neutral zone. They will definitely be worried about giving up a breakaway and as a result may not hold the blue line as tight. The space between the attacking players and defensive players is generally referred to as the gap. On offense, a loose gap gives you a chance to make plays in front of the defensive team and have more time. The defensive team wants to have a tight gap to eliminate time and space.

Center

The center usually plays low in the defensive zone, but as noted in the section on defensive zone coverage, any forward could be the low player. The player who plays low defensively is usually good in coverage and breakout situations. Often the low forward is involved in getting the puck back from the opposition, so other than a dumped-in puck, his position on the breakout seldom varies. The low forward provides the defense with a mid-ice option on all breakouts. If the puck is passed up the boards, the center should be in a support position for the winger, who may bring the puck inside, make a direct pass, or chip it off the boards. The center or low forward must be available for a pass but also in a position to react defensively if a turnover occurs.

When passes are made up the boards, centers need to come from underneath the pass and skate into a support position. The player needs to be cautious in this position because anything could happen, and if a turnover occurs during the breakout, the center or low forward must be ready to defend. In addition, the center shouldn't crowd the winger as the puck moves up the boards; staying in line with the dots is a good guide so that the winger can make an inside pass.

Strong-Side Winger

The strong-side winger on the breakout must be available on the boards for a direct or rimmed puck. We like the winger to be in a higher position above the circles so that the pass from the defenseman or center advances the puck as far up ice as possible. If the other team pinches or closes down on the winger as the pass is being made, then the winger must fight the battle up higher on the boards. He can try to box out the pinching defenseman by backing into him as the puck is being passed. If the winger starts the breakout lower on the boards and not up higher as suggested, then more time and potentially more passes will be needed to get over the blue line, often resulting in turnovers. The winger must be strong in all board battles because a turnover here may be costly, leading to extended time in the defensive zone and often an opportunity for the opposition to create scoring chances. The strong-side winger also must be able to make passes inside to the center or to the backside D. These passes require skill and smart reads.

Back-Side Winger

The back-side winger on the breakout may skate one of three routes:

1. As the puck advances up the far side, the back-side winger may slash across for support. The slashing winger may move all the way across or, as many teams do, slash across and out in line with the center-ice logo. The back-side winger needs to be ready to receive a pass or move to a puck that is chipped off the boards into the neutral zone. The winger coming across creates more options than the winger staying wide and the success of this strategy relies on short passes or chip plays. Short passes or chip plays are definitely easier to execute than long cross-ice passes, which are often intercepted.

2. As the puck advances up the far side, the back-side winger may stay wide to avoid checking pressure from the other team. This wide pass is more difficult to make, but once made it usually provides more skating room for the winger because he will be on the outside shoulder of the opponent's defense and can drive in the wide lane. Breakout passes to a wide winger may be made indirect, off the boards, so that the player can skate into the pass.

3. Some coaches like to give the green light for the wide winger to leave the zone early and be available by moving in the neutral zone. This approach is effective because the opposition will have to back one of their defensemen out of the zone, and, as a result, the back-side winger can more easily move into open ice as the pass is made. The only problem with doing this is that playing four on four in your defensive zone is more difficult than playing five on five.

Goaltender

In most leagues goaltenders are restricted in the area in which they are allowed to handle the puck. At the NHL level, goaltenders may handle the puck anywhere above the goal line and in the trapezoid area below the goal line. Regardless of the level and restrictions, goaltenders must learn to pass the puck up on line changes (figure 1.3), set up the puck for defensemen, and move the puck by forechecking pressure to a waiting teammate or to an area where teammates can get the puck first. When going out to play the puck, goaltenders must check their options first and then listen to the communication of teammates to make the best decision. Strong, confident puckhandling goaltenders are valuable to a team because they provide an extra breakout player and often save the defense from being hit by the forecheckers. In addition, goaltenders are always facing up ice, so they see options sooner. The only problem with goaltenders handling the puck is that their passing ability is usually not as good as a defenseman's because of their restrictive equipment.

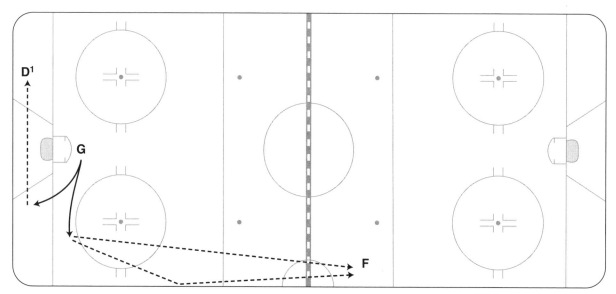

Figure 1.3   Goaltenders must learn to move the puck.

Defense

Coaches may have a different philosophy on this, but we believe that the defense should be prepared to move into the breakout after a successful pass is made. Some coaches believe that the defensemen should "stay at home," or always keep the play in front of them. This philosophy is sound, but it significantly eliminates attack options. The key read is a successful pass. The defenseman who jumps into the breakout should be the back-side D, while the puck-moving D holds a more defensive position after making the pass (figure 1.4*a*). The back-side D is in a better position to read the play because he is not involved in retrieving the puck and is generally waiting at the net for the play to develop. Sometimes in defensive zone cover-

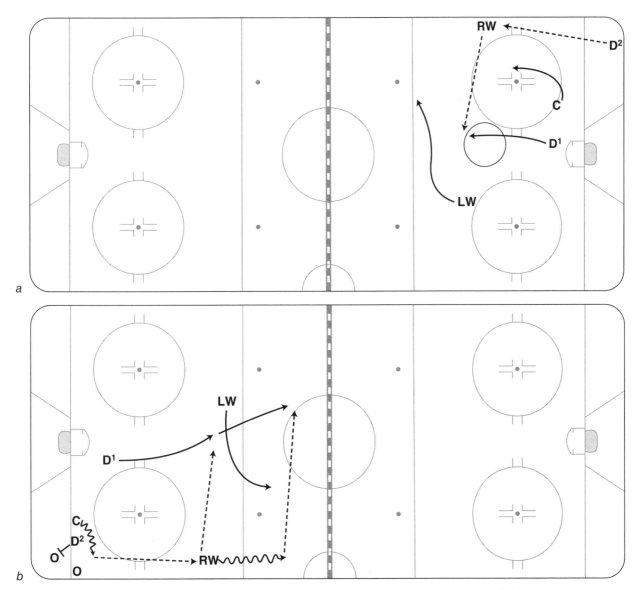

Figure 1.4 (a) The defense joining the breakout and (b) the center caught low.

age and in other breakout situations, the center is caught low, so the net defenseman must be ready and available for a breakout pass (figure 1.4b).

Another common game situation is to get the puck while in defensive zone coverage and then have to initiate a breakout. Players must read and react to the quickest escape option. Often when the defensive team recovers the puck down low, the best option is to break out by moving the puck away from pressure to the back-side D and up the other side. By breaking out on the back side, you take the puck to an area with less traffic and generally less checking pressure (figure 1.5).

Defensemen, especially young defensemen, must learn to make a strong first pass. Coaches and parents often yell to defensemen on the breakout, "Get the puck out!" What they mean is to keep the puck going up the boards or shoot it off the glass. Players do whatever they can to get the puck into

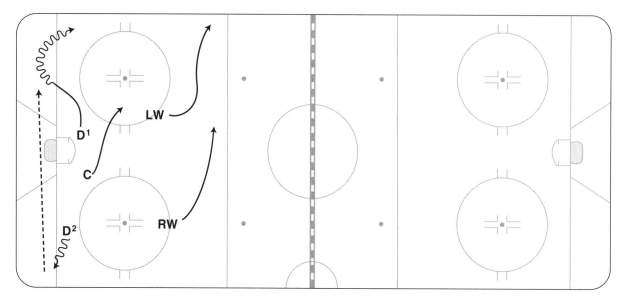

Figure 1.5   Breakout from a defensive alignment.

the neutral zone without turning it over. At certain times in a game, this action may be appropriate, but generally you want the defense to learn to read the play and make a tape-to-tape pass. Defensemen need to learn to make plays by picking the best option on the breakout. Sometimes the best play is an inside pass to the center or a back-side play to your partner because 80 percent of teams on the forecheck take away the boards; therefore, if you use the board option you are essentially passing into traffic and probably creating a turnover. The old saying "Never pass in front of your own net" should be thrown out the window because that is sometimes the only option available and you don't want to be predictable. Make sure you practice these plays often so that the execution level is high and the players gain confidence in making successful breakout plays. As a coach, be careful not to criticize players who make the right play but turn the puck over because of poor execution. Focus on achieving better execution and keep their confidence high. This approach will pay dividends later in the year.

Breakout Plays

When a player goes back to break out a puck, his teammates are his number one resource. His teammates must communicate pressure and make specific calls with regard to the appropriate breakout option to use. Players can make five calls: up, over, wheel, reverse (corner or net), and rim.

■ UP

When D2 calls, "Up," D1 knows right away that when he touches the puck that his primary option is to turn up the strong side and make a play to the board winger (LW) or center (figure 1.6). D2 has read that the other team is taking away the net or back side, so the best option is to get the puck moving right away up the strong side. C supports low, and RW moves across the ice or stays wide.

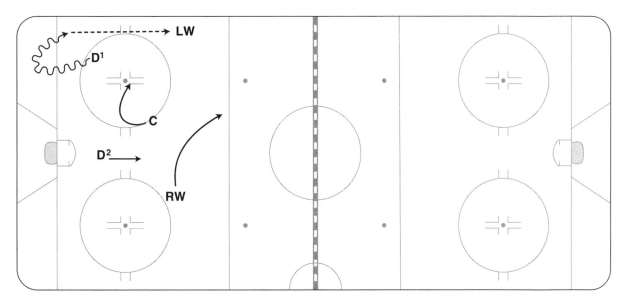

Figure 1.6   Center supports low and RW slashes across on the up play.

■ OVER

When D1 picks up the puck, D2 sees that the other team has flooded one side of the ice, so he moves to the opposite corner and calls for an "over" play (figure 1.7). D1 makes a direct pass or banks the puck off the boards to D2. D1 should move the puck quickly and not make the mistake of carrying the pressure toward D2 and then passing. If that were to happen, the forechecker could easily continue through and get on D2 as he receives the pass. C supports low, RW supports the boards, and LW moves across in support or stays wide.

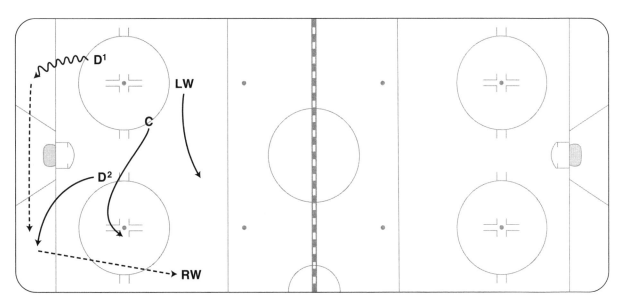

Figure 1.7   Supporting the D-to-D over pass.

■ WHEEL

Here, D1 has a step on the forechecker, so D2 calls, "Wheel." D1 quickly rounds the net, leaving the forechecker trailing. D1 uses the net as a screen for the forechecker by cutting tight to the net on the wheel. D2 should hold the front of the net until D1 makes a play or skates up ice (figure 1.8). C supports low, LW moves across the ice or stays wide, while RW provides a boards-pass option.

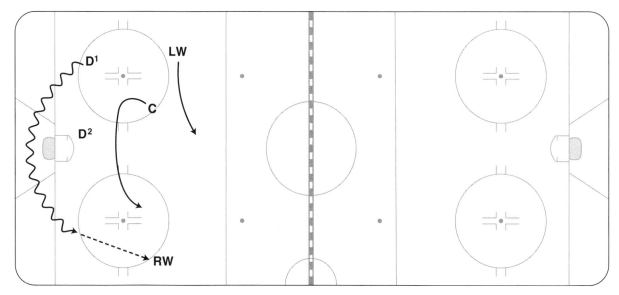

Figure 1.8   D1 wheels the net and passes or skates the puck.

■ CORNER REVERSE, NET REVERSE, AND REVERSE INTERCHANGE

Teams can execute three types of reverses on breakouts.

Corner Reverse

In this situation, D1 picks up the puck and attempts to lose the forechecker by going around the net. D2 sees that the forechecker is right on his partner, so he calls a reverse (figure 1.9). D1 banks the puck off the boards in behind the forechecker to D2. C supports by first moving with D1 and then back low through the slot after the reverse pass is made. LW moves inside and then out to the boards, ready for an outlet pass. RW initially is ready for the up pass from D1, but when the reverse pass is made, RW moves across the ice to support the breakout or stays wide for a direct or bank pass. D2 passes to C or LW.

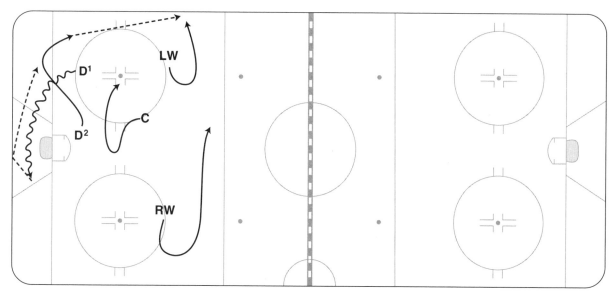

Figure 1.9   D2 reacts to the corner reverse by D1.

Net Reverse

The difference with the net reverse is that the defense or low forward who picks up the puck is moving toward the corner but sees no option up the boards or to the middle and is going to get hit. In this situation, he can reverse the puck toward the net for D2 or the center to pick up. They can then wheel the net (figure 1.10).

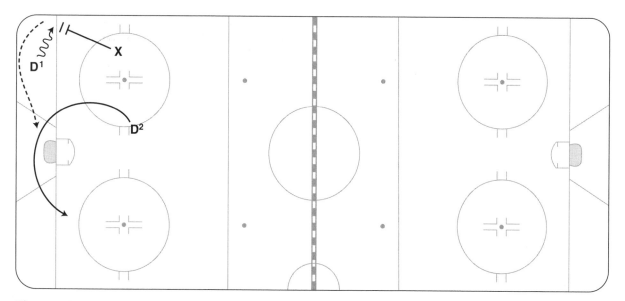

Figure 1.10   D1 uses a net reverse to move the puck away from pressure.

Reverse Interchange

Sometimes coaches like the center and the winger to switch on reverse plays, which allows them to maintain speed, but they must make the exchange quickly to avoid giving up defensive position at a time when a turnover may occur. As noted in figure 1.11, when D1 swings behind the net, C moves to support. If D1 reverses the puck, C can continue moving toward the boards, and RW can move to mid-ice to support the reverse pass to D2.

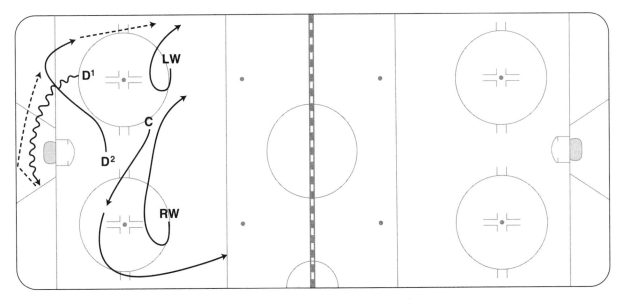

Figure 1.11   Center and winger exchange lanes on the breakout.

The final option for reverse plays is for D1 to reverse the puck to C in the strong-side corner. This action allows the breakout team to spread out and makes it difficult for the forecheckers to take away all options. D2 supports the wide side, looking for an over pass, and D1 reverses the puck to C, who should call this option.

◼ RIM

This option (figure 1.12) is often used when the opposition is forechecking hard with two players. The best choice under these conditions is to bypass the forecheck by passing the puck hard around the boards. D1 goes back for the puck and quickly rims the puck to RW. C supports from underneath, and LW moves across in support. Against teams who pinch down with their defense on rimmed pucks, the wingers who receive the rim must be able to protect the puck, control it, and then move it to support. In this situation, RW must be able to control the puck and make a play, skate with the puck, or chip it behind the pinching defenseman. As mentioned earlier, the ability to get pucks off the boards under pressure is a skill that also involves a component of toughness—especially if the other team's defensemen pinch down quickly to finish the hit.

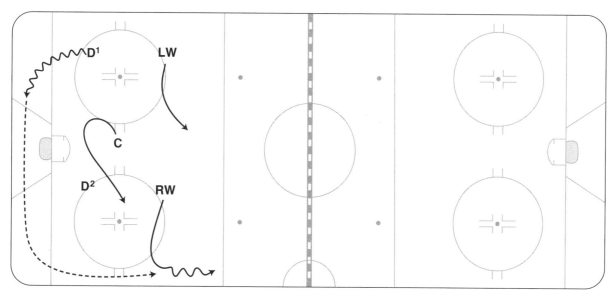

Figure 1.12 D1 uses a quick rim to escape pressure.

■ FLIP

In the last few years, more teams have used a flip pass to escape their zone. This play is often used when under checking pressure, but sometimes it can be used as a strategy to create more offense by getting forwards in behind the opposition's defense. To execute the play, the low center or defense usually gets the puck and flips it high into the neutral zone for the wingers to chase down. The only risk in using the flip pass is the execution of the player making the pass. If this player doesn't get the puck high enough, it remains in the zone while the wingers are in the neutral zone.

Control Breakouts

When your team gets the puck, the opposing players may have already pulled back into a trap forecheck. They are sitting back waiting for the breakout to take place and looking to turn the puck over. Instead of free-lancing your way through the trap and potentially being unsuccessful, a better plan is to move out together in a coordinated fashion. This approach is called a control breakout.

Unless you come out of your zone in a controlled manner with set patterns for the five players, the opponent will have a good chance of creating a turnover. A controlled breakout includes two key factors: (1) the four players without the puck move with speed, and (2) the puck carrier knows the options and picks the best one.

In a control setup, the puck carrier is like a quarterback who knows the routes of the receivers and picks which option is open. This section includes diagrams of three control breakouts in which the effect of moving in a coordinated fashion will provide you with enough options to break the trap. The alternatives can all be equally successful, but learning and executing all three is difficult, so coaches should pick one and practice it repeatedly until it becomes automatic. When these breakouts are run effectively, they often result not only in breaking the trap but also in generating a scoring chance.

In all control breakout situations, the idea is to give the defenseman with the puck more options than the opposition can take away. The defenseman then just needs to make the right choice. The coaching staff must also prepare the team for specific options that may work against certain opponents.

■ BLUE-TO-BLUE STRETCH

D1 waits behind the net for C to move back with speed. C swings with speed behind the net. D2 swings into the opposite corner. LW waits at the corner of the close blue line. RW waits at the corner of the far blue line. D1 has four options. C can pick up the puck with speed and try to weave his way through the trap or move the puck to LW, RW, or back to D1 and up the other side (figure 1.13a). D1 can allow C to go through and then step out the other side of the net and pass to LW or D2 (figure 1.13b). If D1 passes to D2, the next primary option should be a stretch pass to RW moving across the ice or to LW, who bends his pattern through the center of the ice.

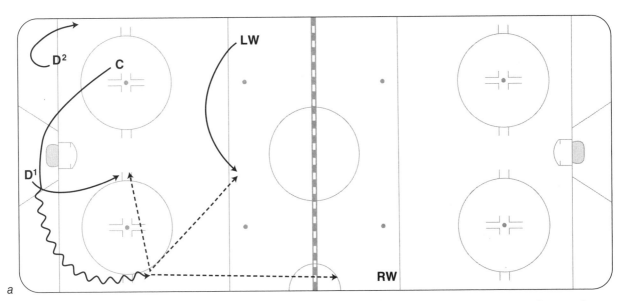

Figure 1.13a   Blue-to-blue stretch control breakout with the center picking up the puck.

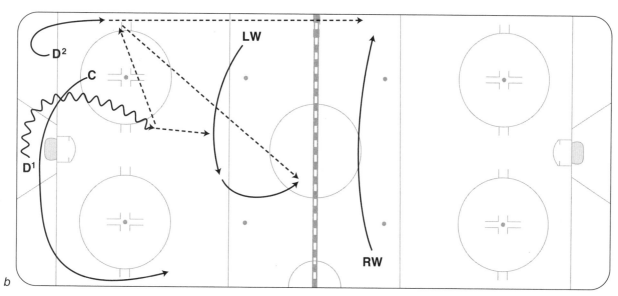

Figure 1.13b   Blue-to-blue stretch control breakout with D1 initiating the play.

■ STRONG-SIDE SLANT

D1 waits behind the net for C to swing. C can swing behind the net or into the far corner. RW swings on the same side with the C. As they move up ice, one slants inside and one stays wide. LW stations himself in the middle of the far blue line ready to move back into the play. D2 waits deep in the corner. D1 now passes to D2, who then has three options as he moves up ice: (1) pass to C slanting through mid-ice, (2) pass to RW wide, or (3) pass to LW off the boards or direct. LW can pass or chip the puck to RW or C. The key players are RW and C as they move with speed to break through the trap (figure 1.14).

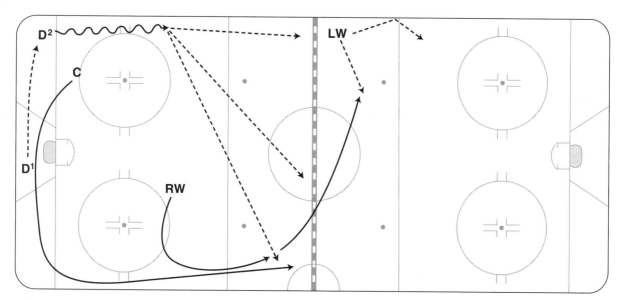

Figure 1.14   Strong-side slant control breakout.

■ THREE HIGH

D1 waits behind the net for a few seconds. All three forwards stay out high in the neutral zone. D2 supports D1 by moving wide into one of the corners. D1 steps out and passes to C curling in mid-ice or to LW or RW, who are moving or posting up (stationary along the boards by one of the lines). If C is under pressure when he receives the puck, he may chip it by and create a footrace for LW or RW (figure 1.15).

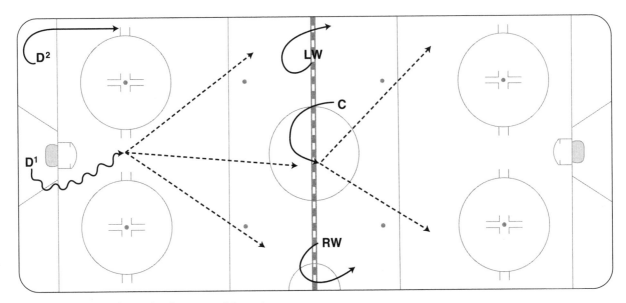

Figure 1.15   Three high control breakout.

Chapter 2
Neutral Zone Counters and Regroups

For the purpose of clarity, this section deals with plays that originate in the neutral zone as opposed to plays that originate in the defensive zone and move through the neutral zone. Two types of attacks involve the neutral zone: (1) the rush, which is a continuation of the breakout, and (2) regroups and counters. All rush plays are covered in the next chapter on offensive zone entries. This chapter focuses on transition plays such as quick counters and regroups. Puck possession in the neutral zone usually results from a turnover or face-off. When the defensive team gets the puck off a turnover, the objective is to move through the neutral zone quickly and catch the opposition behind the play. Advancing the puck through the neutral zone off a face-off is more challenging because the opposing players are initially aligned above the puck. Although the neutral zone is technically between the blue lines, we have expanded this area to include the tops of the circles at the attacking team's end to allow the play to develop (figure 2.1).

Recent NHL analytics have shown that when a team moves through the neutral zone and enters the offensive zone with possession, the odds of generating a scoring chance go way up. Therefore, teams should focus on gaining the offensive blue line with the puck as opposed to dumping

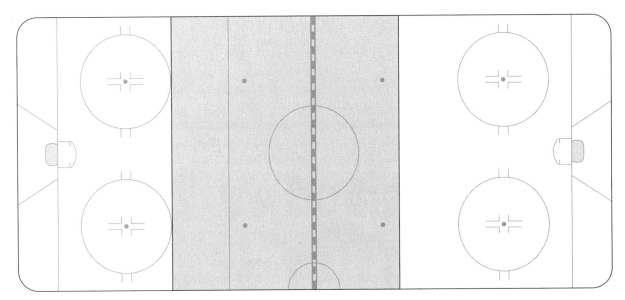

Figure 2.1   The neutral zone.

or chipping it in. We recommend a 60-40 split on entries in favor of possession entries. Track your team's results over several games and see how much of a possession game you are playing.

Counters

The difference between counters and regroups is that counters are quick plays with the intent of catching the opposition disorganized and not set in their neutral zone forecheck. In contrast, regroups are more organized and attempt to navigate through an opponents' neutral zone forecheck.

Quick counters often result in odd-man rushes. When the turnover happens, the opposition is moving aggressively on the attack and often cannot react quickly enough to get back. Therefore, you should practice counters with speed. When a team counters, the intent is to catch the opponent moving toward the offensive zone. You then quickly pass the puck up to the forwards in the hope of getting an odd-man rush. If this happens 50 percent of the time, your team would be considered a good transition team. The other 50 percent of the time the pass is confronted by pressure, and the puck carrier must look for a play or dump or chip the puck into the offensive zone.

Practice repetition will help teach defensemen to read the forecheck and then pick the appropriate option. At times, players counter quickly but the puck carrier is confronted or runs out of space to carry the puck, leaving the player with only two options: either dump the puck in or chip behind pressure.

Dump-Ins

Dumping the puck is a useful counter option when players are confronted at the blue line and have no opportunity to enter with possession. Some teams like to designate where to dump the puck so that skaters off the puck know which area to move toward. Players who are dumping the puck have four options.

1. **Cross-corner dump-in:** This option is effective because it forces the defensive team to switch coverage from one side of the ice to the other and in doing so, they may lose defensive position. Effective cross-corner dumps also give the offensive team a chance to get to the puck first. Make sure when dumping the puck that it does not move into the area where the goaltender can play it. Try to dead corner it by placing the puck in the corner so that it stops close to the boards (figure 2.2).

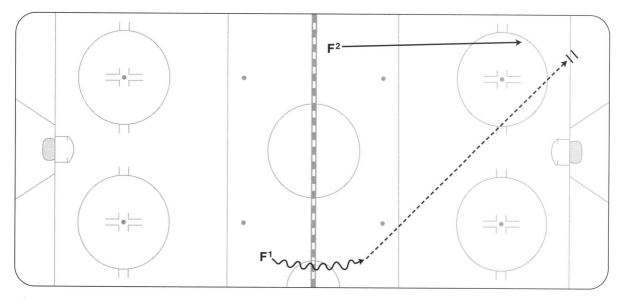

Figure 2.2   Cross-corner dump-in.

2. **Hard, wide rim:** The puck carrier shoots the puck into the zone so that it rims around the boards and comes up the wide side for the wide winger to retrieve (figure 2.3). Make sure that the puck is shot

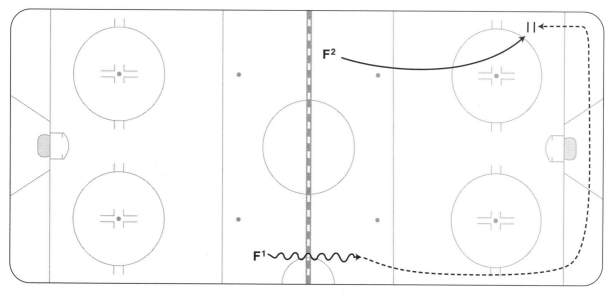

Figure 2.3   Hard, wide rim.

hard enough that the goaltender cannot stop it behind the net. This puck will be difficult for the winger to get off the boards, so he should stop it first, protect it, and look for a play. As in the previous strategy, quickly changing sides with the puck can cause the defensive team to lose their position in the zone when they adjust to the puck.

3. **Same-side dump-in:** As with the cross-corner dump, the intent of this strategy is to have the puck stop in the near corner (figure 2.4). When pressured in the neutral zone, the puck carrier lays the puck behind pressure by shooting it into the near corner for a supporting teammate. Most opposing defensemen will try to stay up on the puck carrier, which will allow the supporting offensive forward to get to the puck first. Often with a same-side dump, the puck carrier has enough speed that he can jump around the defenseman and get to the puck first.

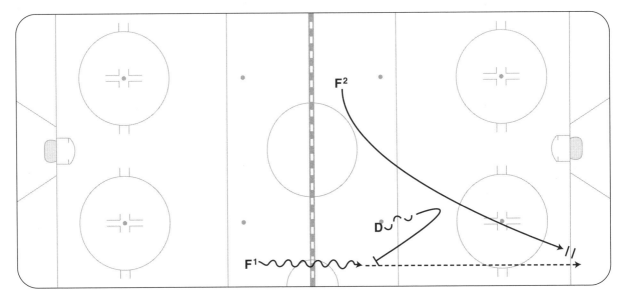

Figure 2.4   Same-side dump-in.

4. **Putting the puck on net:** When watching sports highlights, you will often see a player skating through the neutral zone, faking a dump-in to the corner, and then surprising the goaltender by shooting the puck on net (figure 2.5). At times it will go in, but this result is rare. Employing this strategy catches the goaltender by surprise and forces him to make a play. Many goalies have trouble stickhandling and passing the puck, so this tactic often forces the opposing defensemen to hurry back and receive a below-average pass from the goaltender to start the breakout. If the goaltender you are playing against is a weak passer, this option may be a good strategy. In addition, some shots are hard for goaltenders to handle, so they simply direct the puck into the corner, which creates a difficult play for the defensemen. They have to retrieve the puck and then turn around and make a play while under heavy forechecking pressure. Most of the time when a rebound is created by a long shot on goal, the offensive team has as good a chance of recovering the puck as the defensive team.

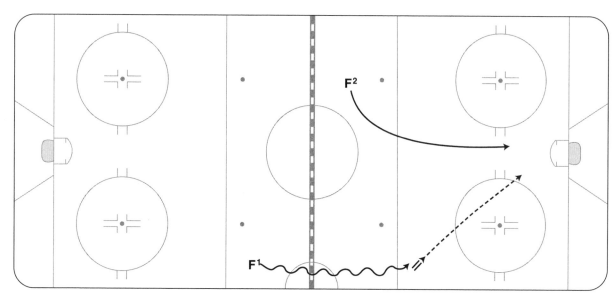

Figure 2.5   Putting the puck on net.

Possession Counters

As mentioned earlier, analytics at the NHL level have confirmed that scoring chances increase significantly when teams carry the puck into the opposition's end. Possession entries cause coverage problems for the opposition and provide the attacking team with a chance to work set plays.

Dumping the puck into the zone is an effective strategy, but the more exciting transition play—and the one that usually results in a scoring chance—involves the defensive team getting the puck in the neutral zone and making a penetrating pass to one of the forwards that results in an odd-man rush or breakaway (figure 2.6). This counter play has two key aspects: (1) the defenseman recognizes the option quickly, and (2) the forward skates into a stretch area with timing and speed. The stretch area is an open space as far from the puck carrier as a skater can go without going offside.

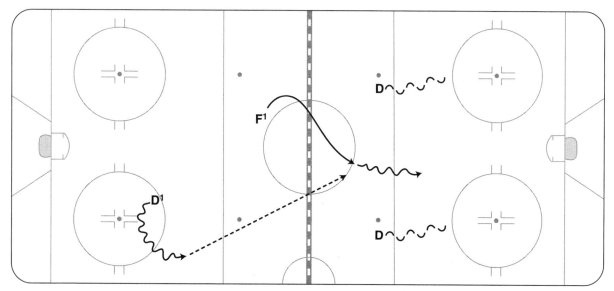

Figure 2.6   Making a penetrating pass for an odd-man rush or breakaway.

The forward off the puck can occasionally get in behind the defense and look for a breakaway pass (figure 2.7). This option will be available more often against teams that pinch up in the neutral zone with their defense. Forwards can look for that high middle area between the opposing defensemen to open up. When his teammate is ready to pass, the receiver should move to that area quickly with good timing. Even if the pass isn't made, having the forward available will pull back the opposing defensemen and open up other areas.

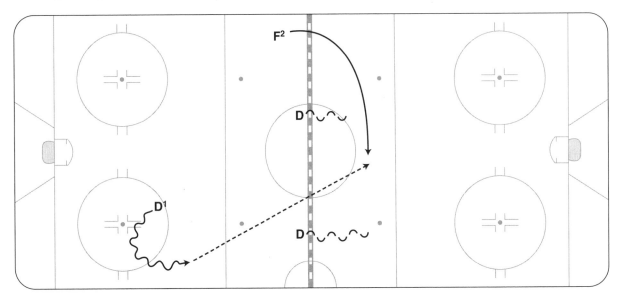

Figure 2.7   Getting open behind the Ds for a breakaway pass.

Tag Up Counters

Almost 50 percent of all counters occur off situations when the defensive team dumps or moves the puck out of the zone and the attacking forwards quickly tag up (get onside by getting over the blue line) while their defense quickly retrieves the puck and turns it up ice. The three forwards should all take a lane to provide the defense with the most options (figure 2.8). Make sure that each forward gives himself enough room to accelerate into the pass before crossing the blue line.

Activating Defense Into the Counter

The other factor to consider when executing neutral zone counters is involving the defense in the attack. In most North American leagues, generating offense is difficult, so coaches should look for ways to get their defense involved. This doesn't have to happen all the time, but your team can practice this strategy and use it according to your need to generate more scoring opportunities. Relying only on the forwards to score limits a team's ability to be a dangerous offensive unit.

Activating your defensemen through the neutral zone offers several advantages:

○ You have one more passing option.

○ The defensive team has one more player to cover, often causing confusion in their defensive system.

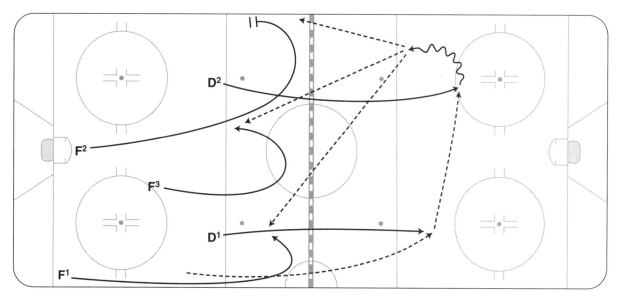

Figure 2.8   Tag up counters make quick up passes to tag up forwards.

○ It prepares the attack to have a late or mid-ice threat from the defense. If the defensemen wait too long to join the attack, they won't be a factor in the offensive zone.

○ Having a defenseman in the play often backs off the opposing defense, therefore giving the puck carrier more time to skate or make a decision. Note that defensemen cannot jump indiscriminately into an attack. The decision to activate must always be based on the quality of puck possession. If the puck carrier has good possession, then the defenseman can move to become an option; if not, he should stay back.

Regroups

If the opponent is already set up in their neutral zone forecheck, then regroups are a more effective way to break through this area and enter the offensive zone. Most teams will have an organized forecheck in the neutral zone to try to prevent teams from successfully regrouping. Knowing before the game which forecheck your opponent is using will help identify what regroup options are available. The coach must decide for all regroups what patterns the forwards should run so that they are consistent. The defense can then identify where potential passing options may exist because the forwards are available in specific areas. The two regroup patterns we will discuss are lane regroups and motion regroups. Both regroups are effective against all types of forechecking pressure. The difference between the two is whether the center stays in the middle or has the freedom to swing wide and exchange with the wingers (figure 2.9).

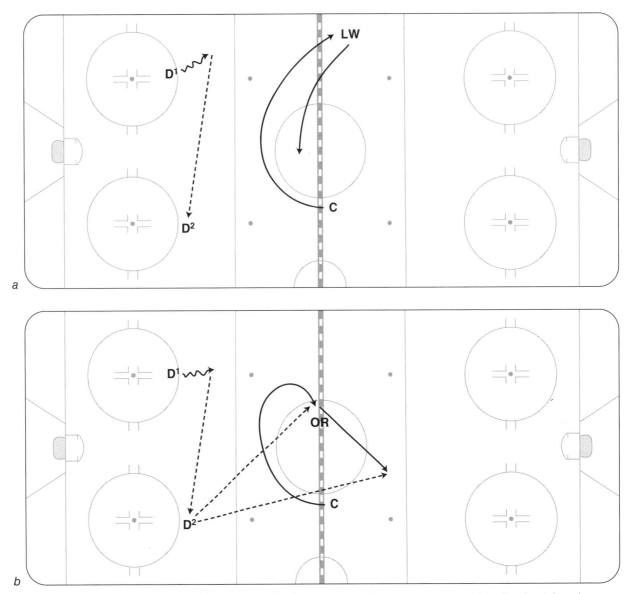

Figure 2.9 (a) Center exchanging with the winger; (b) center supporting both sides (low or high).

Lane Regroups

For the following regroups, the strong-side forward supports the boards while the back-side forward stretches. The center supports both sides, either low or high (figure 2.9b). The sequence of options for defensemen in the neutral zone depends on how the opponents forecheck. Do they forecheck with two forwards in a 2-1-2 system or with one forward in a 1-2-2 or 1-3-1 setup? If they forecheck with one forward, does he take away the D-to-D pass, or does he take away the flat pass to the wide forward? Teams that take away the D-to-D pass eliminate the hinge play, whereas teams that take away the cross-ice pass give up the hinge play. These important reads help the defensemen choose which of the following options to use.

■ QUICK UP

In this situation, D1 gets the puck just inside the blue line and turns it up quickly by passing to LW or C (figure 2.10). This option should be the first for all teams because speed in transition usually results in odd-man rushes. In addition, the quick-up play does not give the opposition time to set up a trap. RW stretches on the wide side and then supports across the ice when the pass is made.

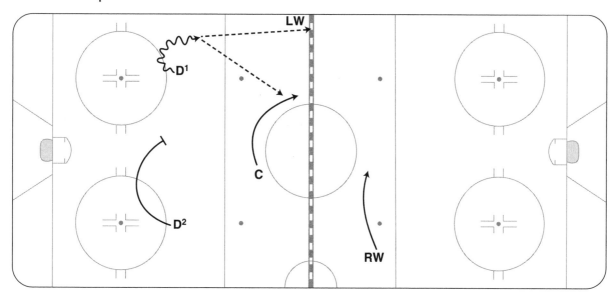

Figure 2.10   Quick up regroup.

■ D-TO-D STRETCH

When D1 gets the puck and the strong-side options are taken away, he should immediately pass the puck to his partner (figure 2.11). After making the pass, D1 should sink back to mid-ice to protect his partner in case of a turnover and to provide an option for D2. D2 passes up to RW, who is in a stretch position by the far blue line, or to C in mid-ice. After the pass is made, LW moves to support.

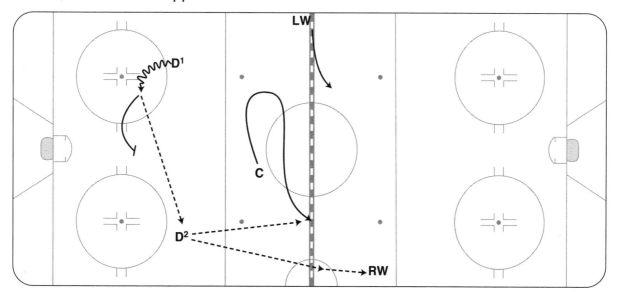

Figure 2.11   D-to-D stretch regroup.

■ D-TO-D FLAT PASS

D1 passes to D2, and now the opposition takes away his options to RW and C. D2 passes across to LW, who sinks low into the open seam (figure 2.12). This option is usually available when the opponents forecheck in a 1-2-2 format and lock the center, leaving the back side open. When D2 initially gets the pass from D1, he should move up ice and look to make a play up the boards or to the center. This deception will open up the wide side to LW. The pass must be made flat across the ice because a diagonal pass might be intercepted.

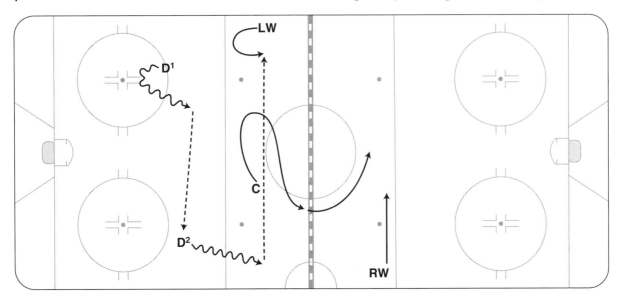

Figure 2.12 D2 using the regroup flat pass.

■ HINGE PLAY

D1 passes to D2 and then slides back to mid-ice to support his partner (figure 2.13a). D2 moves up ice and looks to make a pass. With no option available, he passes back to D1, who is behind and in mid-ice. D1 then moves the puck quickly to LW as the primary option or

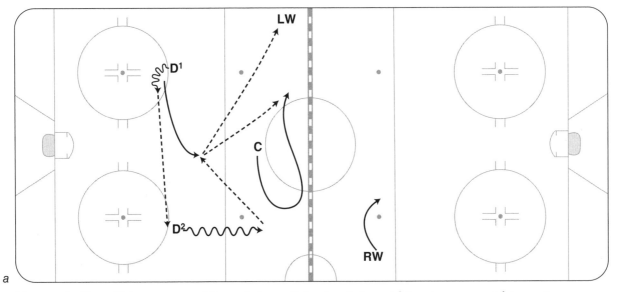

Figure 2.13a D1 passes to D2 and then slides back to mid-ice to support his partner.

to C. Initially when D1 moves the puck to D2, he has the option to drop back deeper and perform a "skating hinge"—in which the supporting defenseman moves back in behind the play and prepares to jump into the hinge pass with speed, catching the opponent off guard. Using the skating hinge also gives this defenseman room to accelerate, time to read the play, and the ability to draw in a checker and move the puck to the best option (figure 2.13b).

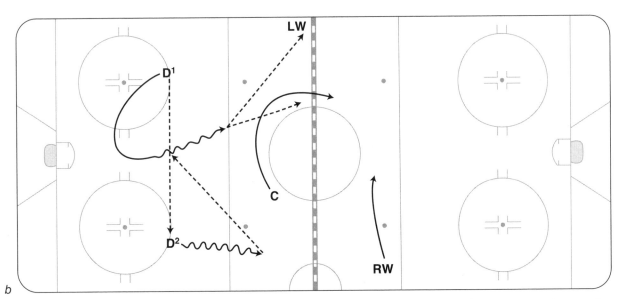

Figure 2.13b   Using the skating hinge. The D-hinge process is critical to support the puck carrier.

■ CENTER STRETCH

When a D1-to-D2 pass is made in the neutral zone, C should have the option of supporting low or moving up into the high seam stretch area (figure 2.14) for a potential breakaway pass. If teams check center on center in the neutral zone, this option is an effective way to lose the check and split the opponent's defense.

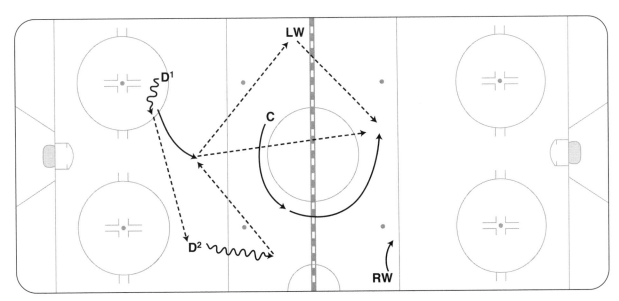

Figure 2.14   The high center stretch regroup sometimes will create a breakaway.

■ CHIP BEHIND PRESSURE

Because most teams use tight-checking systems, there isn't a lot of room in the neutral zone. When a pass is made to a teammate in this area, the receiver must have quick and close support. If the receiver is confronted, he will have the option of chipping the puck into the space behind the checker. The support player can anticipate the chip and get to the puck first. This tactic is very effective if the pass is confronted by the opposing defenseman stepping up to make a hit. In most cases, the center should be the player who is ready to support the chip (figure 2.15).

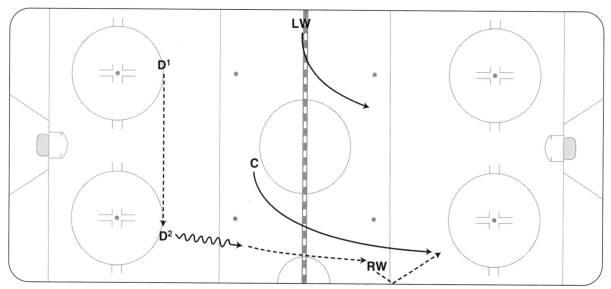

Figure 2.15   Chip to support behind pressure.

■ DEFENSE SUPPORTING MID-ICE

When a pass is made by a defenseman to a forward in the neutral zone, the passing D should be ready to move up through mid-ice and support the attack (figure 2.16). As the partner of D1, D2 must remain in a strong center-ice position behind the attack. D1 must again read the quality of puck possession to determine how far to move up and how quickly.

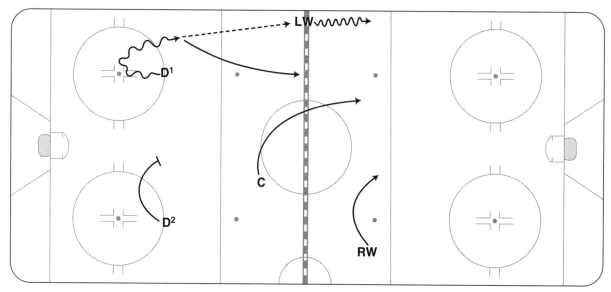

Figure 2.16   D1 moves to support the pass in the neutral zone.

Motion Regroups

The difference with motion regroups is that the center now has the ability to exchange positions with the wingers. Again, the sequence of options for defensemen in the neutral zone depends on how the opponents forecheck. The advantage of using motion regroups is that the players have more speed when getting the pass and often catch the opposition flat footed. The disadvantage is that the positioning of the forwards is not as predictable so the defensemen can't always anticipate where they will be. At times the forwards are so focused on moving and building up speed that they lose eye contact with the passer. The forwards must remember to keep their eyes on the puck. With motion regroups, the center always changes lanes with one of the wingers, and that winger then moves into center ice. If the player in the middle moves to support a pass and it is not made, an exchange occurs with the winger on that side (figure 2.17a). The player in the center may also swing away to build up speed on the wide side (figure 2.17b).

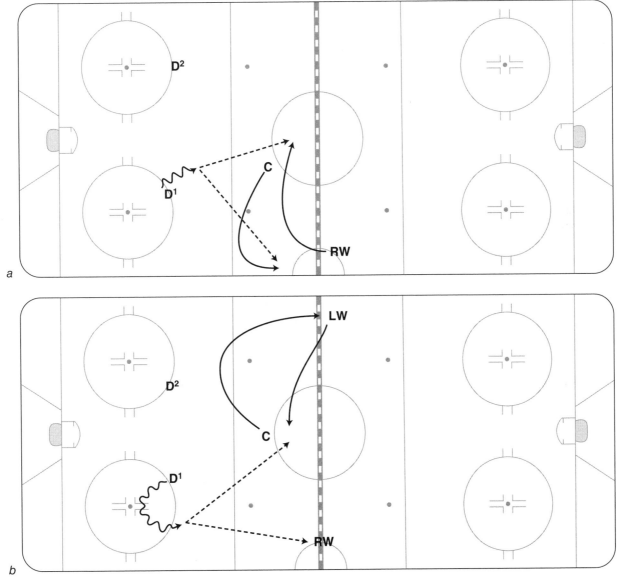

Figure 2.17   (a) Strong-side motion regroup and (b) the wide-side motion regroup.

With motion regroups, if teams check center on center in the neutral zone, having the center move into an outside lane often results in coverage confusion.

Using the same options presented for lane regroups, we now look at how the passing options change with the center leaving the mid-ice lane.

■ QUICK UP

In this situation, D1 gets the puck just inside the blue line and turns it up quickly by passing to LW or RW, who has moved off the wide boards as C swings to that side (figure 2.18). The exchange between the center and RW must be made quickly to provide immediate support for D1.

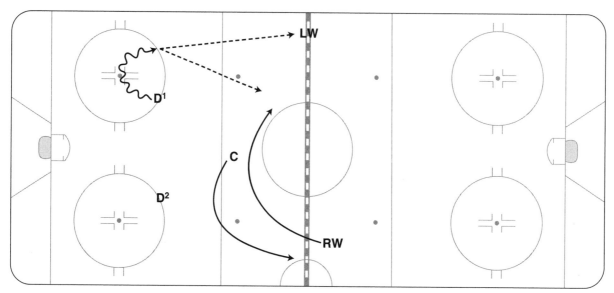

Figure 2.18   Center and wing exchange lanes to create regroup speed.

■ D-TO-D STRETCH

When D1 gets the puck and the strong-side options are taken away, he then passes to his partner (figure 2.19). C again swings away to the wide side. After the pass is made, D1 should sink back to mid-ice to protect his partner in case of a turnover and to provide an option for D2. D2 passes up to RW or to LW, who has moved off the boards and is available in the middle of the ice.

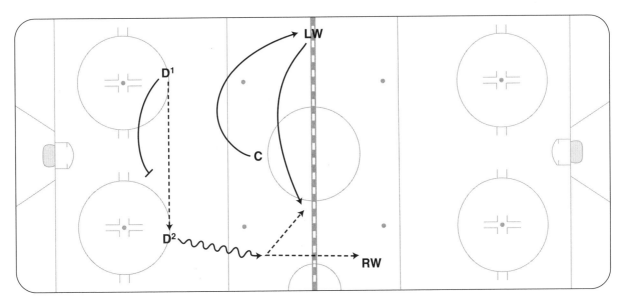

Figure 2.19 D-to-D motion regroup.

■ D-TO-D FLAT PASS

D1 passes to D2, and now because of how the opponents are forechecking, the main option is to make a flat pass to C with speed in the wide lane (figure 2.20). This is one of the more effective options in the motion regroup sequence because the center tends to build up a lot of speed in the wide lane and can often enter the zone easily. This option is usually available when the opponents forecheck in a 1-2-2 formation and lock the center of the ice, leaving the back side open.

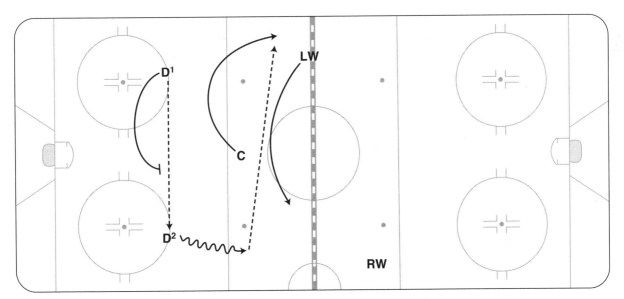

Figure 2.20 D2 passes to C who gains speed in the wide lane.

■ HINGE PLAY

D1 passes to D2 and then slides back to mid-ice to support his partner. D2 moves up ice and looks to make a pass. With no option available, he passes back to D1, who is behind and in mid-ice. D1 then moves the puck quickly to C, who again has a lot of speed built up in the outside lane (figure 2.21). LW may also be available in the middle of the ice. D1 may perform a skating hinge and accelerate up the middle of the ice while looking for options.

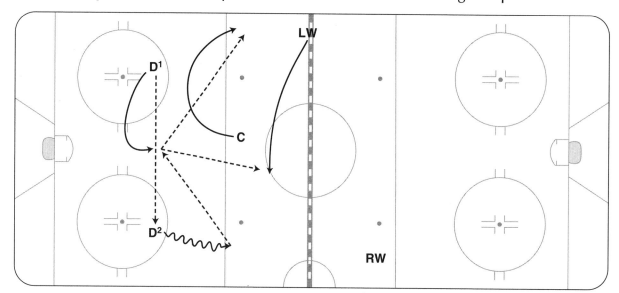

Figure 2.21   Hinge play to center or winger.

■ STRETCH PASS

When a D1-to-D2 pass is made in the neutral zone, C exchanges with the wing, and RW now has the option of moving out higher in behind the opposing defense (figure 2.22). Because the center swings lower, the defense has an alternative safer option if the stretch play is not there. RW must time it to hit the open space behind the opposition defense when D2 is ready to pass.

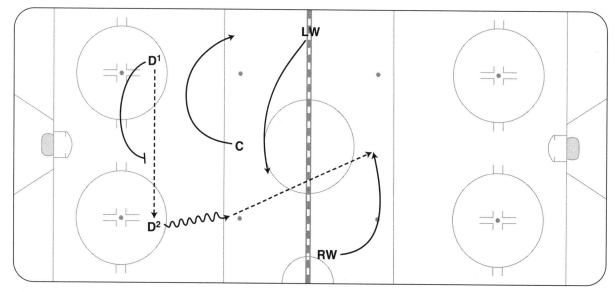

Figure 2.22   RW provides the stretch pass option.

■ HEAD TO HEAD

Teams sometimes face opponents who defend with a stationary or deep trap. In that case you should consider a motion regroup strategy like the head-to-head regroup, which provides you with the best chance of getting through with possession. After D1 gets the puck, he delays for a few seconds and then moves to mid-ice with the puck (figure 2.23). C and RW swing low to one side. D2 moves to the opposite outside lane. LW stretches in mid-ice at the far blue line. All four low players move together against the trap. D1 has the option of passing to any of the forwards or D2. The advantage of this strategy is that F1 in the trap gets frozen by D1 and the speed of the players coming from behind allows them to be able to navigate through the trap.

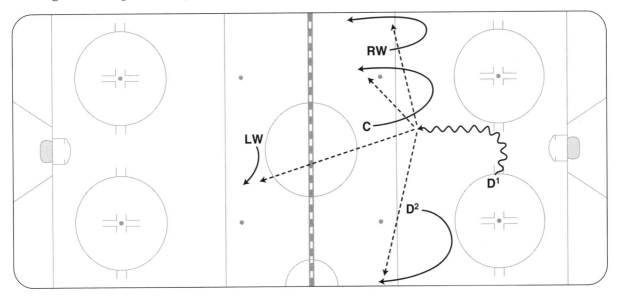

Figure 2.23   Beating the deep trap with back speed.

Chapter 3
Offensive Zone Entries

In this chapter, we deal with plays entering the offensive zone. Whether the rush starts from a successful breakout in the defensive zone or results from a counter or regroup in the neutral zone, offensive zone entries are a key strategy for generating successful scoring chances.

Entering the offensive zone in control of the puck is every player's goal. Not turning the puck over when entering the offensive zone is every coach's goal. Let's face it. We play this game to battle for and enjoy possession of the puck. Puck possession needs to be a key underlying philosophy, not only for playing hockey at a high level but also for enjoying it.

Coaches universally become disappointed with players who needlessly lose possession of the puck in two areas. The first is the 7 or 8 feet (2.1 or 2.4 m) just outside the blue line, and the second is the 7 or 8 feet just inside the blue line. Players turning over pucks in these two critical areas tend to hear about it. Why? When the puck is turned over here, the opposing team can counter quickly and create outnumbered attacks. This result happens because the two forwards without the puck tend to be anticipating the puck going deep, and they are in that "flat" vulnerable position along the blue line with no speed (figure 3.1).

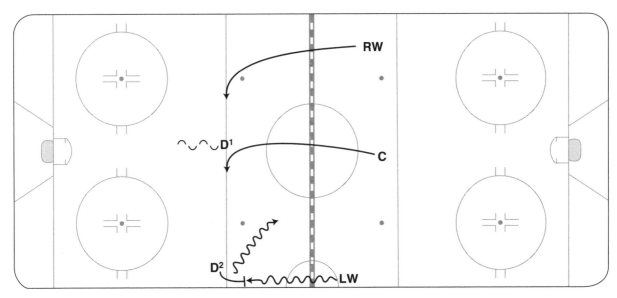

Figure 3.1   Turnover at the blue line.

Taking Advantage of the Hybrid Icing Rule

With the recent hybrid icing rule being incorporated at the professional and many amateur levels, teams are now taking advantage of early area plays. Although these plays may go for icing, they usually create a foot race between the attacking forward and the defenseman. Coaches often allow or encourage one of the forwards to stretch early and then to use a flip pass, bank pass, or long direct pass to try to get in behind the opposition's defense (figure 3.2a). If the stretch player misses the pass, he must

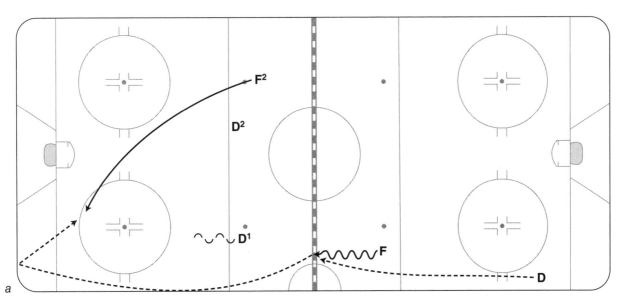

Figure 3.2a   Taking advantage of the hybrid icing rule.

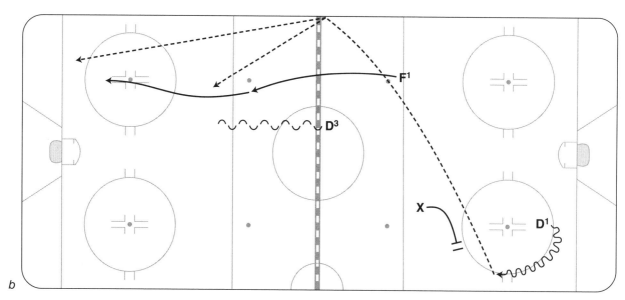

Figure 3.2*b* Bank pass to speed forward.

get to the face-off dot before the opposition defense so that the icing will be waived off. If the pass doesn't connect but the forward wins the foot race, possession will be obtained low in the offensive zone.

As mentioned in the chapter on breakouts, many teams now use indirect breakout passes to try to spring one of the wingers into open ice or get an odd-man rush. These passes are often made off the boards and into an area that the winger is skating toward. The player receiving the pass can often adjust his skating and get to the puck before the defensive team has a chance to adjust. Again, missing the pass is usually not a problem because of the hybrid icing rule and the advantage for the offensive team to win the race to the puck (figure 3.2*b*).

When playing five on five, the player with the puck must read the opponent's pressure when entering the offensive zone. If the gap between the player in possession of the puck and the defender is large or adequate, obviously the attacking player keeps possession of the puck and enters the attacking zone. If the player with the puck senses pressure, his first option is to pass, but if that isn't available, the cross-ice dump or chip are two tactics that can reduce this pressure and create a chance for puck possession deeper in the zone. Coaches should set up practice drills that incorporate this read. Drills that allow the puck carrier to react to varying gaps by the defender and varying pressure help to make these decisions with the puck more automatic and successful in game action.

Dump-In Entries

The cross-ice dump (figure 3.3) works best under two conditions:

1. Defensive pressure is read, and the offensive team is changing.

2. Defensive pressure is read, and the puck carrier has no support option.

The perfect cross-ice dump hits the boards halfway between the net and the side boards and angles away from the goalie toward the half boards.

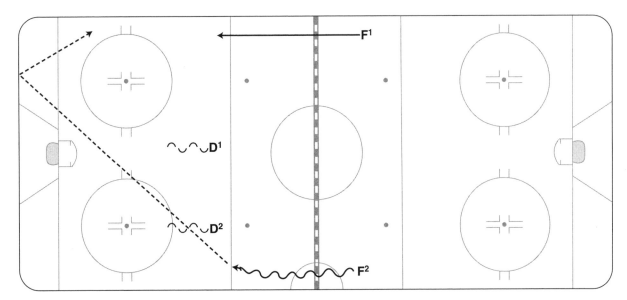

Figure 3.3   The cross-ice dump.

Rims

A second tactic when the offensive player reads pressure is to rim the puck to the wide side. The player entering the zone senses that his teammate skating wide can retrieve the puck. Therefore, the player with the puck rims it hard around the boards (figure 3.4). To increase the probability of the puck making it by the goaltender, he takes a quick wrist shot. If he uses a slapshot, it has to be hard enough to clear the back of the net because most goaltenders will read a rim when the player winds up for a slapshot.

At the top levels of hockey, this tactic has limited success. Goalies in today's game are so mobile and so good at trapping the rimmed puck that few pucks get around to the desired teammate. Most are stopped behind the net and turned over to the opposing defense. Before using this tactic, know the opposition goaltender. If he isn't mobile or is poor at trapping the puck off a rim, then use it more often. Conversely, if he gets out of his net quickly and is able to handle the puck, rimming it will only result in a turnover.

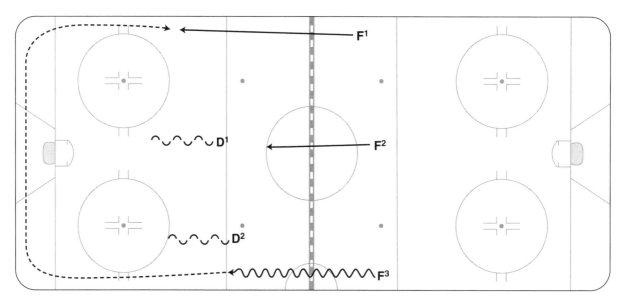

Figure 3.4   The basic rim.

Chips

The chip tactic (figure 3.5) is used in many areas of the ice, but it may be most effective during an offensive zone entry. Chipping the puck can be considered a pass if done correctly. Chipping refers to banking the puck off the boards to a space behind the defender. The chip works well because it puts the puck in better offensive position (behind the pressuring defender) and gives the player chipping the puck a good chance of retrieving it. Younger players make a monumental mistake by not pulling the defender off the boards slightly toward the middle of the ice before chipping the puck. If players are close to or right next to the boards, angling the chip to a place where it can be retrieved is nearly impossible. The goal of the chip is puck placement.

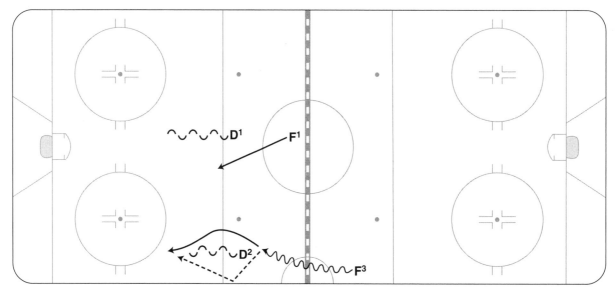

Figure 3.5   The basic chip.

Chipping the puck past the defender forces him to turn and try to catch the offensive player. Because the offensive player is moving forward with speed and his supporting teammates are moving to that area, the defender is often caught in a difficult position. Several years ago the defender would have been able to hook or hold up the offensive player for a few seconds but not anymore; the obstruction rules have eliminated that tactic. Therefore, the defender's inability to pressure the player with the puck creates the opportunity for puck possession deeper in the offensive zone.

The chip has two options for retrieval. The first is to chip the puck and have the same player retrieve it. The second and most effective is to chip the puck into the space behind the defenseman and have a teammate with speed pick it up (figure 3.6). The chip to a teammate should always be used when the puck carrier has no room to carry the puck but has a teammate moving to support the space behind the defense. This strategy is also commonly referred to as attacking the space behind the opposing defense. Get your players to visualize this tactic and constantly talk about the space behind.

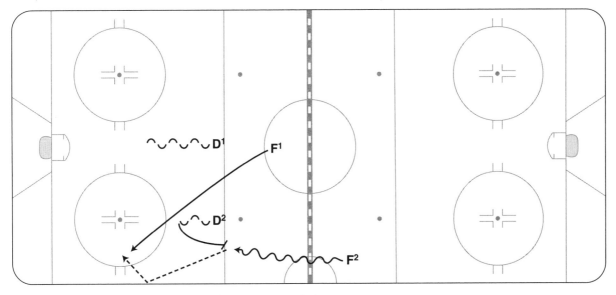

Figure 3.6   Chipping the puck behind the defenseman to a teammate.

Mid-Ice Entries

Most coaches prefer outside-drive entries because a dangerous turnover is less likely to occur. Players who enter the offensive zone with the puck in the middle often face several risks. The major concern is that any sideways movement in the middle of the ice brings with it the opportunity for the defenseman to stand up and make an open-ice hit. Most major open-ice hits occur as players are carrying the puck into the middle of the ice on offensive zone entries (figure 3.7).

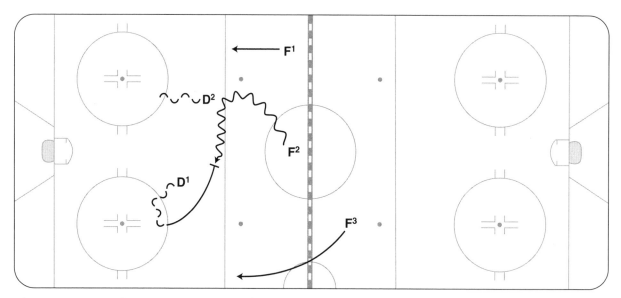

Figure 3.7   Mid-ice entry open-ice hit.

Midlane to Late Speed

Many talented and offensively gifted players use this middle-ice space to pass off to teammates coming from behind the play with speed. This entry tactic is exceptional when executed properly because backspeed—players moving from behind the puck carrier with more speed than the puck carrier—can catch defenders completely off guard.

The back-side pass upon middle entry (figure 3.8) is the most difficult to execute because it requires more skill, but it is always the most effective. Players gifted with the puck often carry it across the middle of the

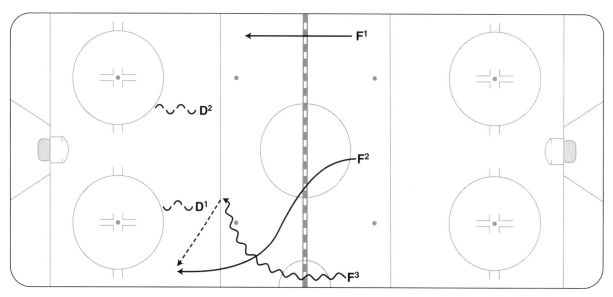

Figure 3.8   Mid-ice entry back-side pass.

offensive zone just inside the blue line and then pass back toward the space where they have just come from to a player with vertical speed. The effectiveness of this entry comes from shifting the defenders sideways, with the puck carrier thereby opening up space for the player on the back side to enter the zone.

Kick and Run Play

A second option for the puck carrier in mid-ice (F1) is to use a kick and run play by driving across the line through the middle and then bumping the puck to the outside player stationary at the blue line (F2). As F1 continues to drive to the net, he will push the opposition defense back. This action will free up space and time for F2 to shoot or make a play. F2 will have the option to pass back to F1, shoot with F1 screening the goaltender, pass across to F3, or hit the late D1 moving in. If no options are available, F2 can lay the puck behind the net to F1 for low puck possession. This kick and run play is one of the most effective plays for drawing the defense in tight as F1 enters the zone and then pushing them back as F1 passes off and drives to the net. It definitely creates a lot of confusion in defensive coverage (figure 3.9).

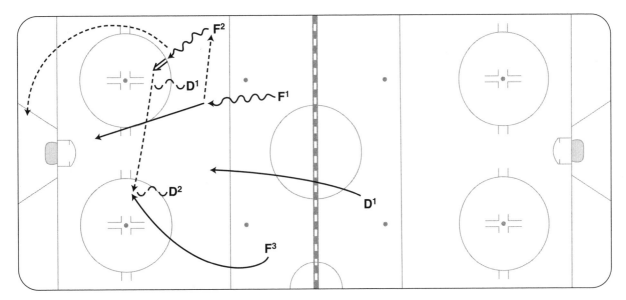

Figure 3.9   Mid-ice kick and run play.

Wide-Lane Drives

The wide-lane drive is the most used offensive zone entry because this space is most often available to the puck carrier. When the puck carrier enters the zone wide, he may have the option to drive deep and try to go around the defenseman or behind the net. Defensemen are usually intimidated by speed and want to protect the space inside, so they will initially give the puck carrier room on the outside and then try to cut off the puck carrier deeper in the zone. The puck carrier may also delay by driving deep and then cutting back up ice to the space where he came from. The puck carrier may also drive and cut inside. He must be able to read options quickly as he enters the zone wide with speed. The puck carrier going wide needs to read where the open space is; if it is deep, he drives around the defenseman; if it is in front, he cuts laterally across in front of the defenseman; if the defenseman closes quickly on the puck carrier, then the best option may be to spin off and delay (figure 3.10).

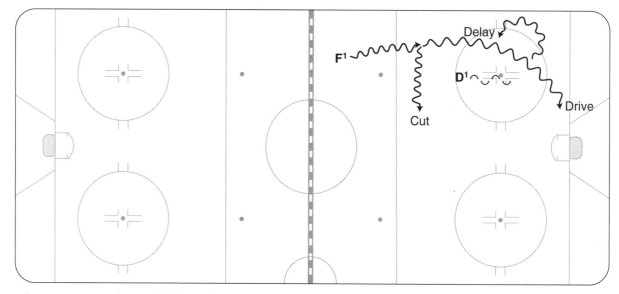

Figure 3.10   The wide-lane drive with options to cut, drive deep, or delay.

Funneling Pucks

Sometimes coaches need to have in their back pockets a tactic or philosophy that simplifies the attack options. Funneling pucks to the net is a basic yet effective tactic (figure 3.11). The funnel philosophy says that after a player

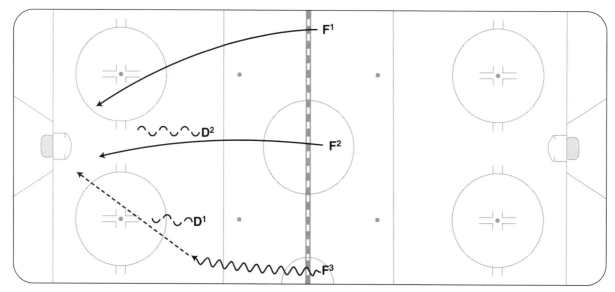

Figure 3.11   The funnel.

carrying the puck crosses the top of the offensive face-off circles, that player has only one option: placing the puck toward the front of the net. Under these instructions, the other two offensive forwards should not be trying to get open for a pass but should be driving hard to the net looking for a second-chance rebound. In other words, everything—the puck and the players—is funneled toward the front of the net. If 70 to 80 percent of all goals scored come off a second chance created by a rebound, then the funnel simplifies how to make this happen. In every league the leading scorers are the ones who take the most shots. They understand the funnel philosophy—get the puck to the net. Volume of shots is key.

The funnel opportunity is maximized if the player carrying the puck into the offensive zone and placing the puck toward the front of the net is an offensive defenseman (figure 3.12). Obviously, this option frees up all three offensive forwards to skate into prime position and jump on any loose pucks to create second shots. When shooting from the outside, players should recognize that they aren't trying to score. At most levels the goaltending is too good, and few are beat from those wide angles. The main objective is to hit the net. Shots should be low for the goaltender's pad to create a rebound for the players going to the net. Goaltenders usually cannot deflect this type of shot to the outside.

If the defenseman on the rush has speed to attack the net off the rush and the team's strategy is to funnel pucks, then many coaches give the attacking defenseman permission to go directly to the net, with one rule— after the play turns from a rush to a forecheck, the attacking defenseman must return quickly and directly to the blue line.

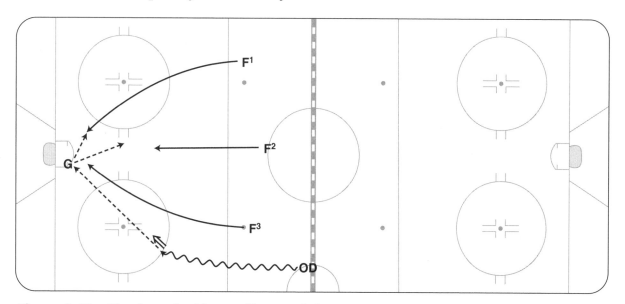

Figure 3.12   The funnel with an offensive defenseman.

Two-on-One Attacks

When the offensive team realizes they have a potential two-on-one opportunity in the neutral zone, they should attack quickly with speed (figure 3.13). Initially they may cross, but they must attack with speed so that the backcheckers don't catch them and nullify the odd-man rush. If it is a wide two on one, players should try to get closer to mid-ice right away. Regardless of which side the puck carrier is on when he crosses the blue line, he should get the puck into a triple-threat position—in shooting position at his side so that he can either pass, shoot, or make a move. The puck carrier now needs to read how the defense and goaltender might play the situation and pick the best option. The second offensive player must have his stick in a position to shoot or deflect the puck into the net.

A team can use several strategies when attacking two on one. First, they can try to move the puck once side to side when they cross the blue line to shift the goaltender and the defenseman. Second, they need to recognize whether the D is going to slide. Coaches should include in the scouting report whether the other team has a tendency to slide when facing a two on one. When a D slides, the puck carrier can cut inside quickly or wait out the D and pass around the sprawling defenseman. The puck carrier needs to have patience and poise to prevent the sliding D from being successful.

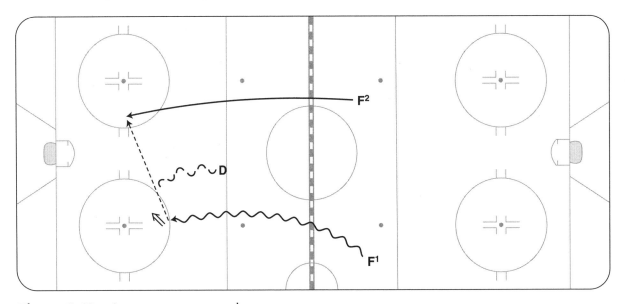

Figure 3.13 A two-on-one attack.

Two-on-Two Attacks

Three basic strategies can be used for a two-on-two rush. There are no set rules about when to use each, but they give the offensive players options. Although the choice may be dictated by the coaches' philosophy of play, practicing each option is important. The key principle for all two-on-two rushes is for the offensive players to isolate and attack one defender.

■ TWO-ON-TWO CRISSCROSS

The first strategy is for the puck carrier (F1) to crisscross with F2 and isolate one of the defensemen (figure 3.14). If properly executed, the crisscross creates a lateral move that develops a sense of uncertainty in the defender's mind. The key to the crisscross is for the player with the puck to initiate the lateral movement and be closest to the defenders; the player without the puck crosses in the opposite direction behind the puck carrier. Young players often mess up this sequence and put themselves offside because the player without the puck is too anxious and goes ahead of the puck carrier. The puck carrier should make the decision about which way he will go.

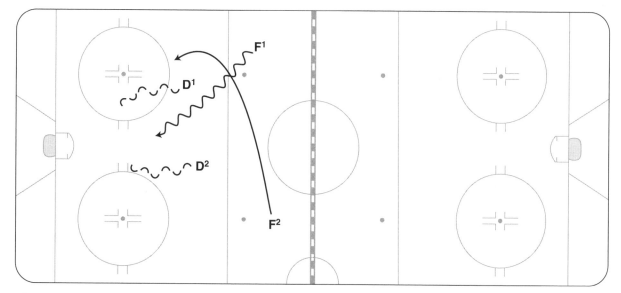

Figure 3.14   F1 and F2 use a two-on-two crisscross.

■ TWO-ON-TWO MIDLANE DRIVE

The second option for the two on two is for the player off the puck (F2) to drive through the middle of the two defensemen, allowing F1 to cross in behind (figure 3.15). This action must be executed just inside the blue line so that the player without the puck doesn't go offside. Driving between the two defensemen creates a brief hesitation by the defenseman playing F1. This hesitation by the defender will allow F1 time and space to cross and shoot or make a play.

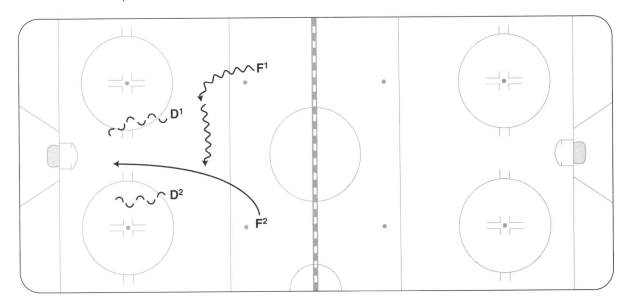

Figure 3.15   F2 drives the middle to give F1 room.

■ TWO-ON-TWO DOUBLE DRIVE

The third option is for both players to double drive. F1 may lay the puck to F2 in the space behind the defender. F2 must move to that space on the inside shoulder of the defending defenseman (D2) (figure 3.16). With the double drive, F1 might choose to shoot off the drive as F2 goes to the net for a rebound.

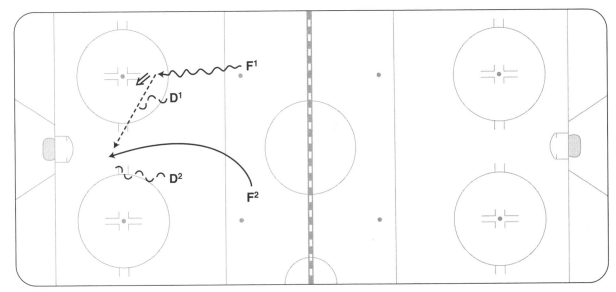

Figure 3.16   Both players drive on the two on two attack.

Three-on-Two Attacks

When the offensive team catches the opposition in a three on two, they should be able to generate a scoring chance. Although not as good as a two on one, it is still a great offensive opportunity. Because three players are involved in the attack, several options are available to create a great chance. Teams should practice and use all four attack options: the high triangle, the midlane drive, the triple drive, and the drive and delay.

■ THREE-ON-TWO HIGH TRIANGLE

Let's start with the traditional option. Most often in three-on-two situations, the attacking team wants to force the defenders to play man on man with one player and isolate the other defender two on one. F1 drives wide with the puck, and F3 drives wide without the puck (figure 3.17). F2 now trails, looking for a pass from F1. The options available for F1 are to pass to F3, to shoot and create a rebound for F3, or to pass back to F2 for a shot from the high slot. The key read for F1 is whether the opposing defenseman goes with F3 on the wide drive. This movement will give an indication of what is open.

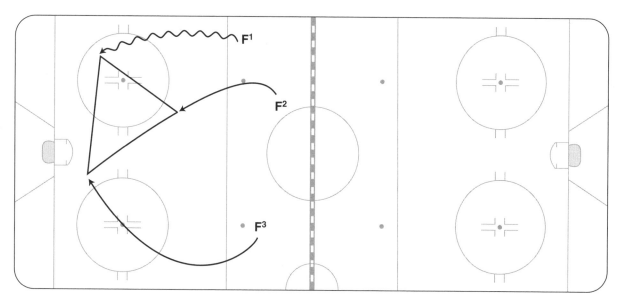

Figure 3.17   The high triangle creates a back pass and wide pass option for F1.

■ THREE-ON-TWO MIDLANE DRIVE

A three-on-two entry with a midlane drive gives the puck carrier even more options. Before entering the offensive zone, players should get the puck to the outside of the ice. Because the two defenders must respect the outmanned situation they find themselves in, their tendency is to back off and allow the entry. After the puck is to one side or the other, the middle attacking player drives hard toward the net (figure 3.18). F2 drives through the mid-ice seam on the inside shoulder of D2. This is the moment when defenders get confused and make mistakes. Because the middle player (F2) is seen as attacking the net and has position to do so, D2 has to vacate the prime scoring area. The middle drive completely neutralizes that defender's ability to get involved in what now has turned into a two on one. The far-side winger (F3) stays available on the wide side or closer to mid-ice. F1 now has the option of driving and shooting as F2 goes to the net, passing through to F2 for a tip or chance to shoot, or passing to F3 for a wide shot or high slot shot. This attack allows the potential shot to come from the perfect scoring area and forces the goaltender to look through the screen provided by F2.

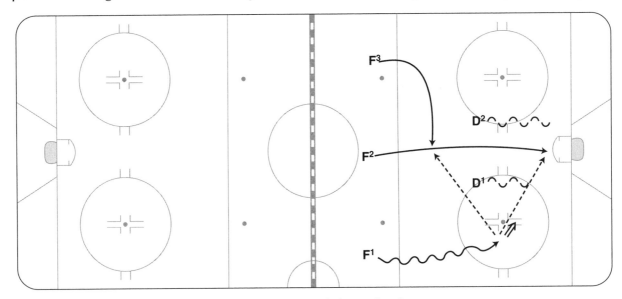

Figure 3.18   F2 drives the middle to push the defense back.

■ THREE-ON-TWO TRIPLE DRIVE

In the triple drive, a variation of the midlane drive three on two, all three players initially drive deep (figure 3.19). The puck carrier (F1) takes the puck wide with lots of speed. The middle-ice attacker (F2) continues to drive to the net. This time instead of slowing down, F3 attacks the net. The player with the puck (F1) drives outside the near defender and then immediately cuts hard inside. This action creates separation and a chance to make a variety of plays or take a shot against the grain from the prime scoring area. F2 and F3 need to drive hard to allow F1 more space to work with. If F1 is skating down his off side (left-hand shot skating down the right wing), he will be in a better position to shoot and make a play because he will have the puck on the forehand.

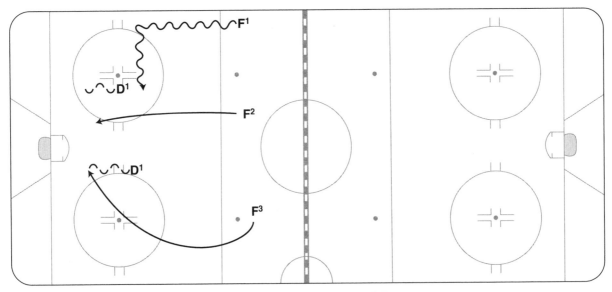

Figure 3.19   The triple drive allows F1 to cut to the middle.

■ THREE-ON-TWO DRIVE AND DELAY

In the world of hockey, as in most sports, speed kills. Outside offensive zone speed has a tendency to back off defenders, and this is where our next offensive zone entry tactic works wonders. The player driving outside with the puck looks as if he will drive the puck hard toward the net, but then just at the right moment, this player pivots or tight turns (always to the outside or away from the defender) and skates back toward the blue line (figure 3.20). This delay creates what every hockey player wants: time and space to make the next move. Initially, the defender will have to give space because he is afraid of the deep drive, and as a result he will take a second or two to react to the delay.

A couple of teaching keys allow this excellent offensive tactic to work. The outside-drive player (F1) must sell the drive to the net. The perfect time to turn up is when the offensive player is level with or forcing the defender to pivot toward the offensive player. Today's high-speed, high-pace game gives players with the puck little time to make good plays. Therefore, creating offensive gaps between the player with the puck and the defenders is critical. Wayne Gretzky, an amazing player, scored a high percentage of his goals off this tactic of driving, pivoting, gaining middle ice, and shooting.

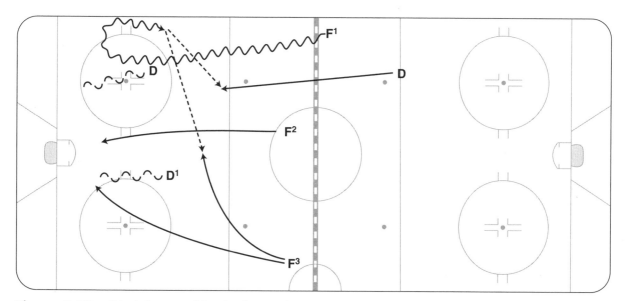

Figure 3.20   F1 delays and looks for options.

■ PRESS-AND-PULL PLAY

A wrinkle in this outside-drive play is being executed often at the NHL level. As the middle-drive offensive player (F2) drives toward the net, he doesn't stay in front of the net but pulls away and finds a shooting soft spot (not in the middle of the slot) toward the side of the net where the player with the puck (F1) is turning (figure 3.21). As F1 turns back up ice, he makes a quick inside pass to F2.

This play is effective off the rush because it drives the defender to the net and then creates separation from this defender, who is reluctant to leave the front of the net. Rush plays like the press and pull are effective because of their drive north and then pull south effect.

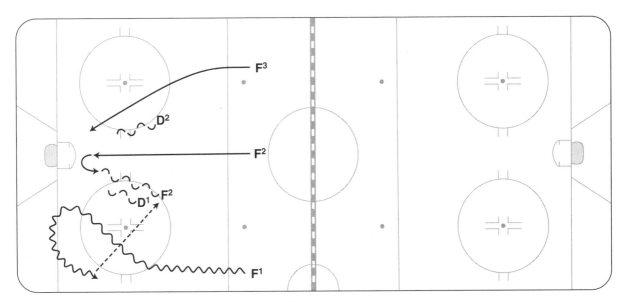

Figure 3.21   F2 uses the press and pull play to get open.

■ FOUR-PLAYER ATTACK, DEFENSEMAN IN THE RUSH

Figure 3.22 illustrates the perfect attack with four players involved. At all times on the attack, your players should work hard to establish a four-player attack at the offensive blue line. Attacking with four players definitely backs up the defenders. The defenseman joining the rush may be in any of the four positions. Crossing the blue line, the attack formation should look like a diamond, thus giving the puck carrier a wide pass, net play, pass to the late player, or cut off the drive.

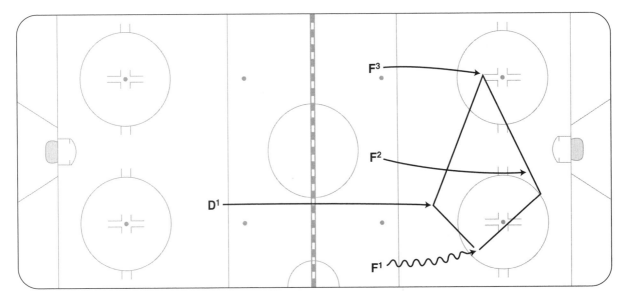

Figure 3.22   Four-player attack; defenseman joins the rush.

Offside

Entry into the offensive zone can create one of a coach's many pet peeves—the offside. High-level coaches speak often about controlling the controllables. John Wooden, the great basketball coach, said, "I don't worry too much about winning and losing. I worry a lot about practicing the details that deliver the win." One of the details that deliver the win is never, never, never to put yourself or your team offside. Offside comes from selfish possession of the puck or lazy actions when the puck carrier waits too long to make a play and his teammates go offside while trying to anticipate a pass. Yes, opponents can have a positional influence on the offside, but more often than not the offside is created by the team with the puck instead of the team without the puck. Puck possession is hard to get and hard to keep, so why would a team easily give up a puck that they fought so hard to retrieve?

Activating Defense Into Offensive Zone Entries

After a successful breakout or regroup, with the puck in possession of the forwards, one defenseman should follow up as a late-wave option or as one of the three attacking players. As mentioned in the breakout chapter, the center may at times get caught low in coverage, so one defenseman needs to be in the rush. When a defenseman moves up to join the rush, he should read the quality of puck possession. Does a teammate have the puck under control while advancing up the ice? If so, then one defenseman must be activated into the rush. Is it risky to have an active defense? Well, the answer is no. The responsibility is in the hands of the puck carrier; he must make good decisions and pick the right options. A defenseman should join and stay in the rush from the breakout, through the neutral zone, and then read the quality of puck possession at the offensive blue line.

By joining the rush and staying in as the third or fourth attacker, the defenseman creates confusion as opponents try to figure out their coverage on the backcheck. In addition, an active defenseman usually results in more odd-man rushes because he can get up the ice quicker than the other team backchecks. If the quality of puck possession is good, defensemen should have the green light to go to the net, but they must know that they cannot stop and hang out in front for the puck—they have to get back to the blue line. Allowing your defense to join the rush is a good strategy, but you don't want it to cost you the other way and give the opposition a chance to get an odd-man rush.

Chapter 4
Attack Zone

Cycling. Setting up behind the net. Activating the defense in the offensive zone. Stretching the zone. Exploiting the high seam area. Protecting the puck low to buy time and find players who are open. Getting open off the puck. Screening the goaltender. Making tight plays to sticks at the net. All are tactics and strategies used in the attacking zone.

When an attacking team has possession in the offensive zone, the brilliant coaches in the game of hockey really turn on their creative juices. The goal of every attacking team is to create offensive chances. What constitutes a chance differs from coach to coach, but in essence, a chance is a shot taken from inside the scoring area. Three general philosophies can be used to create these offensive chances:

1. Shooting through traffic
2. Creating separation
3. Creating deception

Taking shots through traffic (players in front of the goaltender) will obviously distract the goaltender or deny him the opportunity to see the puck. Goalies are so good these days that a shot without traffic between the shooter and the goalie is usually a giveaway. All the top offensive teams make sure that one player is always in the net area and moving across the sight lines of the goaltender or planted in front of him. Often this tactic results in the opposition trying to clear the net by moving this player, which results in a double screen or possibly a penalty. Both favor the offensive team.

In the separation tactic, the puck carrier creates the time and space needed to make successful plays and create shots. Players away from the puck have to work to get open and separate from their check. They should move to areas where they can receive a pass and be ready to one time the puck or shoot quickly. Sometimes players off the puck can move into an area and then push off their check or push back into an open space. Separating from your check sounds like a simple task, but we find that many offensive players off the puck skate into their check and essentially check themselves. Smart players, however, always seem to be able to get open, and as a result they always have the puck.

The puck carrier also needs to be deceptive so that the defending team doesn't know whether he is going to shoot or pass. Deception tactics include faking a shot or pass or simply looking the defender off. Looking the defender off the puck means looking at an option, making a motion to pass in that direction, and then skating or moving in another direction. Usually the defender will turn his feet toward the first look, giving the offensive player room to move by. Coaches often talk about the triple-threat position, and we mention it several times in this book. When an offensive player has the puck, he should always keep it by the hip on his forehand side, which gives him the option of passing, shooting, or making a move on the defender. This triple-threat position creates deception simply by the location of the puck and the options available. All these tactics play themselves out through many practiced and set plays that we will now explore.

Cycling

Many offensive strategies include cycling the puck. Younger, inexperienced players often get the cycling process wrong, so let's start with this basic tactic. The cycle works best when the player with the puck deep in the offensive zone begins to bring the puck up the boards toward the blue line (figure 4.1). Generally, a defender will press this puck carrier toward

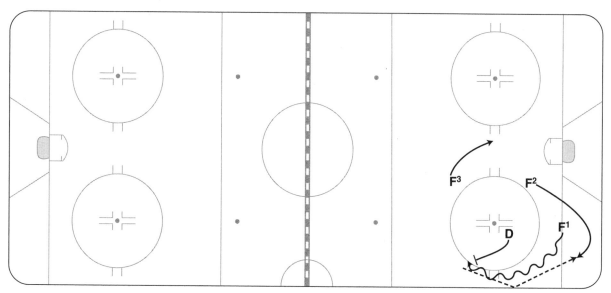

Figure 4.1 Cycling.

the boards and work to remove the puck. The key to the cycle setup is the second offensive forward. This forward mirrors the positioning of the puck carrier but stays 10 or 15 feet (3.0 to 4.6 m) away from the puck carrier on the boards, toward the goal line. This player calls for the puck. Here is where inexperienced players mess up. The tendency is for players to pass into open ice, but the cycle doesn't work best this way. It works best when the puck is angled off the boards, away from the defender's stick, so that it bounces off the boards and onto the stick of the second offensive forward. Cycling is an effective tactic when executed correctly.

The purpose of the cycle is to keep possession of the puck and take it to the net to create a scoring chance. If the initial player with the puck can gain a lane to the net, he shouldn't cycle—he should take the puck to the net. Many coaches become upset when players cycle for the sake of cycling and don't read when to exploit the defenders. If the puck carrier feels pressure and knows the lane is shut down, he should lay the puck back to the corner where he came from. His support player (F2) needs to read this and move to support the cycle pass. After this play is made, F2 may continue the cycle with a pass back to F3.

The three forwards should move in sequence from the boards to the slot to the net and back to the corner to support the cycle, a sequence that accounts for the name. The goal of the cycle is to pull a defender out of position and then attack the net or the seams with a quick pass to the open player. Opponents often get their coverage confused because of the quick rotation of players who cycle with the puck, lay it to the corner, and work to get open. The cycle is not easy to defend continuously, and a missed defensive assignment means an offensive chance. The cycle works best along the side boards but can also be used near the back of the net.

The net cycle (figure 4.2) is another cycling option. If well executed, the net cycle pulls defenders from the front of the net toward the corner

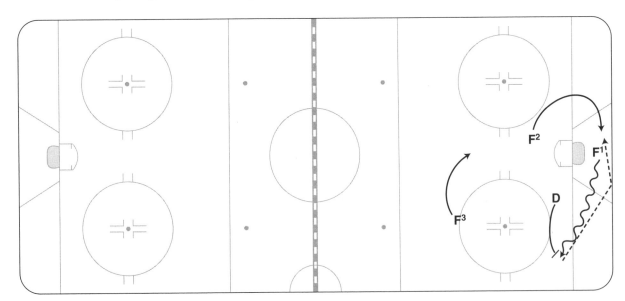

Figure 4.2   The net cycle.

or behind the net, and this movement often opens up passing lanes for excellent scoring chances. It is similar to the side board cycle in that one player skates behind the net with the puck and when pressured passes the puck back behind the net. In addition, it forces the goaltender to follow the play behind the net while trying to keep track of options in front, which is difficult.

Off any cycle play, getting the puck to the net quickly is important. Whether the cycle is on the side boards or behind the net, as soon as the first cycle pass is made that player should look to take the puck to the net or shoot the puck at the net right away. Quick plays like this catch the defensive team off guard and catch the goaltender trying to adjust. In most situations a quick shot will result in a rebound because the goaltender is not set. The other players going to the net should have their sticks on the ice ready to play the rebound or make a potential shot pass play.

Playing Behind the Net

Wayne Gretzky played behind the net so effectively that this area became known as his office. Gaining offensive positioning behind the net opens up many opportunities for direct-shot (high-percentage) chances. To use the back of the net effectively, teams should automatically move the puck to this space when they don't have another option. The offensive player at the net now reads that his teammate is in trouble and moves to the back of the net area. When a pass is made to the back of the net, the offensive team will always get there first because the defensive team never overplays this area. Using the back of the net forces the opposing defense and goaltender to focus on that area while losing track of where players are in front. Sometimes two defenders can be drawn into this area; if the defensemen are unsure who should be covering the player behind the net, both may jump in at the same time. Now at least one offensive player will be open in the dangerous scoring area in front of the net.

One of the most effective plays from behind the net occurs when an offensive defenseman skates hard from the point (blue line) looking to receive a pass in the slot (figure 4.3). If the defenseman pressing the net is unable to receive a clear pass, the second option off this play becomes very dangerous. As this defenseman moves to the front of the net—pulling as many defenders with him as possible—the boards-side forward steps into this soft spot vacuum and often gets to take a dangerous shot through the traffic created by the pressing defenseman.

The second play selection from behind the net (figure 4.4) is also hard to defend. The big decision that defenders must make about the offensive player standing behind the net with the puck is when or how they should flush him out from behind the net. If the defending defenseman attacks the offensive player from one side of the net, two options open up. The

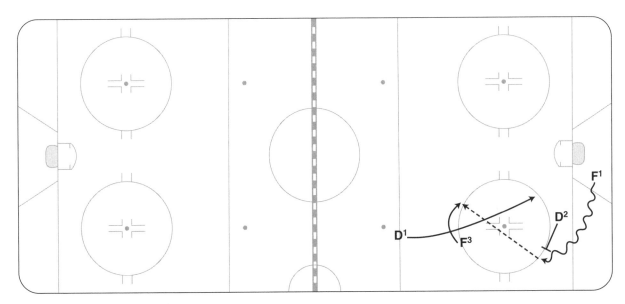

Figure 4.3   Pressing the net.

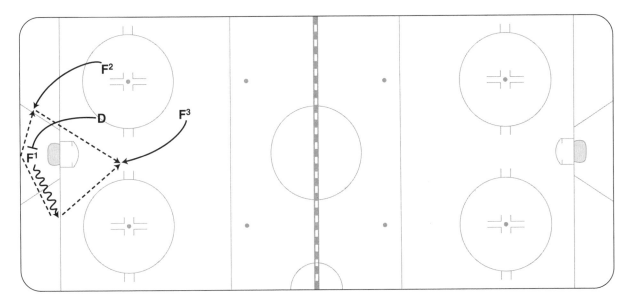

Figure 4.4   Options for a player being flushed from behind the net.

first is that players in high-percentage scoring areas may be left open. The second option is for the player with the puck to reverse the flow and create some back-door deception. When flushed out, the player with the puck angles the puck (similar the half-boards cycle) to a teammate filling this flushed-out position. Defenders who were focused on the player being flushed out must now divert their attention back toward the other side of the net. This refocus often opens up back-door or back-side plays.

Activating Defense in the Offensive Zone

As with other aspects of offensive play, coaches have to decide how comfortable they are with getting their Ds involved in the offense. Basically, they need to determine how much risk they want to take. If the offensive team has quality puck possession, allowing the defense to move in offensively presents little risk. You have to teach your players to make good decisions with the puck and trust that they will make a safe play rather than a dangerous play. The key rules for defensemen that will help minimize risk are as follows:

1. Only one D at a time goes deep into the offensive zone.
2. Ds must read the time of the game and the score; they should be more cautious when moving in offensively late in periods or when their team has the lead.
3. The forwards must have quality puck possession for the defense to activate.
4. When a D moves in, if a pass is not made, he does not hang out but gets back to the blue line quickly.

■ SCISSOR CYCLE

Deception and speed are key offensive weapons to increase offense in our game. When teams can combine these two weapons in our structure, our offensive numbers increase. One play that combines these two tactics is what coaches call the scissor cycle (figure 4.5). The scissor cycle can happen anywhere in the offensive zone, but it may be most effective when F1 generates behind the net speed skating hard toward the blue line. F2 (defenseman or forward) starts near the boards and backs up looking for a one-timer pass, while F3 uses across the blue line speed to slide down the boards to receive a short shuttle or drop pass. Obviously, if F1 can fake a pass to F2 just before dropping the puck to F3, the execution is enhanced by this deception.

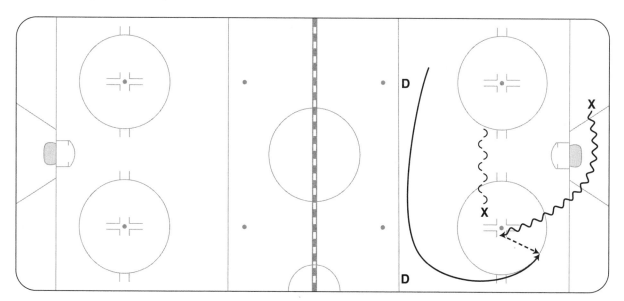

Figure 4.5   The scissor cycle.

Stretching the Zone: Low–High Plays

With many teams playing a collapsing defensive style (one in which all five defenders play low in the offensive zone), penetrating the net area in the attacking zone is often difficult without using low–high plays. Low–high plays spread out the defense and create opportunities to get the puck to scoring areas with more time and space. This strategy must be identified before a game as part of the game plan.

Offensive players with the puck make a quick pass to the point (F1 to D1) when they get the puck low or possibly recover a loose rebound in the corner (figure 4.6). D1 can now make a decision to shoot, move the puck to D2, or pass back to one of the forwards. Having the puck move from down low to the blue line creates a gap in the defensive alignment because the defensive wingers try to rush to their point coverage, leaving space between them and their defense. When all five defensive players are down low, the scoring area is crowded; getting the defensive wingers to move out high creates more space in the slot. Each time defenders scramble to defend the high blue line area, offensive players have an opportunity to find more time and space to create better offensive chances low. In addition, the shot from the point, through traffic, is still a primary option to create scoring chances.

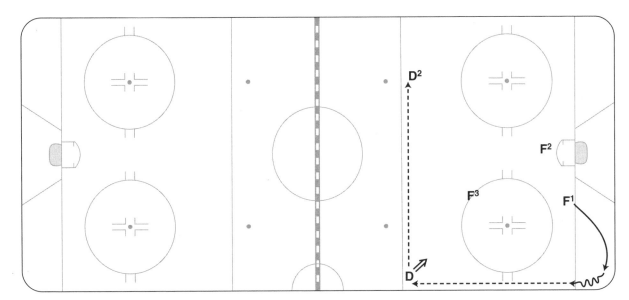

Figure 4.6 Stretching the zone.

Attack Zone Plays

This section describes special plays made in the offensive zone using an active defense. The plays are all effective and provide a variety of options.

■ STRONG-SIDE SLIDE

D1 reads that F1 is cycling out of the corner, so he slides down the boards and receives an exchange pass from F1. The exchange is like a handoff in football; the puck carrier protects the puck and gives it to D1. D1 now has the option of driving the net with the puck or cutting behind the net with possession and looking for a passing option (figure 4.7). F1 should cycle out high and remain in a defensive position until D1 recovers.

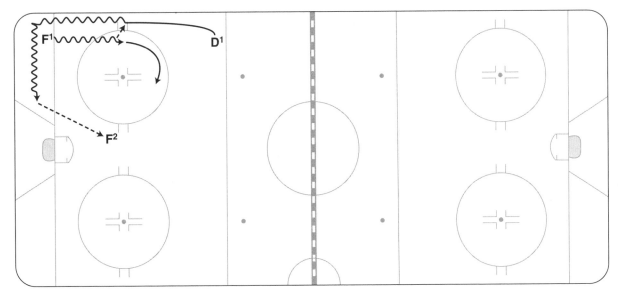

Figure 4.7   Strong-side slide play.

■ MIDSEAM PENETRATION

When D1 sees the defensive team overplaying the boards, he should slide into mid-ice and down through the slot toward the net. F1 should use deception by looking as if he will pass to the point and then making a quick pass to D1, who is moving through the middle of the slot. D1 may have an opportunity to shoot quickly or move in deeper (figure 4.8). Again, F1 should move out to a higher defensive position after the pass in case of a turnover.

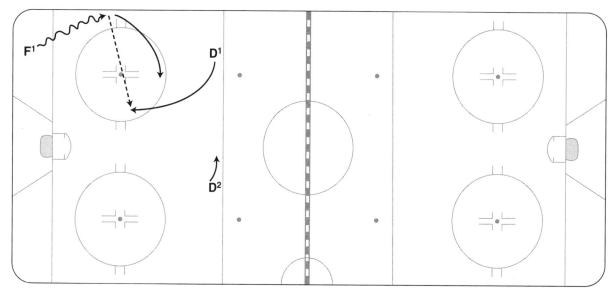

Figure 4.8   D1 jumps into the midseam.

■ BACK-SIDE SLIDE

When the offensive player (F1) has the puck and D2 reads that the defensive team is over-playing one side of the ice, D2 should quickly move down the back side and be ready for the pass. F1 tries to find an open seam to thread the pass through to the wide side. If D2 doesn't get the pass when moving in, he should get out immediately. Again, this play should be made quickly and with deception so that attention is not drawn to the defenseman moving in. This play is riskier because of the length of the pass and the number of players in the area, but if D2 gets the pass clean he will have a great scoring chance (figure 4.9).

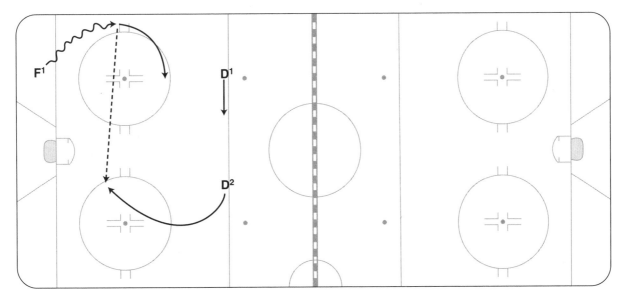

Figure 4.9   Back-side slide option with D2.

Chapter 5
Power Plays

When developing the power play, the coach must go through several steps including selecting a formation, describing the skills necessary for each position, slotting players into positions, developing drills to practice the skills, and finally allowing players to offer input as they mature and possibly select their own options within the framework. Most coaches go through these steps before the season starts after they know the makeup of the team. As a coach, you should follow these steps and review them from time to time as your lineup changes or when you are looking for improvements.

1. **Select a formation.** We will discuss three formations in this chapter. Identify which formation is suited for the abilities of the players available to you. Certain players are more suited to execute one formation better than another. The differentiating factor is usually the skill level and how good they are at passing, seeing the ice, and shooting off the pass.

2. **Describe skills necessary for each position.** Make a list of all the skills needed to play each position in the formation selected. Keep this list when working on the power play in practice. You can also use it to decide which players in your lineup are best suited to play each position. For example, the following six skills are critical for defensemen on the power play: deception, walking the blue line on the forehand and backhand, shooting, one-timing the puck, seeing the opening and making a pass through the box, and skating into the open seam at the right time. Under the section on zone setup, you will find the skills listed for each player. This list should help you decide which players are best suited for a particular position.

3. **Slot players into the positions.** Decide based on the skills required where each player should play in the system. On the power play some interchange will occur, but generally each player will become proficient in one of the five positions. One of the harder positions to play is the front of the net. You would like someone with size who also has good hands to corral a rebound or quickly release a shot off the pass. This player cannot be afraid of being hit with the puck and needs to have a touch for deflecting and redirecting pucks.

4. **Develop or select drills to practice skills.** Develop a bank of drills to work on the skills of the chosen power-play alignment and the breakout options. Sometimes the power-play breakout drills can be included with regular breakout practice. When developing in-zone skills, start with no resistance and progress to working against penalty killers. Players of all ages need to focus for the first month or so on constant repetitions with no resistance to get their puck movement and timing down before progressing to resistance. If penalty killers are introduced too early in practice situations, frustration is likely the result.

5. **Allow players freedom to choose the right options.** Much like a quarterback in football, one or two players on the power play should take the lead and pick the best available play or shot. As you will see in the specific alignments, there are five or six set plays to choose from. Having set options is better than allowing the power play to freelance. After the players become familiar with the alignments and have practiced them enough, the options will become instinctive. Let the power-play group watch video on a regular basis so that they become familiar with the options that arise with various penalty-kill alignments and pressure.

6. **Repeat for specific situations.** All the previous steps must be repeated for five-on-three and four-on-three situations.

When developing and monitoring the power play, coaches should remember that small details create a successful power play.

O **Outwork the penalty-killing unit.** The tendency of players on the power play is to rest in their manpower advantage. Strong discipline and intense practice is needed to train your power play to outwork their penalty-kill opponents.

O **Encourage your team to gain momentum** by getting scoring chances and shots. At all levels the best power-play units score on only 2 out of every 10 power plays, but your team should create momentum on every power play.

O **Players should look confident and never show dejection or defeat.** Body language is important in sport. Your team should not give any signs that they don't think they can score. They should leave the ice with the attitude that they didn't score this time but will definitely score next time.

O **Have two units with two looks.** Confuse the other team's penalty-killing units by having a different setup for each of your units.

○ **Win the draw!** Face-offs are key on special teams. If the other team clears the puck, the power-play unit will need 15 to 20 seconds to get set up again in the zone.

○ **Try to give other players on your team an opportunity to go on the power play**—doing this will do wonders for their confidence. Make sure in practice that all players work on power-play skills.

Power-Play Breakouts

Discussed here are five breakout options and two neutral zone regroup options. All breakouts are diagrammed with D1 starting behind the net, but at times D1 will pick up the puck and look to skate or advance it quickly, depending on the penalty-kill pressure and forecheck alignment. Lack of up-ice pressure or a change of penalty killers is a cue for D1 to turn up ice quickly. In other situations the power-play unit starts from behind the net and comes up as a coordinated unit. To execute the plays perfectly and efficiently, teams should have only one breakout for each unit or use the same breakout for both.

■ SINGLE SWING

D1 gets the puck behind the net (figure 5.1). D2 swings in one corner, and F1 swings in the other. F2 waits at the near blue line, and F3 is at the far blue line. As D1 begins to advance up the ice, F2 and F3 start to move across the ice. Both players look to get open early. Options for D1 are to pass to F1 with support from F2, pass to D2 with support from F3, pass to F2 or F3 early (may use a long bank pass to F3), or skate the puck and rim it to either side.

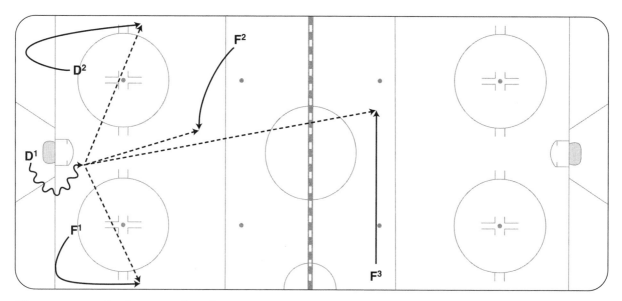

Figure 5.1   Single swing breakout.

■ DOUBLE LATE

Teams at the highest level of hockey tend to use late-speed breakouts, and the double late is one of the best. D1 carries the puck from behind the net directly up the ice. D2 or a forward and a second forward swing deep and late. D1 wants to skate hard at the penalty kill forwards and then immediately drop the puck back to his backhand-side late player. The double late creates the lateral option for the late player now carrying the puck to continue with the puck or to pass to the second late forward. Second-speed or late-speed breakouts are very effective if your team desires to enter the offensive zone with possession of the puck (figure 5.2).

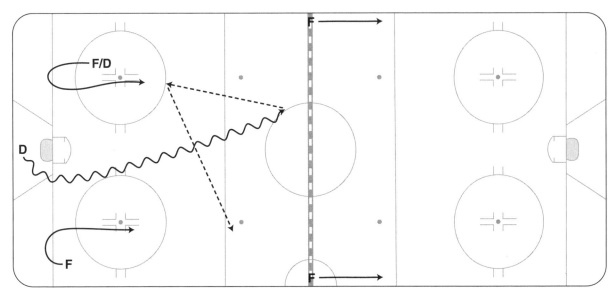

Figure 5.2   Double late breakout.

■ DALLAS CUT

D1 stops behind the net with the puck (figure 5.3). D2 swings in one corner. F1 and F2 swing in the other, with F1 slightly ahead. F3 stretches. The primary option and one that sometimes can result in a breakaway is for D1 to pass to F2 on the inside angle, trying to split the seam between the defenders. This pass is effective because when D1 fakes a pass to F1 wide, the opposition defense freezes and a quick pass to F2 on the inside allows F2 to split the seam with speed. D1 also has the option of passing to F1, who carries the puck in with support from F2. D1 can also pass to D2, who gets support from F3; pass to F3 early if uncovered; or rim the puck to F1 or F2 (figure 5.3).

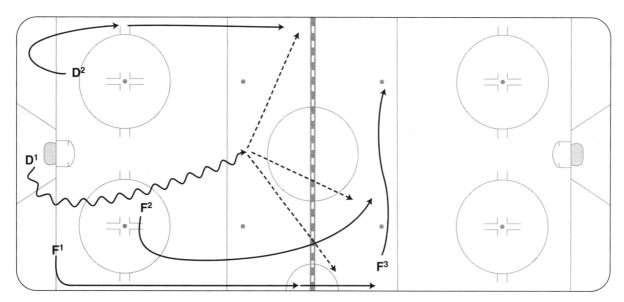

Figure 5.3   Dallas cut breakout.

■ SLINGSHOT

Speed is a key weapon to allow power plays to enter the offensive zone with possession of the puck. Many top power plays in today's game create ways to increase their team speed while at the same time slowing down their penalty-kill opposition. The slingshot breakout is one of these plays.

As is common with many power-play breakouts, D1 carries the puck up the middle of the ice. D2 and F1 time their speed to stay almost lateral with D1. D1 times his pass to F1 who relays (almost a lateral drop) the puck to F2, who is now picking up speed in the opposite direction. As with many power-play breakouts, the timing of each player is critical and must be practiced often. As you can see by viewing the diagram, the slingshot breakout creates amazing second speed or under speed and often allows a clean entry through a penalty kill, who at this point are close to standing still (see figure 5.4).

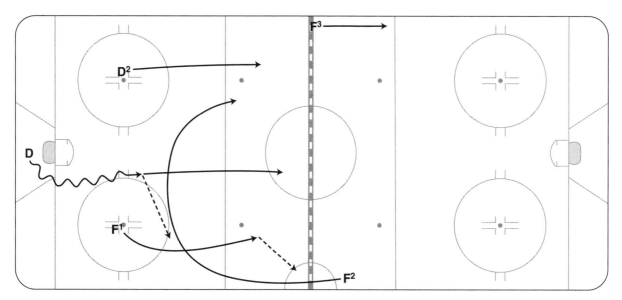

Figure 5.4   Effective sling shot breakout with F2 moving back.

■ CANUCK CENTER-LANE OPTION

D1 starts with the puck (figure 5.5). F1 and D2 swing to opposite sides. F2 swings slightly higher on the same side as F1 and looks to get the puck in the middle of the ice. F2 carries the puck through the middle and uses F1 or D2 for support. F3 clears a lane for F2 by stretching across the far blue line. F2 tries to enter the zone with possession and then lays the puck to the outside after defenders are drawn to him.

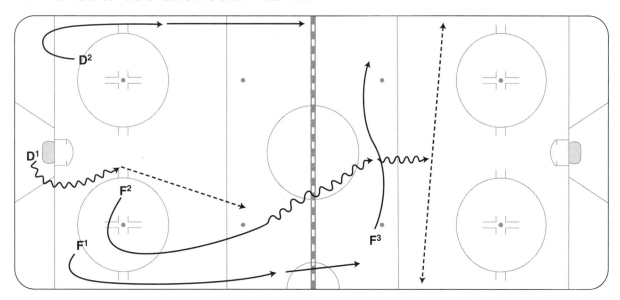

Figure 5.5 Canuck center lane breakout.

■ FIVE BACK

All players come back to the puck. When the last player is back, all five players start to advance up ice together (figure 5.6). F2 and F3 take the inside lanes, while F1 and D2 move up ice along the boards. D1 has the option to pass to the inside players (F2 and F3) or to the outside lanes (F1 and D2). D1 tries to draw the penalty killers into the middle and then dish the puck to speed wide. If D1 skates the puck to center, he can continue into the zone or rim the puck to either side.

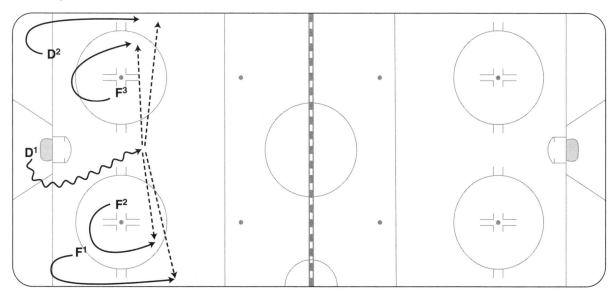

Figure 5.6 All five players come back on this breakout.

■ FOUR CORNERS

This power-play breakout alignment is a good way to show a different look to your opponent's penalty-kill forecheck. The three forwards and the defenseman not carrying the puck stand at all four corners where the blue lines connect with the boards (you will practice where your specific players line up.) As D1 (the puck carrier) skates with speed, all four players react and create north–south and east–west motion for the penalty-kill forecheck to respond to. The goal for the four-corner entry is to be able to skate through the middle to make a short pass to either forward entering with lateral speed (see figure 5.7).

The four-corner breakout is a powerful option that can be used to counter teams who send forecheckers hard and deep after the defenseman carrying the puck. One direct pass bypasses this aggressive forecheck and creates many options for the players now activating off their corners.

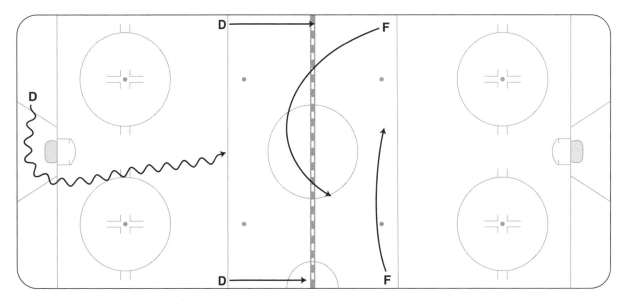

Figure 5.7   Four corner breakout.

■ DROP PASS

The key here is for the late forward to delay long enough to be an option after the defense carries the puck up over the blue line. D1 starts by skating up the middle as F2 and D2 move up the outside (figure 5.8). F3 stretches, and F1 comes late from deep in the zone behind the play. When D1 crosses the blue line, he should try to drag the first penalty killer to one side and then lay the puck over to the area where F1 is skating into. The penalty killers who have been backing up with the initial rush now have to slow down and adjust to F1. F1 has a lot of speed and should be able to weave his way into the zone. F2, F3, and D2 have to be careful not to go offside.

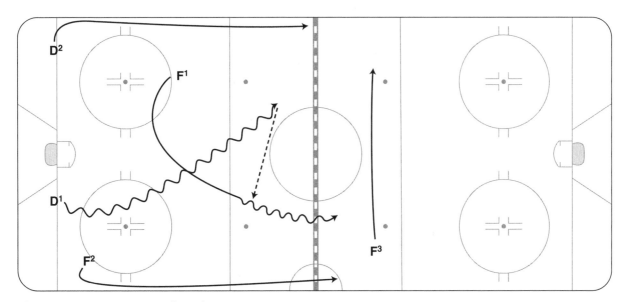

Figure 5.8 Drop pass breakout.

At times on the power play the offensive team doesn't have to go all the way back and break out from their own end. If the puck is in the neutral zone or just inside the blue line, going all the way back behind the net is often a waste of time. Have a plan to break out using half of the ice in a neutral zone counter. The following two plays are great options in this situation.

■ WINGER CROSS

In this option, D1 picks up the puck. F1 and F2 swing to opposite sides and build up speed (figure 5.9). F3 stretches, and D2 supports D1. D1 has the option to pass to F2 or F1 with speed on the outside; pass to F3, who may enter the zone or redirect the puck to F1 or F2; or skate the puck and rim it to F1 or F2.

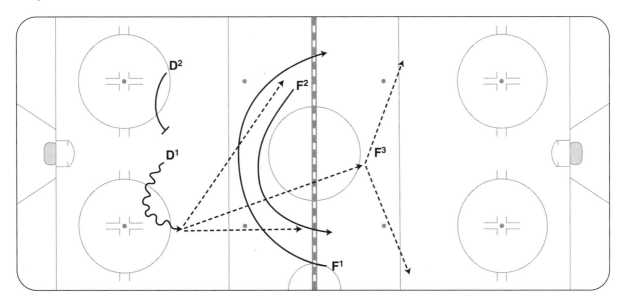

Figure 5.9 Neutral zone power play breakout with wingers crossing.

■ UP THE GUT

In this option, D2 takes the puck up the ice in a wide lane hoping to draw a defender outside (figure 5.10). As D2 advances, he looks to pass inside to F1, who comes from behind the play and moves with speed through the middle of the ice. F2 and F3 stretch. When the first penalty killer is drawn outside, the middle opens up for F1 to skate into. The second option is to use F2 or F3 on the stretch.

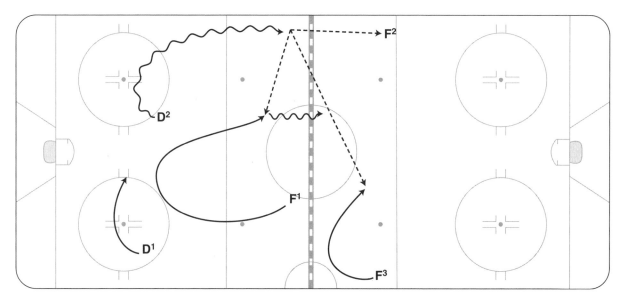

Figure 5.10   Up the gut neutral zone power play breakout.

Gaining and Maintaining Possession Off the Entry

When explaining breakout options to your team, you should discuss how the players set up after they are in the offensive zone. Where do they move the puck to get into the formations they have practiced? Many penalty-killing units focus on denying the setup and prepare various tactics to regain possession of the puck after the power-play unit is in the zone. Listed here are three ways to ensure that the players are able to set up after a dump-in or clean entry.

1. Reversing the puck. When under pressure as he enters the zone, F1 stops or delays and then reverses the puck back up the boards where he came from. This method is successful against teams whose strong-side forward comes down low on the entry (figure 5.11). D1 must get up to the offensive blue line quickly to be ready for this play.

2. Switching sides. As F1 enters the zone, he sees that all four penalty killers are on one side of the ice, so he immediately passes across the ice to F3. F1 will have to thread the puck through traffic, but it may be the only option to get immediate uncontested possession (figure 5.12).

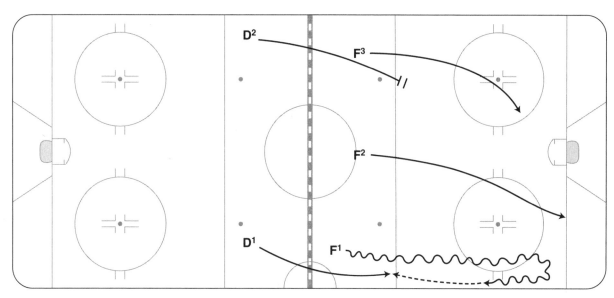

Figure 5.11 Reversing the puck on entry.

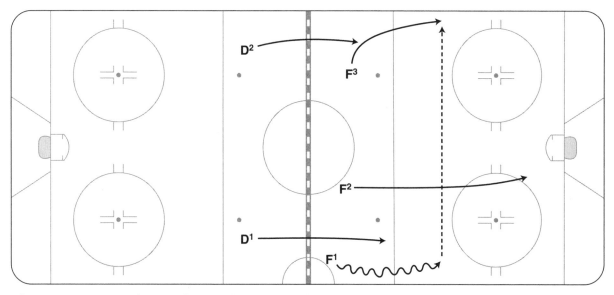

Figure 5.12 Switching sides on the power-play entry.

3. Recovering the dump-in. The key to recovering the dump-in is to get all three forwards quickly to the puck. After the puck is stopped and the forwards are in a battle for possession, F1, F2, or F3 should rim or bank the puck back to the blue line as soon as they get it on their stick. The defensemen should be ready at the corners of the blue line and expect the quick rim pass. The penalty-killing team will probably have three players in the corner for the battle, giving the power play time to set up (figure 5.13).

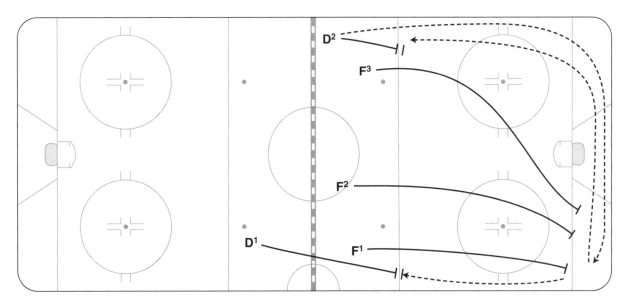

Figure 5.13   Recovering the dump-in.

Zone Setup

After the players gain possession, they can set up in the zone and use one of the following formations. This section discusses the options for three different power-play formations: the overload, 1-3-1, and split power play. Within each are the descriptions of the various plays and responsibilities of each player. As mentioned earlier, coaches can pick which option best suits their players and team. During the season you may change to another setup, but it does take a while to learn all the options and execute properly. Give the players time to get it right.

Overload Power Play

When using the overload power play, either side can be the strong side; left-hand shots quarterback from the half boards on the right side and right shots from the left side. This setup gives the player a shooting and passing advantage from that area. As the name implies, the setup is overloaded to the strong side by having four players on that half of the ice. In this setup, much like most power-play setups, net presence is critical for success. The net player must be in a screen position most of the time but also available to pop out into a scoring area. When setting up the overload and moving the puck, the team should try to twist the box around by having the strong-side D move quickly across the blue line and even go beyond the halfway point before passing back to the half boards or over to D2.

Half-Boards Player

The half-boards player is the key quarterback of this setup. D1 plays a secondary role. The half-boards player must slide up and down the boards, distribute the puck, and shoot from the outside, all while under pressure. He has to be calm and poised with the puck and quick to recognize where to move the puck. Penalty killers will force the half-boards player with either their D from down low or their forward from the top, so this player must be able to move with the pressure, protect the puck, and make a play.

Strong-Side Point Man

The strong-side defenseman is the other key player in this overload setup. He along with the half-boards player will have the puck the most and will be the ones to settle the play down and set up. He should keep his feet on the blue line to create space between himself and the penalty killers. This extra room will give him time to make decisions or step into a shot, while drawing out the penalty killers and creating seams in behind. This player needs to have a shooting mentality and always be a threat to shoot. The number one way to score and create chances on the power play is still to take a point shot with net traffic. Sometimes the shot can be a wrist shot, and other times the D should shoot hard. The penalty killers shouldn't know whether the D is going to shoot or pass; he should have good deception. When pressured, he should move the puck to the half-boards player or the back-side D, or make a quick, low play.

Low Walk Player

The low walk player should have his feet on the goal line and stay close to the net so that he can attack quickly and move in to screen the goaltender or get a rebound. If this player drifts too far to the outside, he cannot do either. The low walk player must be versatile and quick. At times he will switch with the half-boards player, usually when no option is available as the half-boards player drives the net. This tactic forces the penalty killers to adjust quickly and often creates passing options. Before the game, find out how the other team forces—will they pressure quickly with the low defenseman, or will they hold the front of the net? This information will help determine what option might be available and where the pressure will come from.

Net Man

The net player's main job is to screen the goaltender on all shots and then be ready to play rebounds. Although it sounds simple, standing in front of shots requires courage and deflecting those shots takes a lot of skill. When the puck is moved low, the net player should slide out to the low slot or back door (on the back post away from coverage) to wait for a pass. Either option is good, but it should be predetermined before the game so that the low player knows where to pass the puck. Sometimes the net player is so anxious to become available for a low play that he loses the screen position when players above him are ready to shoot. The screen is crucial because you want the opposing goaltender to have to work to see the puck. The idea is to make the goaltender's job tough.

Sliding Back-Side D

The back-side defenseman initially provides a release to get the puck away from pressure and supports the strong-side D when he is under pressure. He will be a threat to score because he is outside the vision of the penalty killers. He sometimes gets lost as the penalty killers focus on the overload side. The back-side defenseman should move up and down the far side of the ice, staying in line with the position of the puck. He can go down as far as the goal line and up as high as the blue line. If he recovers a loose puck on the far side, he should set up on the half boards and then briefly work the setup from there.

Zone Options for the Overload Power Play

The following are the options for the overload power play. All need to become automatic in practice if they are to be executed well in the game. Depending on the skill level of the players involved and on how the opposing penalty killers force, certain options will be more successful than others. Coaches should prepare the players for the resistance they may face from the penalty killers so that they know ahead of time what plays to concentrate on.

■ BACK-SIDE D SLIDE AND SHOOT

Move the puck around to D2, who slides down the back side and looks to shoot and score, shoot for a deflection, or pass across to F1 for a one-timer (figure 5.14). The play back to F1 is a more difficult play to execute because of the skill required to shoot off the pass. F1 should be wide and prepared to receive a pass around the top of the opposite circle.

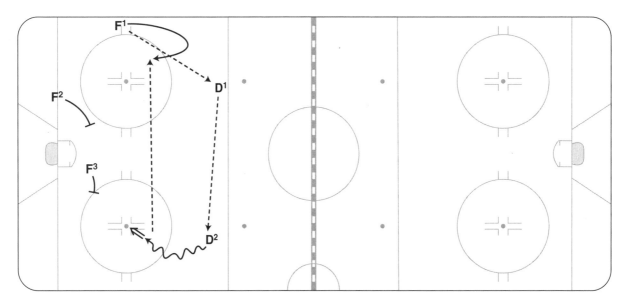

Figure 5.14 D2 decides to pass or shoot.

■ STRONG-SIDE D SHOT

Move the puck from F2 to F1 to D1. D1 slides across the blue line, looking to take a slapshot or wrist the puck through to the net (figure 5.15). F3 must be in a tight screen position. F2, F1, and D2 must be ready to converge on rebounds. D1 must fake the shot against teams that block and look to get the puck by the screen. Establishing a shot from this area on a consistent basis always results in the most power-play chances, but D1 must have deception along with a good shot.

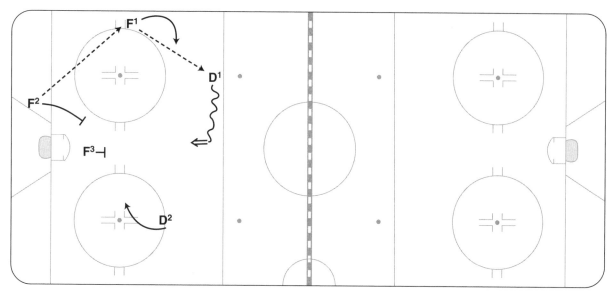

Figure 5.15   Strong-side D slides across the line.

■ HALF-BOARDS SHOT

F2 moves the puck up to F1, who passes to D1. D1 walks across the line, drawing a penalty killer with him (figure 5.16). D1 fakes a shot and passes back to F1. F1 should have followed D1 up the half boards, initially staying wide. After F1 receives the pass, he moves off the boards and shoots. F3 screens, while F2 and D2 converge for rebounds.

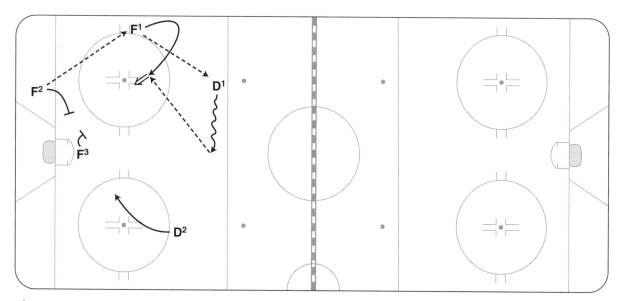

Figure 5.16   F1 rolls high and shoots off the pass.

■ LOW PLAY OPTION

F2 passes to F1, who passes to D1 (figure 5.17). D1 fakes a shot and passes back to F1, who rolls off the half boards, fakes a shot, and passes to F2. F2 now has the option of taking the puck to the net and shooting or taking the puck to the net and passing to F3 on the back side or to F3 in the slot area. The decision for F3 to be on the back door or in the slot depends on how the other team plays this situation. Teams should vary where F3 goes so that the opponent never knows where he is going to be. D2 should move opposite to F3 and move to the slot or back side. F2 also has the option on this low play to take the puck behind the net and pass out to F3 or back to F1 or D2.

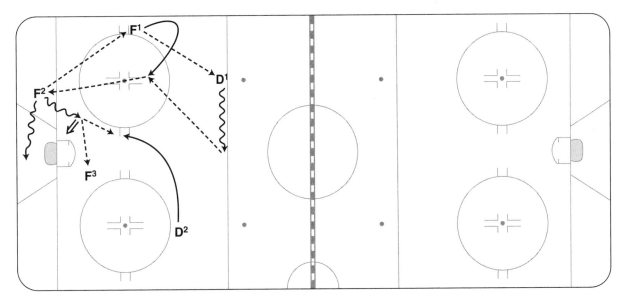

Figure 5.17   Using the low option.

■ HALF-BOARDS INTERCHANGE

After the players learn the previous options, adding some interchange will help make the penalty killers' job more difficult. Whenever F1 passes the puck to F2 and no immediate play results, they should get in the habit of switching positions. F1 passes to F2 and drives the net, looking to get the puck back (which he may). If there is no play, F2 cycles up the boards and starts to look for new options. F1 replaces F2 low (figure 5.18).

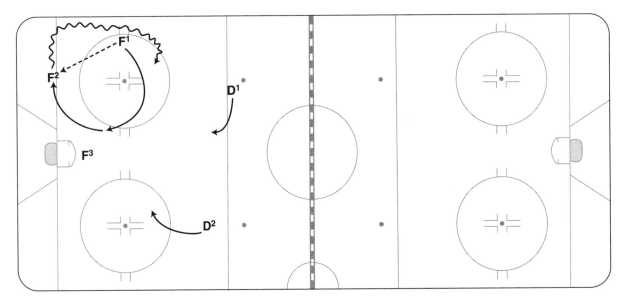

Figure 5.18   Half-boards exchange option.

■ SLIDING D INTERCHANGE

This more complicated maneuver adds a lot of confusion to the penalty killers' alignment. After D1 slides along the blue line and passes back to F1 (figure 5.19), he may move to the net (this should be predetermined). As D1 goes to the net, F3 slides out to the side and D2 moves up top on the blue line. F1 now makes a quick play as this is happening. F1 may use any of the previous options because the alignment is the same. D1 holds a strong position at the net and remains there until a goal is scored or the puck is cleared.

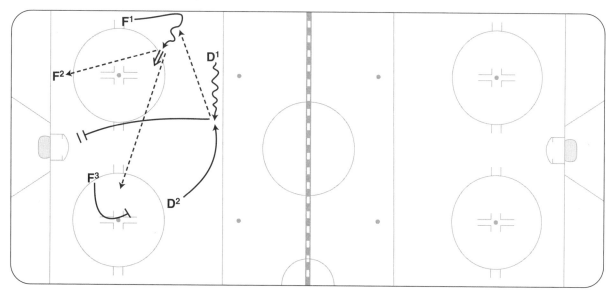

Figure 5.19   D1 creates confusion by going to the net.

1-3-1 Power Play

The 1-3-1 power play is one of the newer power-play formations that several teams use today. Essentially, there are two strong sides, and the puck can be controlled on either half boards. Switching sides is easy, either up top or behind the net to settle the puck out when under pressure or to create chances. Again, net presence is critical. The key to success with this formation is for the top three players to focus on shooting or one-timing the puck. This power play is difficult for pressure penalty-killing units to defend because of the side-to-side options.

Right and Left Side Half-Boards Players

Set up with the right shot on the left boards and the left shot on the right. These two players are definitely the quarterbacks. Both must be a threat to shoot or fake the shot and pass while also being calm under pressure. They should work the puck up to the high D as the number one option and not force plays through the box—often the play through the box will open up after recovering a rebound.

Mid-Ice Point Man

An important strategy for this defenseman is to keep his feet on the blue line to allow more room to make a play or step into a shot. He slides along the line with deception while looking to find an open lane to the net. He quickly works the puck from left to right if the shot isn't there and then looks to shoot again. Wrist shots to the net are also good, but if a chance for a slapshot develops, he should use it. In the 1-3-1 setup, the puck should revolve around this player.

Slot Player

This player can be a defenseman who slides in or a forward who plays defense and then moves into the slot area. He moves into this position after the puck is under control. Depending on whether this player is a right or left shot, from one side he must be ready for a quick release shot and from the other side a shot pass. The shot pass is a play in which the outside players shoot to the stick of the slot player for a redirect on the net. The slot player should move around in the space to distract the penalty killers. This player must be ready to support both half-boards players when they are in trouble.

Net Man

The net man, as the name indicates, plays the net area unless support is needed to settle the puck out. He may release to the strong side for a low pass and the potential to make a quick inside play. This strategy is effective, but the player has to read whether the high players are shooting or whether they need a low option. The net man should stay active and get into shooting lanes at the right time.

Zone Options for the 1-3-1 Power Play

The following four options are used for the 1-3-1 power play. As with the overload power play, all need to become automatic in practice if they are to be executed well in the game. Depending on the skill level of the players involved and on how the opposing penalty killers force, certain options will be more successful than others. Coaches should prepare the players for the resistance they may face from the penalty killers so that they know ahead of time what plays to concentrate on. Note that all options may be run from either side.

■ POINT SHOT

F1 passes to D1. D1 passes to F2, who passes back to D1 for a shot (figure 5.20). This shot may be a one-timer depending on what shot the defenseman is. All players should fake a shot before passing. F3 keeps a tight screen. D2, F1, and F2 converge on the rebound.

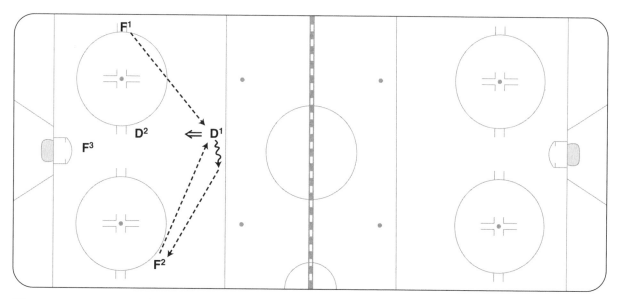

Figure 5.20 Point shot on the 1-3-1 power play.

■ HALF-BOARDS SHOT OR CROSS-ICE PASS

F1 passes to D1 (figure 5.21). D1 passes to F2, who has the option of shooting or passing to F1. At several times during the power play, the cross-ice seam will be available. Remember that this option is more difficult to execute because of the skill level required to thread the pass across ice and one-time the puck. Good deception from F2 will create an open lane to F1. F3 keeps a tight screen. D2, F1, and F2 converge on the rebound.

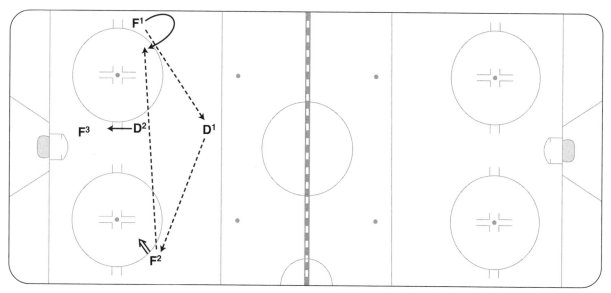

Figure 5.21 1-3-1 power play half-boards option.

■ INSIDE PLAY

F1 passes to D1, who passes to F2 (figure 5.22). F2 fakes the shot and passes inside to D2 for a one-timer or redirect play. This inside play can be made from either side. D2 must be ready for a pass at all times. F3 keeps a tight screen. F1 and F2 converge on the rebound. Depending on which shot D2 is, this may be on opportunity for a quick release shot or shot pass deflection.

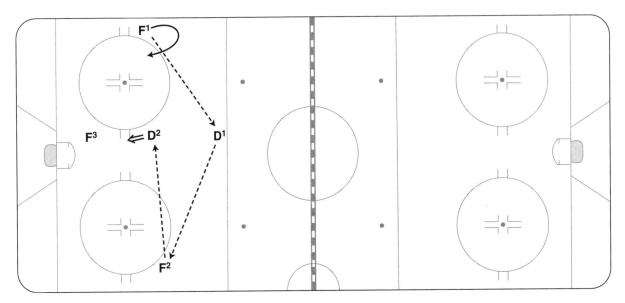

Figure 5.22   Using the slot player.

■ LOW-RELEASE PLAY

F1 passes to D1 (figure 5.23). D1 passes to F2. F3 releases from the net (in this case he would be a left shot). F2 passes to F3. F3 makes an inside play to D2 or a back-side play to F1. F3 could also take the puck to the net. This option is tough to defend against.

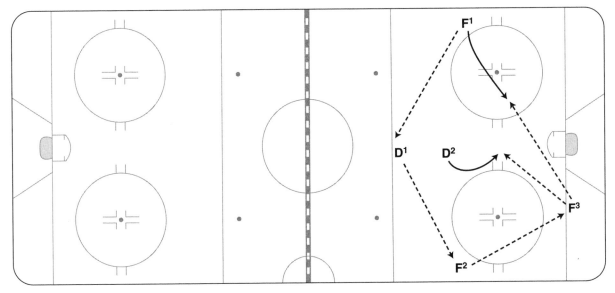

Figure 5.23   Low play on the 1-3-1 power play.

Split Power Play

The third power-play option in this section is the split power play. With two strong sides, it has more of a spread look to it, and as with the 1-3-1, switching sides is easy, either up top or behind the net. Again, net presence is critical. The two defensemen up top must be prepared to shoot. When this happens, they will find that seams will open up for the forwards down low. This power play is also difficult for pressure penalty-killing units because of the side-to-side options. The split power play can easily be twisted into an overload setup and back again.

Two Blue Line Defensemen

The two defensemen on the blue line need to keep their feet on the line to create more space between them and the penalty killers. They should be about dot-width apart. After the puck is moved up top, a quick relay from D to D will spread out the penalty killers. The players work the puck from left to right while looking to shoot. The defensemen may slide along the line with deception to find an open lane to the net. If sufficient time or space isn't available, wrist shots to the net are also good.

Right and Left Side Half-Boards Players

These players set up and operate in a similar way to the setup for the 1-3-1 power play. The left shot is on the right boards, and the right shot is on the left boards. Both players should be a threat to shoot or fake the shot and pass. They need to stay calm under pressure. The number one option should be to work the puck up to the high Ds, especially when being pressured low. They should not force plays through the box—often the play through the box will open up after recovering a rebound.

Net Man

With most of these power-play setups, the net man's job description doesn't change much. This player should stay at the net unless support is needed to settle the puck out, but he may release to either side for a low pass. He should stay active and get into shooting lanes at the right time. He supports the half-boards players when they are in trouble and under pressure by sliding out to the side of the net. To settle the puck out when pressured down low, he simply relays the puck behind the net to the opposite half-boards player.

Zone Options for the Split Power Play

The following are the options for the split power play. Practice all options so that the players can do them automatically. Then in a game, they will be able to pick the best option depending on how the penalty killers react to the puck movement and shots. Coaches should prepare the team for the resistance they may face from the penalty killers so that they know ahead of time what plays to concentrate on. Note that all options may be run from either side.

■ D-TO-D POINT SHOT

F1 passes to D1, who passes to D2 (figure 5.24). D2 slides down a step for a shot. This shot may be a one-timer depending on what shot the defenseman is. F3 keeps a tight screen on the goaltender. F1 and F2 converge on the rebound. Usually if the shot is low, the goaltender will have trouble keeping the rebound from going to one of the side players, F1 or F2.

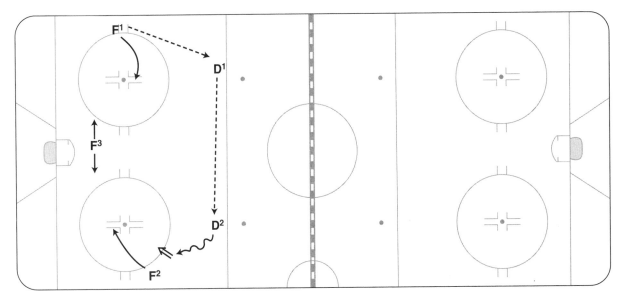

Figure 5.24   Split power play point shot.

■ D-TO-D AND BACK

F1 passes to D1, who passes to D2 (figure 5.25). D2 slides down a step for a fake shot. D2 passes back to D1 in mid-ice for a shot. This shot may be a one-timer depending on what shot the defenseman is. F3 keeps a tight screen. F1 and F2 converge on the rebound.

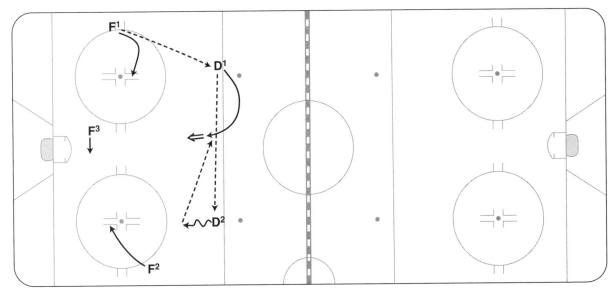

Figure 5.25   D2 sets up D1 for a one timer.

■ D-TO-D CROSS-SEAM PASS

F1 passes to D1, who passes to D2 (figure 5.26). D2 slides down a step for a fake shot. D2 passes to F1 for a one-timer or quick-release shot. F3 keeps a tight screen. F2 converges on the rebound.

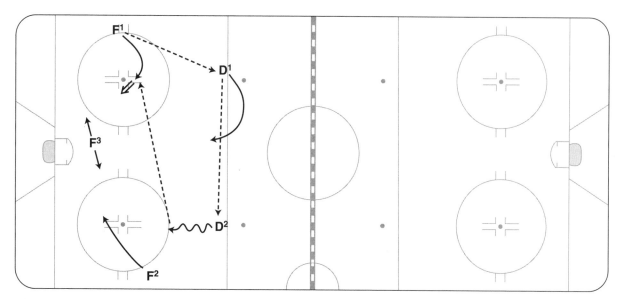

Figure 5.26   Cross seam pass option on the split power play.

■ DOUBLE-SEAM PASS

F1 passes to D1, who passes to D2 (figure 5.27). D2 slides down a step for a fake shot. D2 passes to F1, who fakes the shot and passes cross-ice to F2 for a one-timer or quick-release shot. F3 keeps a tight screen. F1 converges on the rebound.

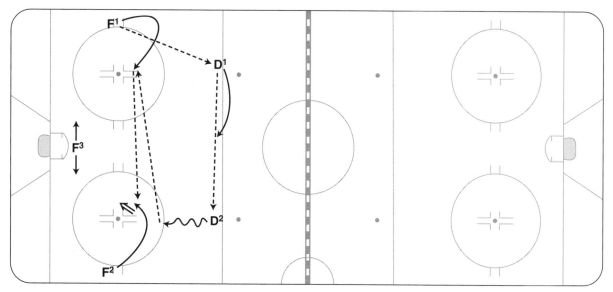

Figure 5.27   Using the double seam pass.

■ LOW-RELEASE PLAY

F1 passes to D1, who passes to D2. D2 slides down a step and passes back to D1 in mid-ice (figure 5.28). D1 fakes a shot and passes to F1. F1 fakes a shot and passes low to F3 at the side of the net. F3 takes the puck to the net or passes to F2 on the back door.

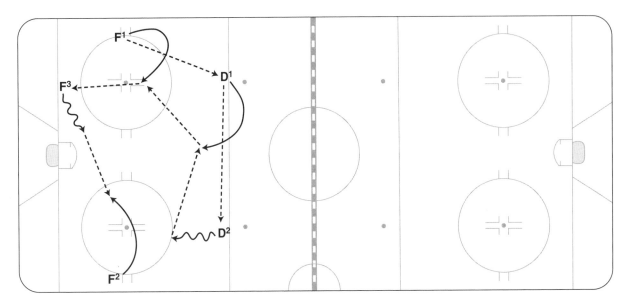

Figure 5.28 Low release option on the split power play.

Five-on-Three Power Play

The five-on-three opportunity is often a turning point in the game because unlike other power-play opportunities, which operate at a 20 percent success rate, a five on three should result in a goal 50 percent of the time. Most fans expect a goal every time, but the thing to remember with the five on three is that you rarely get a full two minutes. Identified here are three options to use—the goal-line 2-3, the motion 2-3, and the umbrella. Pick the one you like best and work on it with your team. Each option has enough plays to have variety, but remember that you want to score and may not have a lot of time, so get your players to execute well.

■ GOAL-LINE 2-3

This 2-3 power-play setup has a number of options. F1 should be a right shot, and F2 a left shot. Some coaches like D1 and D2 to play their regular sides, and others like D1 and D2 to be the same shot. Here are the options with D1 and D2 being left shots: D1 to D2 to F2 and a quick low pass across to F1 (figure 5.29*a*, number 1); D1 to D2 to F2 and a pass to F3 in the slot (figure 5.29*a*, number 2); F1 to D1 to D2 for a one-timer shot (figure 5.29*b*, number 3); or a direct pass from F1 to D2 for a one-timer (figure 5.29*b*, number 4).

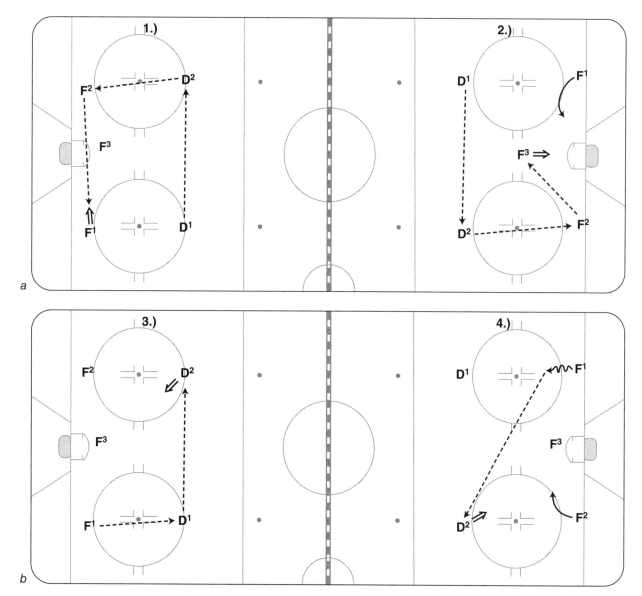

Figure 5.29   Five on three power play options.

■ MOTION 2-3

This setup is the same as the previous one, but it adds motion to create confusion. Penalty killers become so good at staying in lanes that some movement might be needed. D1 and D2 are both left shots in these two options:

1. F1 to D1 to D2. After faking a shot, D2 slides flat across the ice (figure 5.30, number 1). D1 moves behind D2. D2 can shoot, pass down to F1 or F2 for a quick shot, or pass back to D1 for a one-timer.

2. F1 to D1 and back to F1 (figure 5.30, number 2). D1 skates to the front of the net. D2 slides across, and F2 moves up high. F1 can pass to D2 or F2 for a one-timer, to F3 on the back side, or to D1 sliding in.

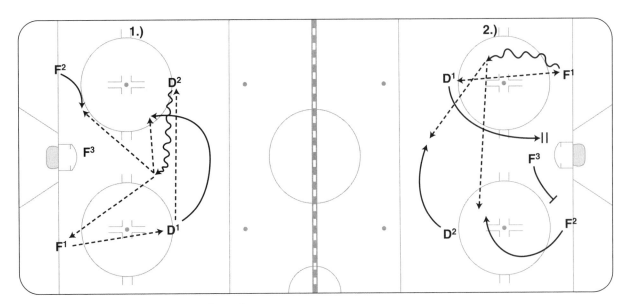

Figure 5.30   Motion 2-3 look and options.

■ UMBRELLA

For this example, D1 is a right shot, D2 is a left shot, and F1 is a right shot. Both low players (F2 and F3) slide in and out as a screen and low pass option. Options on the umbrella setup include the following: F1 to D1 to D2 for a one-timer (figure 5.31a, number 1); F1 to D1 to D2 and back to F1 for a one-timer (figure 5.31a, number 2); F1 to D1 to D2 and back to D1 for a one-timer (figure 5.31b, number 3); or F1 to D1 to D2 and then low to F2, who can pass to F3 or back to D1 (figure 5.31b, number 4).

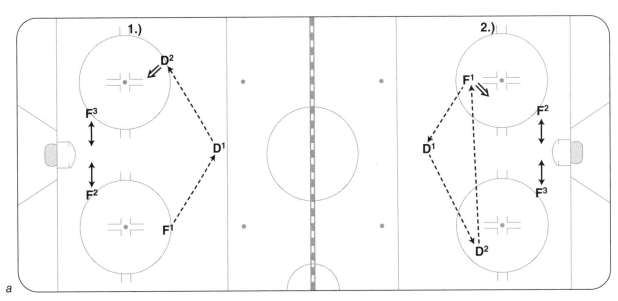

a

Figure 5.31a   Umbrella five on three setup.

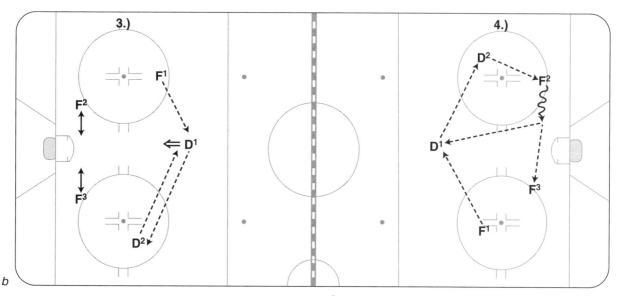

Figure 5.31b   Umbrella five on three plays.

■ BEHIND NET ROLL

Wayne Gretzky was the master of the behind the net power-play movement. F1 posts behind the net with the puck and then skates laterally toward his backhand side to create movement for the opponent penalty killers to react to. When F1 skates back in the opposite direction behind the net on his forehand side preparing to set up a one-timer pass, this movement activates the play. F2 on the left of the net drives toward the front of the net, blocking off the defending D's pathway. The up-top Ds switch positions, rolling into a perfect strong-side one-timer shooting position for D2 (see figure 5.32).

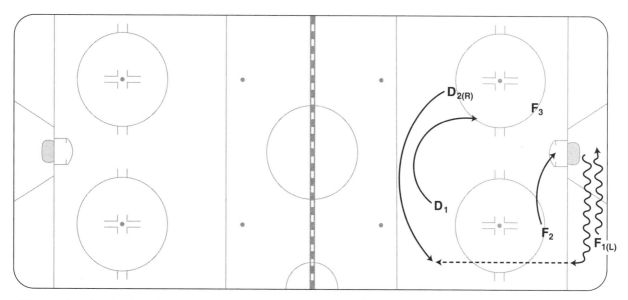

Figure 5.32   Using the back of the net to open up shots.

■ HIGH ROLL

Five-on-three setups often have players standing still and being predictable. Every team defending a five on three wants to allow only outside shots. This high roll option is developed to create movement and generate shots from the middle of the ice. The high roll can start with a box plus one setup with both Ds and the lower Fs positioned for a strong-side shot. The front net forward must be flat and checking his shoulder to stay flat in front of the goalie, reducing his sightlines. Both defensemen pass the puck laterally. After the right-handed D passes to the left-handed D, the right-handed D drives toward the net and then circles back up into a lateral shooting position. As the D drives toward the net, the low forward to the right of the net circles high into the middle of the ice, creating an opportunity for a middle-ice one-timer or as the setup passer to create shots for the two defensemen (see figure 5.33).

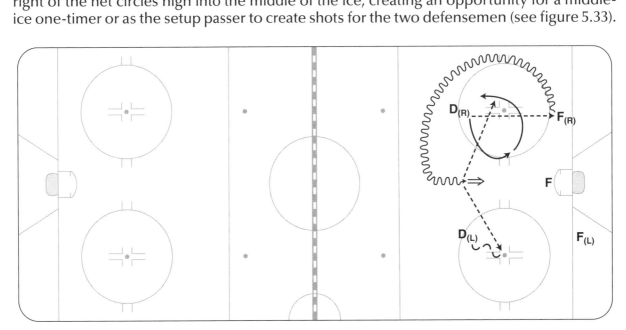

Figure 5.33   High roll play.

Four-on-Three Power Play

The four-on-three power play is the least common of the man-advantage opportunities that occur in a game. The two basic setups are the box and the umbrella. The umbrella is more suited for teams that have a big one-timer shooter up top; the box is better for teams that can make quick, low plays when the shot from the point is taken away.

■ BOX

When using this setup, you need to make sure that one of the low players is in a screen position when D1 or D2 shoots. Both forwards and both Ds should be opposite shots. D1 passes to D2, who passes to F1. F1 passes across to F2 for a quick shot (figure 5.34, number 1). D1 and D2 can also pass the puck back and forth, looking for a one-timer (figure 5.34, number 2). Often the penalty killers will overplay the one-timer shots up top and leave a quick two on one low for the forwards.

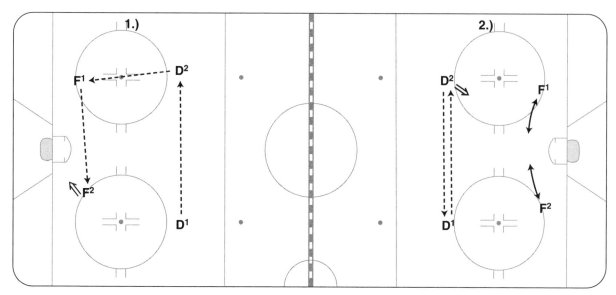

Figure 5.34   Box four on three plays.

■ UMBRELLA

For this example, D1 is a left shot, D2 is a left shot, and F1 is a right shot. F2 screens in front. Options for the umbrella setup are similar to the five-on-three setup; D1, D2, and F1 are looking to get a quick one-timer shot. They may move around slightly but generally stay in the high triangle setup. Here are the options: F1 to D1 to D2 for a one-timer (figure 5.35a, number 1); F1 to D1 to D2 and back to F1 for a one-timer (figure 5.35a, number 2); F1 to D1 to D2 and back to D1 for a one-timer (figure 5.35b, number 3); or F1 to D1 to D2 and then low to F2, who can pass to D1 or across to F1 (figure 5.35b, number 4).

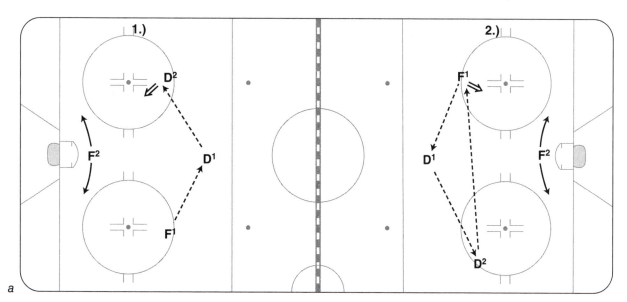

a

Figure 5.35a   Umbrella three on three options.

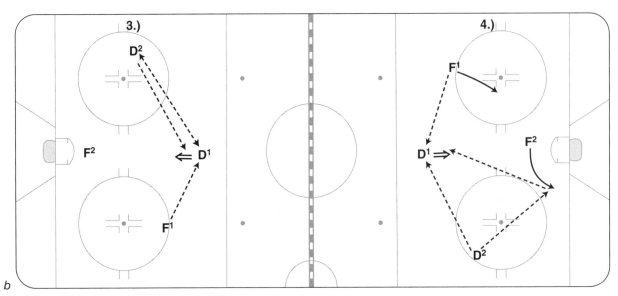

b

Figure 5.35*b* Umbrella three on three options and plays.

■ PHILLY SLIDE

Movement is key to scoring on power plays, especially on a four on three. D2 activates the movement by passing down to F1. After D2 makes this pass, he skates hard down the middle of the ice, circles up, and posts into a strong shooting position. F1 skates outside and toward the blue line with two strong passing options to D2 or D1, who has now rolled into the middle ice for a one-time shot. F2 times his low movement to the front of the net (see figure 5.36).

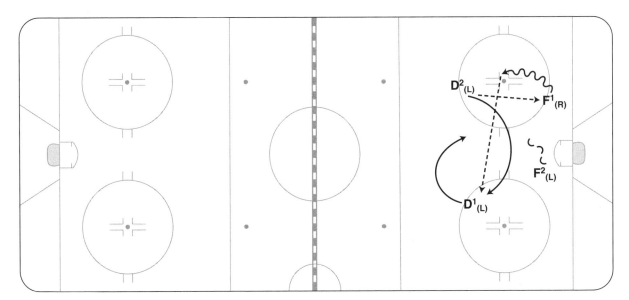

Figure 5.36   Philly slide play.

Part II

Defensive Play for Forwards and Defensemen

Chapter 6
Forechecking

A team applies forechecking pressure in three situations. The most common situation occurs when a team dumps or chips the puck in from the neutral zone and then tries to retrieve it while the opponent tries to break out. The second scenario develops when the offensive team takes a shot that creates a rebound. They then forecheck to get the puck back. The final forechecking situation occurs off a turnover. When the offensive team turns the puck over, they need to apply forechecking pressure to get the puck back. Essentially, there are six keys to successful forechecking pressure:

1. F1 (the first forechecker in) must get in quickly and establish an angle when pursuing the puck carrier. This action will limit the options for the breakout team. Taking away time and space from the breakout team forces hurried plays and mistakes. The quicker that F1 responds to the puck, the less time the offensive team will have to make a play. Coaches often stress the hit, but we believe that the first priority for F1 should be to put a stick on the puck, preferably while separating the puck carrier from the puck by using his body.

2. After the puck is moved, F1 must recover to a high position above the puck while F2 or F3 responds to pressure the pass. If F1 follows through on the hit, he must get off the check right away and move above the circles while observing where the puck is and what is happening.

3. He continues to pressure and recover, pressure and recover until the puck is turned over. The response of the second and third player is key to keeping heat on the opposition and forcing a turnover.

4. If the defensemen are going to pinch (pressure down the boards), they have to get to the puck before it is under control. Pinching defense must read the play and anticipate when the pass is being made to the winger on the boards. One forward must always be in a position to back up the D. Having the high forward in a position to back up the pinching defense will prevent odd-man rushes the other way.

5. Good forecheckers use their sticks to take away passing lanes. They keep their sticks on the ice and in the right lane. The right lane is the one that leads to the best breakout option for the other team. Forecheckers try to take away this option or make it difficult to make the pass by having an active stick. A common mistake with players on the forecheck is that they are in a rush to get in and finish the hit so they lose stick position. Most of the time their stick is in the air when they check.

6. Players need to finish hits when appropriate. Physical play on the forecheck often forces the defense to move the puck quicker next time. A hit is not always the best choice. When the forechecker is within striking distance of the pass, he should continue to pressure the puck instead of hitting the first opponent.

Forechecking Systems

This section describes five forechecking systems that a team can use to get the puck back. Which one you use may depend on the level you are coaching. For example, pressure forechecks work well against younger teams who have difficulty making quick decisions or sequential passes. Your choice will also depend on the risk you want to take as a coach. Conservative coaches like to employ a system in which one player is in on the forecheck but all other players are above the puck. Aggressive coaches will have their defense pinching on a regular basis. Again, the key is proper execution. Therefore, any of the five systems could be used from novice to pro. All these forechecking systems can be incorporated off a dump-in, chip-in, or rebound situation.

1-2-2 Forecheck

This forecheck involves hard pressure from the first forward (F1) and then as the puck is moved, quick pressure from F2 or F3 while F1 recovers. When F1 initiates pressure, he should angle the puck carrier to provide F2 and F3 a read on where the puck may go. Some coaches like F1 to stop the puck carrier from getting the back of the net and turn him up the strong-side boards, whereas other coaches encourage F1 to angle—to steer and get a hit to separate the puck from the puck carrier. If F1 pressures the puck carrier and the puck is moved in the direction he is skating, then F1 should avoid finishing the hit and continue on to pressure the pass.

Usually in a 1-2-2 system, the defensemen never pinch on direct passes to the opposing wingers but come down on long wide-rim plays (in which the breakout team rims the puck from one corner to the other half boards). F2 and F3 should initially be wide to take away passes to the boards and then react to mid-ice passes as they happen (figure 6.1).

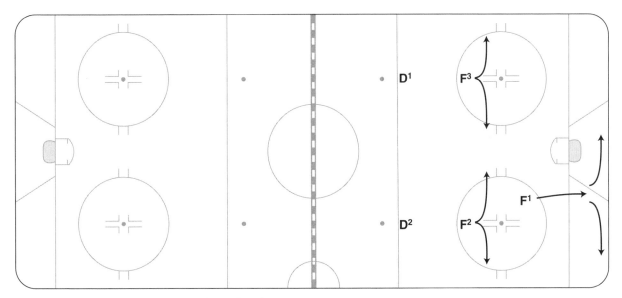

Figure 6.1 The basic 1-2-2 forecheck.

The strength of this system is that the other team is enticed to bring the puck up the boards and then the boards are taken away. In addition, if the opponent breaks out, usually only one forechecker is committed deep in the zone. The weakness in the 1-2-2 system is that the opponent has slightly more time to make plays on the breakout and teams with good passing defensemen can hit the middle of the ice.

As mentioned in the breakout section, the opponent can break out in four ways, so a discussion of forechecking systems should outline how to shut down each breakout. Listed here are the various breakout options and the specifics of how to react when forechecking in a 1-2-2 formation.

Up

F1 pressures O1. F2 and F3 position themselves in line with the dots, even with the opposing wingers, and ready to take away passes up the boards. Initially, the wingers can also line up wider to prevent any quick rim plays, but we prefer that they stay inside to minimize mid-ice space and then move to an outside position. If O1 passes to O4, then F2 closes quickly and F3 moves across, locking the middle (preventing passes to the center) (figure 6.2).

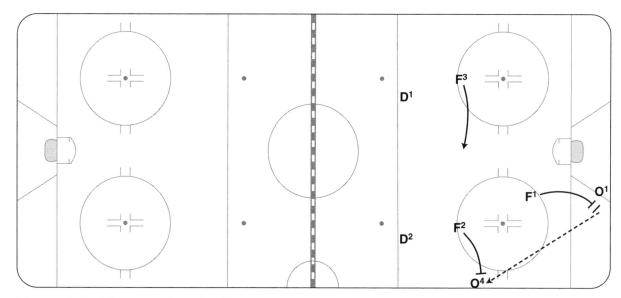

Figure 6.2   The 1-2-2 forecheck versus up.

Over

F1 pressures O1, and on the pass, F3 moves down to take away the pass to O2. F2 moves across to take away the pass up to O5. F1 recovers quickly and locks the middle (figure 6.3). If the puck is moved in the same direction while F1 is chasing O1, then F1 should continue to pressure O2 while F2 and F3 hold their positions.

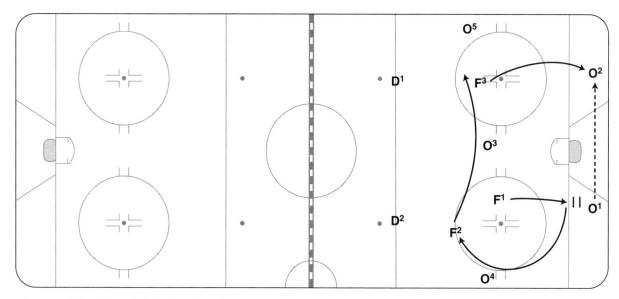

Figure 6.3   The 1-2-2 forecheck versus over.

Wheel

F1 forces O1 as he wheels the net, while F2 locks across the middle. F3 backs up while staying inside the dots and is ready to take away the boards. F1 should force only if he is within one stick length of O1. If not, he should cut across the front of the net and pick up O1 on the other side (figure 6.4).

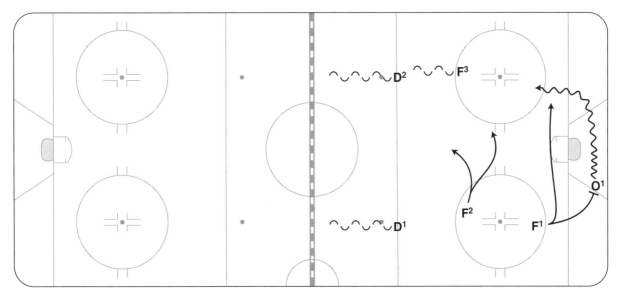

Figure 6.4 The 1-2-2 forecheck versus the wheel.

Reverse

F1 forces O1 as he wheels the net. Then as O1 reverses the puck, F2 closes on the pass. F3 moves across to lock the middle. F1 must recover high on the back side (figure 6.5).

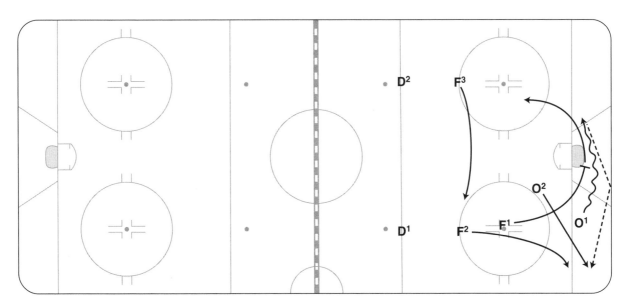

Figure 6.5 The 1-2-2 forecheck versus a reverse.

Rim

F1 pressures O1. If the puck is rimmed to the wide side, then D2 moves down to pinch on the winger. F3 covers up for D2 by moving up to the corner of the blue line. If the puck is rimmed up the strong side, then F2 closes down on the winger (figure 6.6).

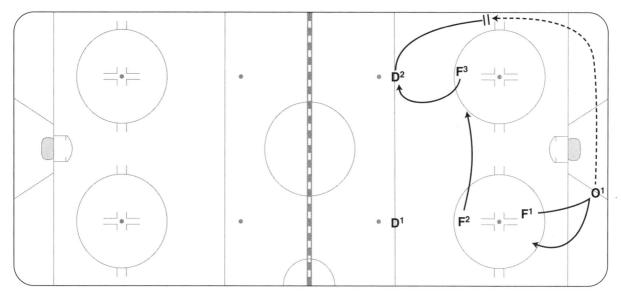

Figure 6.6   The 1-2-2 forecheck versus a rim.

2-1-2 Forecheck

This type of forechecking system was made famous by the Edmonton Oilers of the 1980s, who used their high-powered attack to pressure teams hard and recover the puck. This system forces the opponent's defense to handle pressure while also taking away all options up the boards. This system is a physical forecheck because F1 and F2 are in deep and looking to finish hits while the defensemen are set to come down the boards when the puck is moved to the opposition wingers. The 2-1-2 forecheck forces teams to use the middle of the ice to escape the zone. The strength of the system is in applying high pressure and giving the opponent only certain areas to break out of the zone. The weakness of the 2-1-2 system is that at times a defenseman is pinching and a forward is back on defense accepting the rush when the opponent breaks out. Most forwards are weaker than any of the six defensemen at defending the rush. Figure 6.7 shows the details of the system.

F1 pressures O1 to put the puck up the boards or across to his partner. F1 generally has an opportunity to finish his hit on O1. After the puck is moved and F1 has finished the hit, he recovers on the same side of the ice. F2 moves down on the weak side, anticipating a pass to O2. If the puck is moved up to O4, then F2 starts to recover on the same side.

F3 maintains a high position between the two defensemen. When D1 or D2 pinch down on a pass, then F3 moves out to the blue line on that side and backs up the D. If the opposition starts to break out, then F3 will have to back up like a defenseman. F3 is available in a solid defensive position, but after the puck is turned over, he is ready to receive a pass in the prime scoring area.

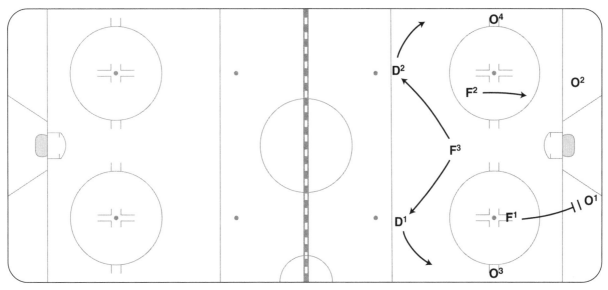

Figure 6.7 The basic 2-1-2 forecheck.

Both defensemen must read the play and anticipate when the puck may move up the boards. When they see that a pass is being made, they should pinch down on the winger (move toward the winger quickly, not letting him get by). They finish hits on the winger but remain in control. When the puck moves away, they get back to the blue line. Sometimes coaches talk about a pre-pinch position in which the defensemen are one-third of the way down the boards when the puck is on that side. This position reduces the distance to pinch on the winger.

Listed here are the various breakout options and the specifics of how to react when forechecking in a 2-1-2 formation.

Up

F1 pressures O1 to move the puck up the boards (figure 6.8). F2 moves down halfway on the wide side ready to close on O2. F3 stays in the middle of the ice. D1 moves down quickly on the pass to O3. F3 fills in for D1.

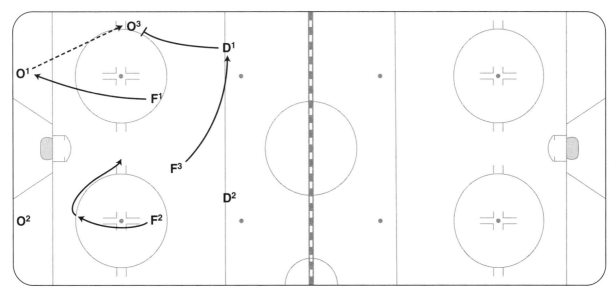

Figure 6.8 The 2-1-2 forecheck versus up.

Over

F1 pressures O1, and on the pass, F2 closes quickly on O2 (figure 6.9). If O2 passes the puck up the boards to the winger, then D2 moves in and finishes the hit on O4 while F3 fills in on the blue line. If O2 tries to pass to the middle of the ice, then F3 takes away O5.

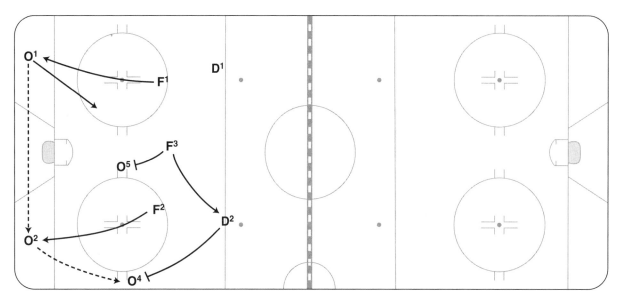

Figure 6.9　The 2-1-2 forecheck versus over.

Wheel

F1 forces O1 as he wheels the net, while F2 moves down to prevent O1 from rounding the net and makes him pass to the boards (figure 6.10). D2 closes down on the board pass, while F3 fills in on the blue line.

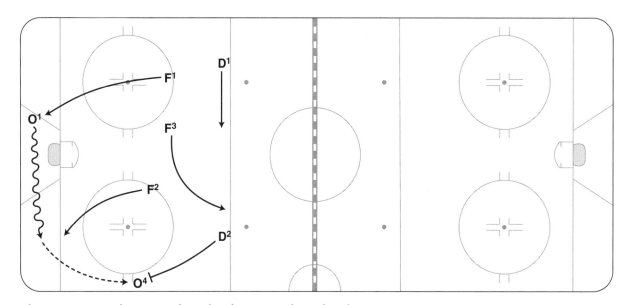

Figure 6.10　The 2-1-2 forecheck versus the wheel.

Reverse

F1 forces O1 as he wheels the net (figure 6.11). F2 is ready to stop O1 from wheeling, and then when he sees the reverse to O2, he moves in quickly to that side. F3 takes away the mid-ice pass and is ready to fill in for D1 if he pinches on a pass to the boards.

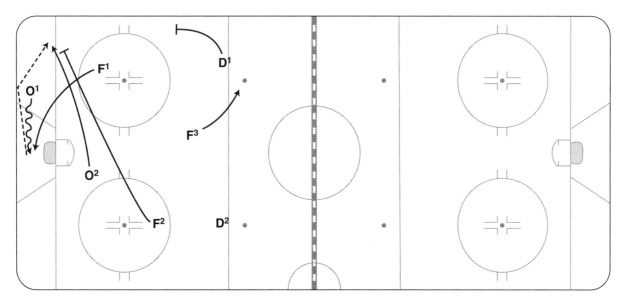

Figure 6.11   The 2-1-2 forecheck versus a reverse.

Rim

F1 pressures O1. If the puck is rimmed to the wide side, then D2 moves down to pinch on the winger (figure 6.12). F3 covers up for D2 by moving up to the corner of the blue line. If the puck is rimmed up the strong side, then D1 pinches with F3 again filling in.

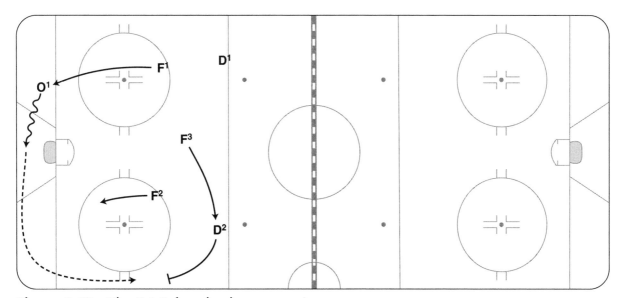

Figure 6.12   The 2-1-2 forecheck versus a rim.

2-3 System or Left-Lane Lock

In the 2-3 system, the key component is the pressure exerted by F1 and F2. They pressure the defensemen and each pass by skating constantly, finishing hits, and recovering quickly. The harder they work, the more hits they finish, and the quicker they recover, the more effective the system is. The 2-3 system is often referred to as the left-lane lock because one forward (F3) stays back on the left side of the ice—eliminating breakouts up those boards. The reason the left side was originally picked is that left wingers are traditionally better defensively than right wingers, whereas right wingers are traditionally the scorers. The defensemen shift to the right side; the left D plays in mid-ice, and the right D plays the right boards (figure 6.13).

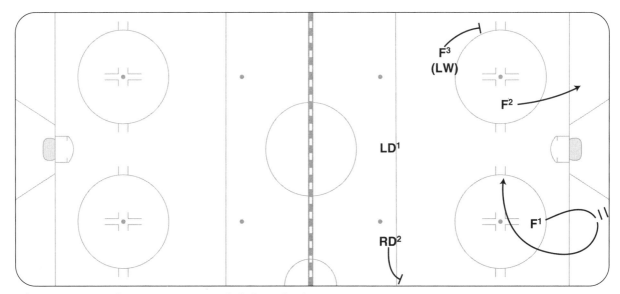

Figure 6.13   The 2-3 system or left-lane lock.

When the puck is turned over, the left winger can move in offensively, but then he has to move back when the puck is in doubt or turned over. The lock player doesn't always have to be the left winger; teams may decide to use their top defensive player in that role. If you leave it up to the players to read and react to filling the lock position, confusion will occur. The result will likely be either no one there, two players there, or players moving to the area late. Listed here are the various breakout options and the specifics of how to react when forechecking in a 2-3 or left-lane lock system.

Up

F1 pressures O1 to move the puck up the boards (figure 6.14). F2 moves down halfway on the wide side, ready to close on O2. F3 is on the far boards. D2 is in mid-ice. D1 moves down quickly on the pass to O3. D2 covers up for D1, and F3 fills in wide on the blue line.

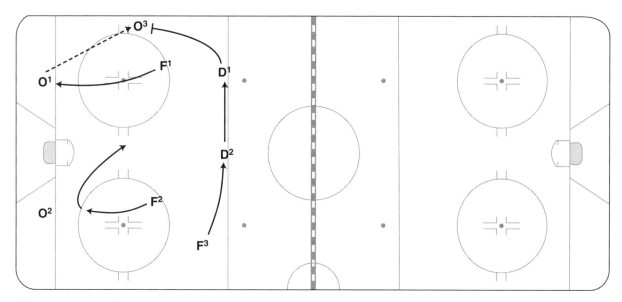

Figure 6.14   The 2-3 versus up.

Over

F1 pressures O1, and on the pass, F2 closes quickly on O2 (figure 6.15). If O2 passes the puck up the boards to the winger, then F3 moves in and finishes the hit on O4 while D2 fills in on the blue line. D1 moves to mid-ice.

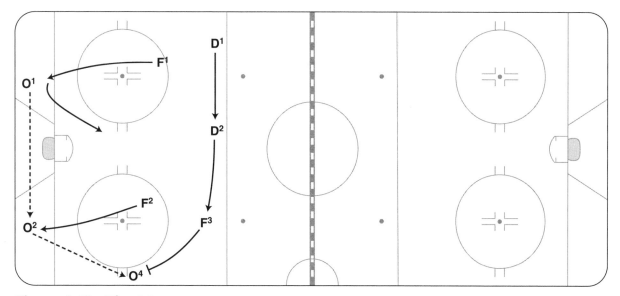

Figure 6.15   The 2-3 versus over.

Wheel

F1 forces O1 as he wheels the net, while F2 moves down to prevent O1 from rounding the net and makes him pass to the boards (figure 6.16). F3 closes down on the board pass, while D2 fills in on the blue line and D1 moves to mid-ice.

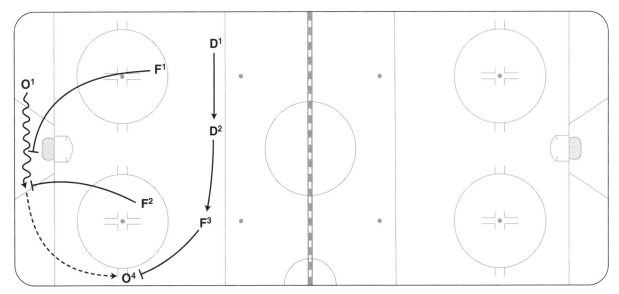

Figure 6.16   The 2-3 versus the wheel.

Reverse

F1 forces O1 as he wheels the net (figure 6.17). F2 is ready to stop O1 from wheeling and then once he sees the reverse to O2 moves in quickly to that side. D1 takes away any pass to the strong-side boards. D2 fills in if D1 pinches on a pass, and F3 stays in mid-ice on the blue line.

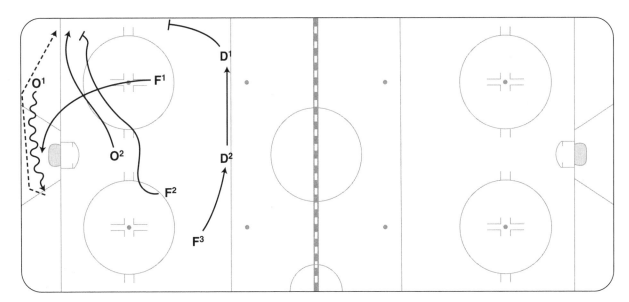

Figure 6.17   The 2-3 versus a reverse.

Rim

F1 pressures O1. If the puck is rimmed to the wide side, then F3 moves down to pinch on the winger (figure 6.18). D2 covers up for F3 by moving up to the corner of the blue line. If the puck is rimmed up the strong side, then D1 pinches and D2 again fills in.

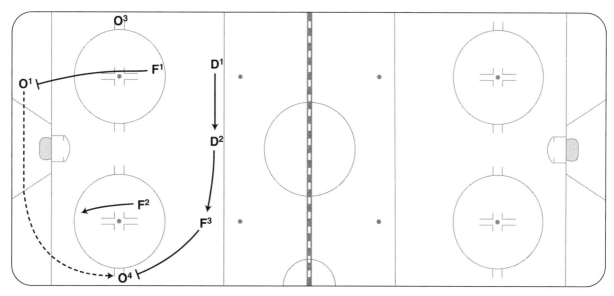

Figure 6.18   The 2-3 versus a rim.

Torpedo System

This interesting system was developed in Sweden and is not commonly used in North America. It is similar to the left-wing lock system but different in strategy.

The system is called *torpedo* because the first two forwards in on the forecheck buzz from corner to corner, pressuring the puck. The third forward (F3), who is usually the center, stays high on one side. The defensive defenseman stays in the center of the blue line and is more of a safety. On the opposite side of F3 is the offensive defenseman. The offensive defenseman and the center have the freedom to pinch down hard on all passes up their boards and move in offensively when F1 and F2 have puck possession. Some coaches allow F3 and D2 to pinch all the way down the boards to the goal line on that side (figure 6.19).

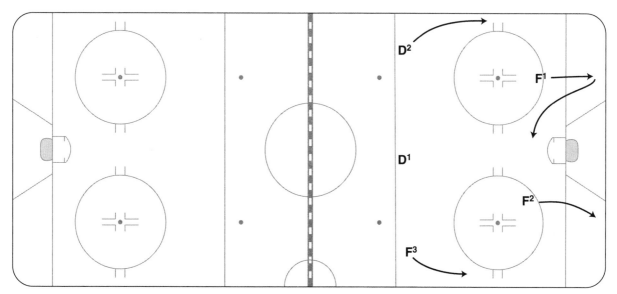

Figure 6.19   The torpedo system.

The advantage of this system is that F1 and F2 always provide pressure on the opposing defense while F3 and D2 shut down passes up the boards. In addition, when the puck is turned over, F1 and F2 have two potential passing options. Offensively, F3 and D2 are always ready to jump in to receive a pass or take a shot. For this system to work effectively, the center (F3) must be good at playing back defensively because if D2 gets caught in the zone, F3 will have to play defense with D1. Few teams are as comfortable with their centers playing back as they are with their defense. In addition, the wingers who get in on the forecheck must be good, quick skaters who can buzz from side to side. As with other systems, the weakness in the torpedo system is that the middle of the ice is available for breakout plays. Although the torpedo is nontraditional and therefore sometimes overlooked, if you have the personnel to fit the descriptions of the positions, trying it is definitely worthwhile.

Diagrams and descriptions for the breakout options have not been included here because the rotations are the same as those used in the 2-3 system. The one variation is that the center is back on the far side and the outside players F3 and D1 pinch aggressively on any passes up the boards. They even try to anticipate the pass being made and pinch early, not giving the wingers any opportunity to get the puck.

Control Forecheck

A control forecheck is used when the opposing players are set up behind their net with full control of the puck. This may happen off a line change or when the opponent gains the net and stops before you can apply pressure. When the opponent stops behind the net, you can forecheck off the control setup in a couple of ways.

Deep Trap

Much as in the neutral zone forecheck, all five players back up and meet the attack at the blue line. F1 takes a shallow angle and steers the puck carrier to one side. The forward on that side (F2) stands up and prevents the team from gaining the red line. F3 can lock across or stay wide. This more conservative strategy forces opponents to move through the neutral zone against a lot of traffic with five defenders in this area. The opposition will have time and space to build up speed, but when they hit the blue line, it will be taken away and turnovers often result (figure 6.20).

Swing With Speed

Most offensive teams on a control breakout will swing one and sometimes two players behind the net or in the corner to build up speed while also having a stretch forward. One way to neutralize this speed is to move in and swing with the players building up speed. In this case F1 stays in to deter the defense from passing, while F2 and F3 swing with and lock onto the player or players swinging deep. If the opposing D holds onto the puck and moves out from behind the net, F1 would move in on an angle to force the puck carrier to one side. The defense must be aware of any stretch players and eliminate the threat of the long stretch pass. This control forecheck is effective in eliminating the opposition's speed, but it does open up some areas of the ice for them to make plays (figure 6.21).

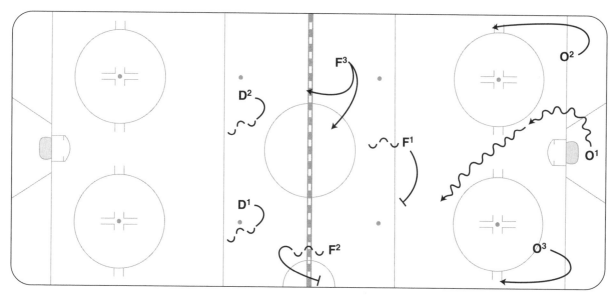

Figure 6.20 The deep trap.

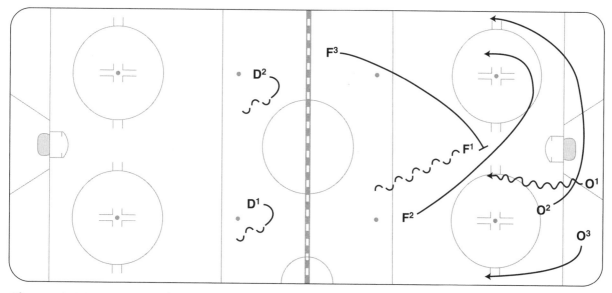

Figure 6.21 Swing with speed.

Quick Flush

When the other team sets up behind the net, they usually need 5 to 10 seconds to coordinate their control breakout. During this time they are often out of sync. We believe that the forechecking team gains an advantage by striking quickly whenever possible. When F1 sees O1 stop behind the net, F1 should quickly force him to come out one side, ideally on his backhand side. After F1 initiates the force, then F2 also comes in on an angle and confronts O1, doubling up the pressure. This quick flush will create some confusion and panic. F3, D1, and D2 move back to take away any longer passes that O1 might make (figure 6.22).

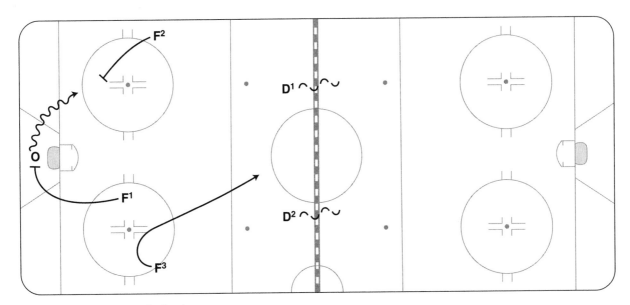

Figure 6.22   Quick flush.

Chapter 7
Neutral Zone Forechecking

Teams and coaching staffs constantly talk about how much pressure they want to apply versus how passive they want to be in the neutral zone area. Whether the forecheck starts off a face-off, a turnover, or a puck that is dumped out of the zone, there is a lot of space to cover in the neutral zone. Therefore, a strategy must be employed to shut down possession plays through this area.

If you pressure, opponents have less time and may make mistakes, or they may take advantage of the extra space to work with. Conversely, if you sit back, opponents have more time to read and make a play but less space to work with. What do you do? Coaches have several options when designing the neutral zone forecheck.

All neutral zone forechecking systems must allow the ability to shift quickly as the puck moves from one side to the other. The key player is F1 with regard to his angle and stick placement. With his stick on the ice and proper skating angles, F1 can take away passing lanes from the opposition and steer them into a space where they don't want to go. F1 can also move the stick into different lanes to take away options. When the puck is moving up ice and then back or passed from side to side, both defensemen must be good at regaining their gaps. Teams that tighten their neutral zone gap (the distance between the defending defensemen and the attacking forwards) create havoc for attacking forwards trying to enter the offensive zone. Another key skill of strong neutral zone forechecking teams is that all three forwards are able to skate backward and face the play to make their reads easier. You should practice this with all five defensive players moving in unison.

Neutral Zone Forechecking Systems

Teams may employ seven forechecking systems: 1-2-2 wide, Tampa 1-3-1, pressure 2-1-2, 2-3 deep lock, traditional 1-2-2, retreating 1-2-2, and the maritime sweep. Each system is described and discussed in this section.

1-2-2 Wide

This system is the simplest to teach and is effective in clogging up the neutral zone. The most important factor in making it work effectively is the play of F1. He should never forecheck too deep or too wide and give up mid-ice space. F1 should take a shallow angle and steer the puck carrier to one side. If a D-to-D pass is made by the opposition, then F1 reattacks on a shallow angle again. F1 must stay within 6 feet (1.8 m) of the blue line when initiating the push and take away the mid-ice pass with a well-placed stick. He can let the opposition have the return D-to-D pass. Essentially, F1 remains between the dots through this sequence to take away mid-ice space (figure 7.1). After the puck starts to move up the outside lanes, F1 should skate through the middle.

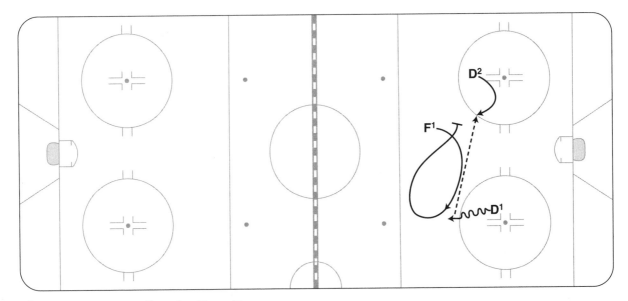

Figure 7.1 F1 angling the D-to-D pass.

F2 and F3 have simplified responsibilities. They stay on their side of the ice and lock the wide lanes (by staying in their specific lanes and skating backward to take away passing options). If the puck carrier comes up F2's side, then he stands up (doesn't back in) and keeps the opposition from gaining the red line (e.g., forces him to ice the puck). F3 takes the wide lane and makes sure that no pass can get to a player in that lane. D1 and D2 keep a tight gap in the middle of the ice, ready to adjust to the puck (figure 7.2a).

If the puck is moved to mid-ice or up the boards, then all five players react. D1 would overplay the boards when the puck comes up F2's side. D2 stays in mid-ice, and F3 takes the wide lane (figure 7.2b).

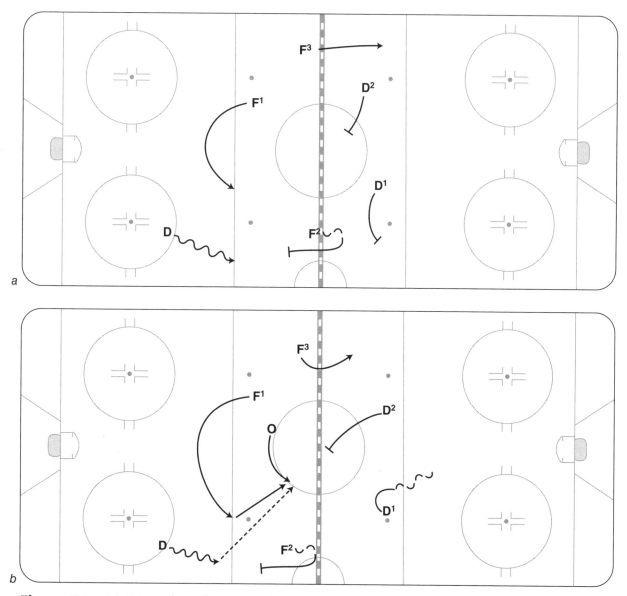

Figure 7.2   (a) D1 and D2 keep a tight gap in the middle of the ice ready to adjust to the puck; (b) if the puck is moved mid-ice or up the boards, all five players react.

Tampa 1-3-1

European teams commonly used this system when they began playing without the red line, which was several years before it was removed in North America. After the red line was removed, teams had more space to cover and this system was developed in response. In the 1-3-1, the three players across the middle of the ice definitely eliminate any room up the middle, but they give up space behind on the far blue line. The theory is that making the long pass is more difficult, especially through traffic. The 1-3-1 can be played in two ways, by either designating which defenseman is up in the middle of the ice or having the defensemen react depending on which side the puck is on. We recommend that one D be designated as the up player and the other as the back player (figure 7.3).

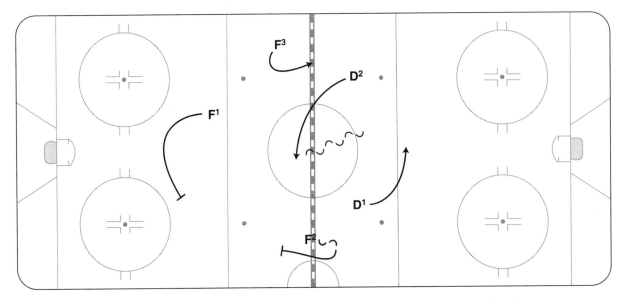

Figure 7.3   The 1-3-1 with one D as the up player and one D as the back player.

F1 has the freedom to go a little deeper (and press or angle the opponent with the puck) in this system because three lanes are covered in behind. F2 and F3 play their sides of the ice. If the puck carrier comes up F2's side, then he stands up and prevents him from gaining the red line. F3 makes sure that the wide lane is locked up and prevents any passes from going to players in behind D2.

D2 tightens up in the middle of the ice, playing as far up as the top of the center circle. D2 may skate forward or accept the rush skating backward. Regardless, D2 must keep a tight gap in the middle. D2 may close on any pass to the middle of the ice. D1 sits back and plays like a rover in football; he stays in the middle initially and then reacts to wherever the puck goes (figure 7.4).

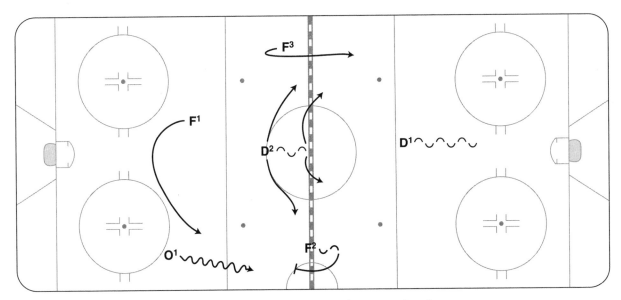

Figure 7.4   D2 keeps a tight gap in the middle and D1 sits back.

Pressure 2-1-2

This system is a common neutral zone forecheck off a lost draw, but it is also used effectively by many teams who want to apply more pressure in this area (when trailing in the game or in need of a more offensive approach). The 2-1-2 system is one of the more aggressive neutral zone forechecks. It is basically a man-on-man system in the neutral zone. F2 and F3 attack the opponent's defense in a staggered fashion. Therefore, if O1 has the puck, F2 will force and F3 will be halfway to O2. If a pass is made to O2, then F3 will jump immediately. F1 locks onto the other team's center, making sure that no passes can be made to the middle of the ice, because both defensemen have outside responsibility. F1 also backs up the defense if they pinch up on the outside. D1 moves up on any passes to O4, and D2 does the same for passes to O5. One D must remain in the middle of the ice at all times when the other D is forcing the outside (figure 7.5).

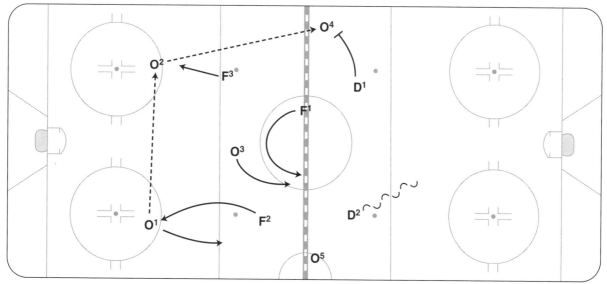

Figure 7.5   The 2-1-2 forecheck.

2-3 Deep Lock

The 2-3 system is similar to the 2-1-2, but it splits the deep ice into three lanes to eliminate the possibility of long stretch passes being made. F2 and F3 attack the opponent's defense, again in a staggered fashion. F1 now slides back with the defense and takes a lane. We believe for consistency sake that designating one side is better. In the diagram, F1 is on the right side, D2 is in mid-ice, and D1 takes the left lane. This setup creates a wall in front of the blue line, which will be hard for the offensive team to penetrate with possession. All three players in back need to keep a tight gap with the opposition forwards (figure 7.6).

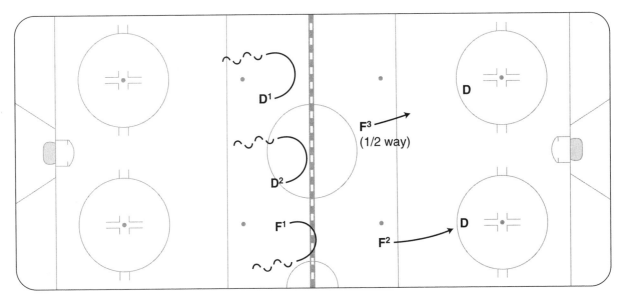

Figure 7.6   Deep lock 2-3 forecheck.

Traditional 1-2-2

This system is common at many levels because it denies teams the ability to bring the puck up the middle and forces them to move the puck wide and try to enter up the boards. F1 starts by steering the puck to one side, and unlike in other systems mentioned, he may take away either the D-to-D return pass or the wide-lane pass, depending on which is a priority (figure 7.7). This decision will influence the angle that F1 takes and the position of his stick. F2 challenges O1 before the red line, forcing him to ice the puck or chip in behind. F3 locks across hard on the opposing player in mid-ice. F3 does not allow passes to any player in mid-ice and forces the opposition to make the long, wide pass to gain entry to the offensive zone.

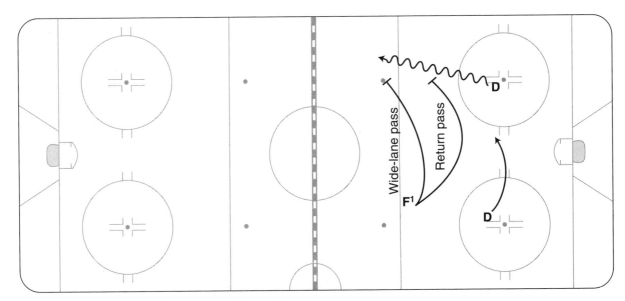

Figure 7.7   The F1 taking away the wide or return pass.

D1 is ready to recover any chips in behind F2 and ready to challenge any bank passes to O3. D2 is responsible for any wide passes to O4. D2 must be alert because the wide pass is the way that teams try to break the traditional 1-2-2—they pass wide to O4 and try to have him pick up speed before the pass is made (figure 7.8).

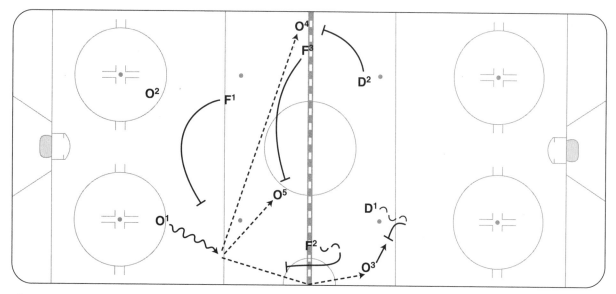

Figure 7.8   Defending all passing options with the mid-ice lock.

Retreating 1-2-2

This system is a defensive setup and is similar to the 1-2-2 mid-ice lock. The primary difference is that all five players tighten up. F1 moves down to the top of the offensive zone circles, and the two defensemen sit back no farther than the center red line. As the offensive team advances up ice, all five players skate backward and retreat in a tight pack (figure 7.9*a*). This setup creates the visual of limited space for the offensive team. F2 and F3 initially remain wide but align themselves with the dots, giving up space along the boards and taking away space inside. D1 and D2 must be aware of the long stretch pass. A pass to the outside is not dangerous, but they have to protect against being too wide and allowing the long mid-ice pass.

F1 starts to angle the puck carrier as soon as the puck advances above the offensive circles (figure 7.9*b*). Again, F1 takes a shallow angle at the puck carrier and tries to steer the puck up one side of the ice. F1 stays between the dots, allowing the puck carrier to move into the trap. F2 now stands up from the inside out, taking away the red line so that the puck carrier cannot dump the puck in. F3 starts to lock across the middle and is ready to take away any passes to that area. D1 stays in behind F2 in case the puck is chipped to the far blue line. D2 stays back in mid-ice but is ready to confront any wide-lane passes. All five players should move as if tied together by a rope.

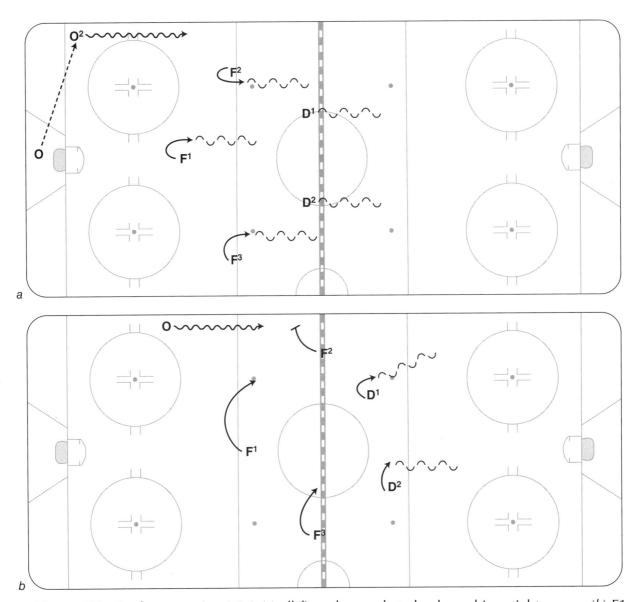

Figure 7.9   In the retreating 1-2-2 (*a*) all five players skate backward in a tight group; (*b*) F1 angles the puck carrier as soon as the puck advances above the offensive circles.

Maritime Sweep

This system is unique but effective. Your team will need several practices to get everyone's roles and responsibilities set so that the players can react and not think about it in a game.

F1 takes away the boards, forcing the opposition defenseman O1 to move the puck D to D. As the puck is moved D to D, F1 makes sure that no return pass can be made to the original defenseman O1. F2 sits in the center circle and on the D-to-D pass starts to move down to pressure O2. With no return pass option to O1, O2 will have to move the puck to one of the forwards.

D1, D2, and F3 create a wall at the far blue line similar to the wall in the 2-3 deep lock system and deny any passes to the forwards. The small space in the middle of the ice, if used, will have to be closed off by the middle D. F3 must always lock one of the wide lanes. The easiest thing for F3 to do would be to fill the lane closest to where he is when the forecheck is initiated. F3 must communicate this to the defense so that they can adjust (figure 7.10).

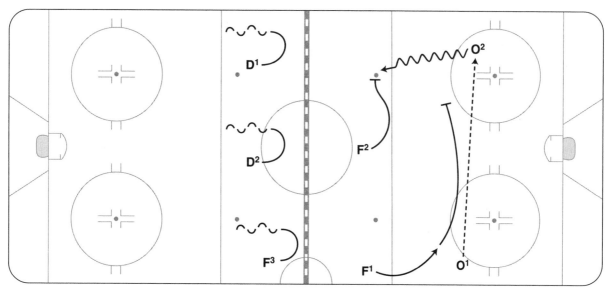

Figure 7.10   The maritime sweep movement.

Chapter 8
Backchecking

Every team wants to be known as a hardworking team. Well, nothing is more reflective of a team's work ethic than the players' willingness and commitment to backcheck. The backcheck starts after the puck is turned over in the offensive zone and doesn't end until you either regain puck possession or shift into defensive zone coverage. All three forwards need to be involved in the backcheck. Some teams rely mainly on one backchecker; the other two forwards coast back and watch that the other team's Ds don't jump by them. This strategy allows for quick counterattacks using long stretch passes after the puck is turned over, but it does not result in as many turnovers. Our philosophy is that when all three forwards hustle back, more turnovers will result and transition off the turnover will be faster. In addition, this strategy provides the offensive team with more space to work with as they advance up the ice.

The backcheck is set up in the offensive zone off the forecheck when players away from the puck recover above the puck to reattack (figure 8.1*a*), back up a pinching defenseman (figure 8.1*b*), or initiate the backcheck by being in a high offensive position (figure 8.1*c*). Players in the offensive zone need to recognize the potential for loss of possession and quickly get themselves into an appropriate backchecking position.

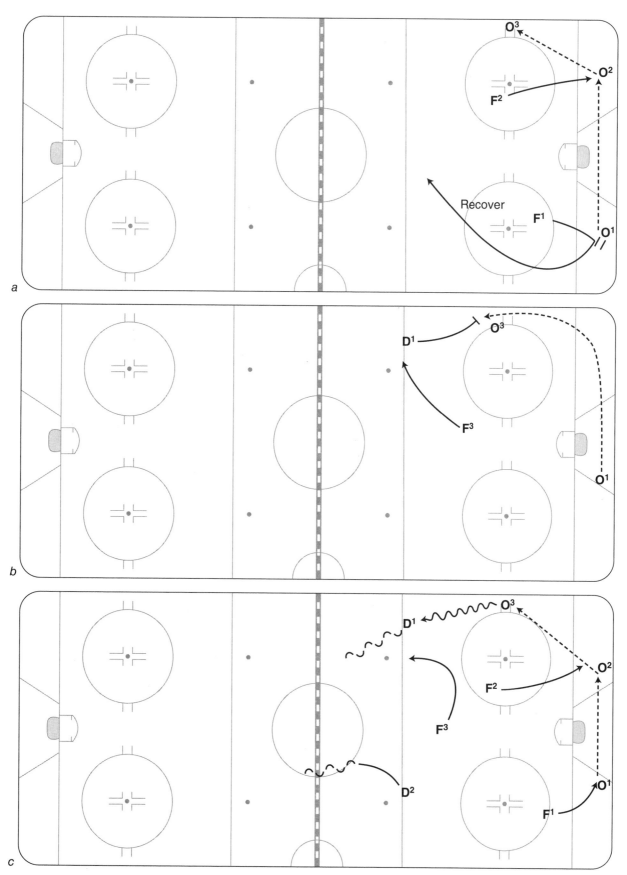

Figure 8.1 The backcheck set up by (*a*) recovering or (*b*) backing up a pinching defense; the backcheck being set up by (*c*) being in a high offensive position.

Late in games, a strong F3 (high forward) position in the offensive zone is key to eliminating odd-man rushes against. This strategy should be used throughout the game. When in a high position, F3 has two choices on how to force the breakout. The first is to pressure the pass immediately if he has support from a teammate who is recovering to the high slot. If he doesn't have support, the second option is to "soft lock." This concept refers to F3 not going for a hit but instead angling the offensive player up ice (toward his own net) and running him out of room or making him rush the pass (figure 8.2). In this way, he keeps in the rush and not behind it. If the offensive player makes a good pass up ice, F3 is still in good position to apply backchecking pressure and chase down the rush.

If your team is giving up odd-man rushes, the first place to look is at your forecheck position and backcheck commitment. Players might end up in a good position on the forecheck but react slowly to the other team's breakout and as a result miss players jumping by them.

Let's discuss the keys to an effective backcheck.

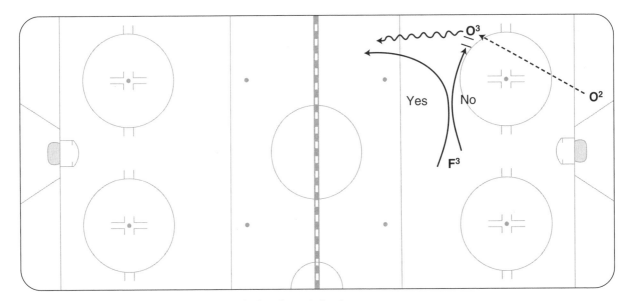

Figure 8.2   The neutral zone backcheck soft lock.

○ **Move into a high recovery position**. First and probably most important is that all forwards on the forecheck move immediately into a high
recovery position when the puck is moved away from them in the offensive zone or after they make a hit (figure 8.3). The high recovery area
is the top of the circles in the offensive zone; coaches always want the
forwards to move there. This positioning sets the stage for an effective
backcheck. If the forwards don't get in the habit of recovering, then
your backchecking strategy won't matter because they will not be in
a position to help.

○ **Pressure the attack from behind.** All forwards come back hard
through mid-ice. They backcheck hard and prepare to move in transition with speed after the puck is turned over. Coaches must rein-

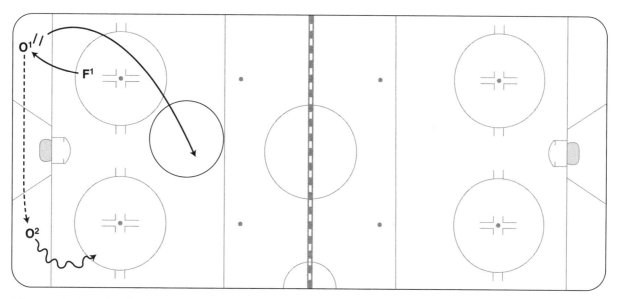

Figure 8.3   The high recovery area off a forecheck.

force with their players that all three forwards must come back hard; backchecking is not the responsibility of only the high forward or the closest forward (figure 8.4a).

O **Try to strip the puck from behind.** The backcheckers should try to lift the stick of the attacking player to steal the puck and counterattack quickly. Players need to work on the skill of being able to lift a player's stick while skating at full speed without taking a penalty.

O **Outnumber them at the line.** By maintaining pressure on the attack from behind and at the defensive blue line, you should outnumber the attacking team. Squeeze the attack from both sides; the forwards press from behind, and the Ds keep a tight gap on the other side (figure 8.4b). If you were to look at an overhead picture of the opposition attack at your blue line, you should see more of the defending team than the offensive team. Show your team a freeze frame at the defensive blue

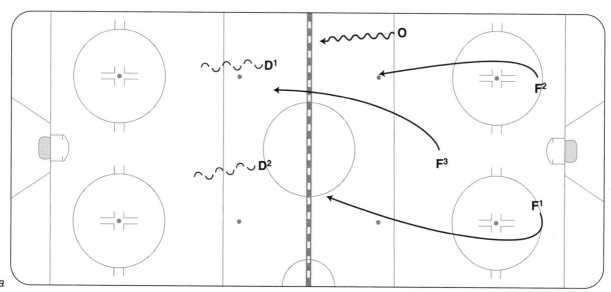

Figure 8.4a   Pressuring the attack from behind.

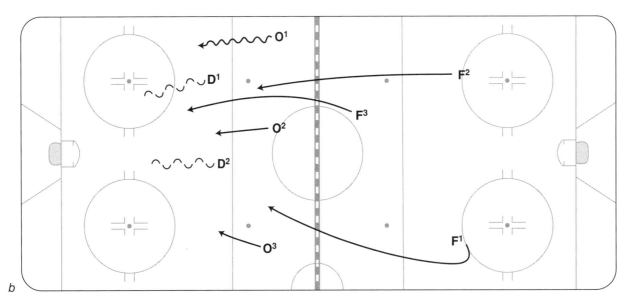

b

Figure 8.4*b*   Outnumbering them at the line.

line. If you have five players in the picture and the opponent has three, then the players are doing a great job of squeezing the attack. Often the puck will be turned over in this area, or the opposition will be forced to dump the puck in.

O   **Have set rules for F1 and D1.** Make sure you have rules for which player plays the puck carrier after the play advances to your blue line and which player holds inside position. You can do this in two ways.

1. F1 pressures the puck carrier hard, trying to catch him and turn the puck over before they reach the center line. But after reaching the center line, F1 releases the puck carrier to the defense (D1). Now F1 holds inside position and supports the defense while looking for late players. D1 calls that he has the puck carrier and stands him up at the line, knowing he has inside protection from F1 (figure 8.5).

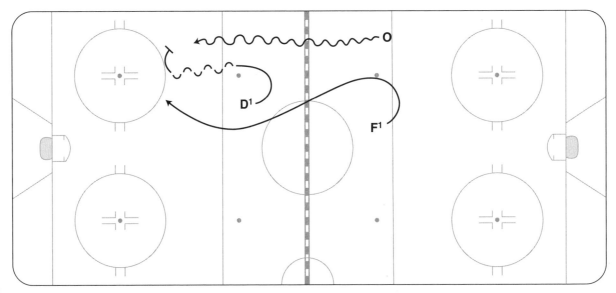

Figure 8.5   D1 stands the puck carrier up at the line while F1 protects mid-ice.

2. F1 pressures the puck carrier hard from behind and continues to try to steal the puck and keep the puck carrier wide all the way into the zone. D1 recognizes that this is the strategy used and now holds inside position and supports F1 while looking for late players (figure 8.6).

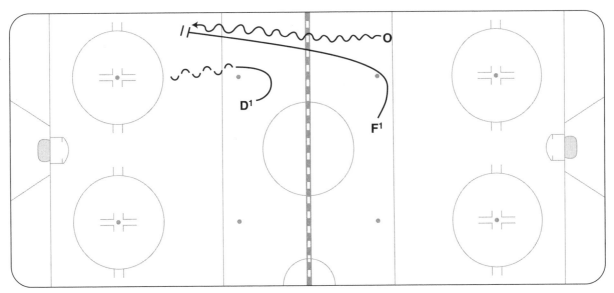

Figure 8.6   D1 holds the inside position, while F1 pressures the puck carrier.

3. F1 pressures the rush from behind but stays away from the puck carrier and locks the mid-ice to wide lane. If you employ this strategy, then the strong-side defense (D1) always knows that the puck carrier is his responsibility (figure 8.7).

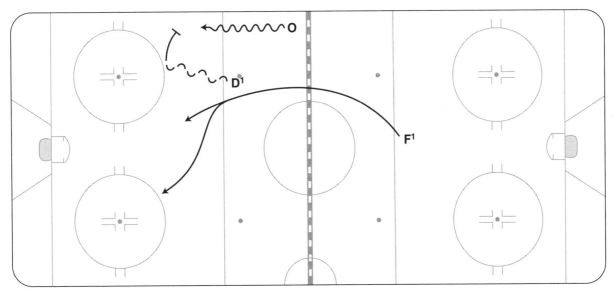

Figure 8.7   The strong-side defenseman owns the puck carrier.

○ **Watch for stretch players.** With no red line, the defense must be aware of the stretch player. Generally, this is the responsibility of the defense, but at times and in certain systems such as the 1-3-1 or 1-2-2 wide neutral zone forecheck, the wide forward has this responsibility. When forechecking or in possession of the puck in the offensive zone and the other team sends a player out early into the neutral zone, the closest D must drop back in coverage and hold mid-ice. When covering a stretch player, you do not have to skate close to the player—just maintain mid-ice position and equal depth. If a quick pass is made up, make sure you have support before going out to play the stretch player. Do not allow the stretch player to bump the puck into mid-ice to create an odd-man rush (figure 8.8).

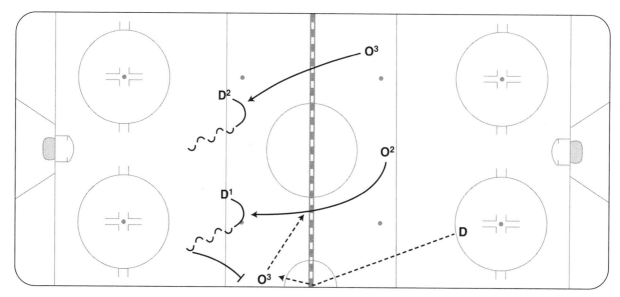

Figure 8.8   The stretch player bumping the puck into mid-ice as D1 overplays.

Backchecking Systems

Teams can employ four backchecking systems: defense early strike, wide-lane lock, midlane backcheck, and hound the puck. Each system is described and discussed in this section. Each has a different emphasis on where and how the offensive players are confronted.

Defense Early Strike

Teams have started to employ this system and concept in the last few years. Generally, it starts in the offensive zone. With more teams sinking down in defensive zone coverage, if the defensemen don't tighten up early, the opposition has room to break out. As noted in figure 8.9a, the two defensemen tighten up early and at times may sit up on the opposition forwards.

When the other team breaks out, the wide D will usually strike across, almost like a soft lock that the forwards employ on the forecheck. When

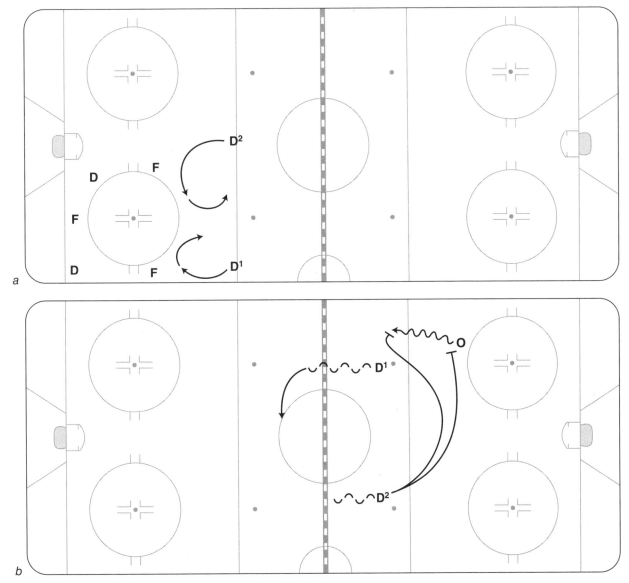

Figure 8.9 *(a)* Defensemen tighten up early; *(b)* D2 Strikes across.

the wide D2 strikes, the strong-side D1 can shift inside. This strategy often surprises the opposition and reduces the time and space they need to make a play (figure 8.9*b*).

Wide-Lane Lock

In this system, the first forward on the backcheck immediately moves to an outside lane. After the forward gets into the wide lane, he may skate backward or forward but must always be able to see the puck and any opposing skater in that lane. This forward is responsible for any opposition player skating between the dots and the boards on that side. D1 now moves to mid-ice, assuming responsibility for this lane, and D2 takes the strong side where the puck carrier is. Essentially, the ice is divided into three parts, and each of these players protects a zone (figure 8.10). The offensive team will have a difficult time getting across the blue line in possession of the puck with three players protecting the line. All three defensive players (D1, D2, F1) attempt to stand up the attack at the blue line, while F2 and F3 continue to pressure the attacking players from behind.

The responsibility of F1 is to prevent any passes to that side and to stay close to his check. He should always try to be deeper than the opponent, which is usually called good defensive side position.

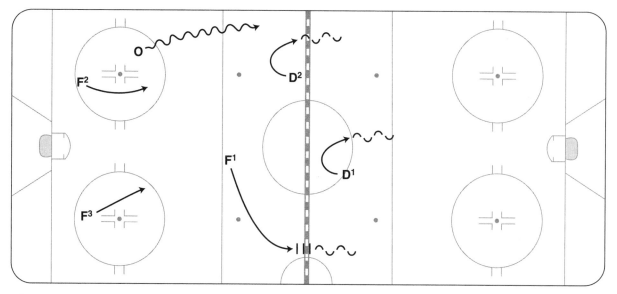

Figure 8.10   Neutral zone backchecking wide-lane lock.

Midlane Backcheck

After the puck is turned over in this system, the first instinct of the high forward should be to get to mid-ice and come back hard through the center seam. All forwards come back through the middle, allowing the defensemen to play the outside areas. The first forward back protects the defensemen from being beaten inside by always staying between the puck and the net (figure 8.11). Therefore, if a defenseman makes a mistake, the forward is

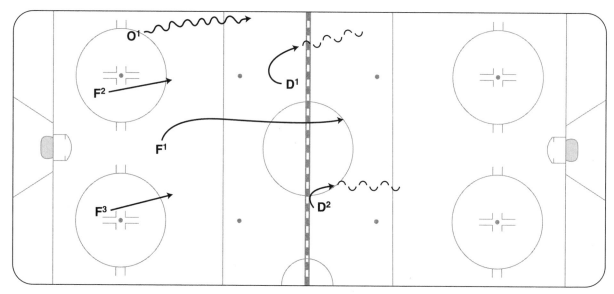

Figure 8.11   The midlane neutral zone backcheck.

always in a position to cover up. In addition, having the forward in the middle intimidates the puck carrier and forces him to stay wide because of the lack of space inside.

When the first forward comes back through the middle, he should come all the way back to the low slot area and then move out to support the defense. The second and third backchecking forwards should again come back hard; they look around for any late players entering the zone and stop at the top of the circles in good defensive position.

Hound the Puck

This system is the opposite of the midlane backcheck. The first forward hounds the puck (backchecks toward the player with the puck) as hard as he can, and if a pass is made, the forward continues to pressure the puck (figure 8.12). The forwards limit the time and space for the opposing players as they move through the neutral zone, and the defensemen hold inside position, protecting the space between the dots. Coaches who like this system generally have a pressure philosophy and want to deny time and space in all areas of the ice.

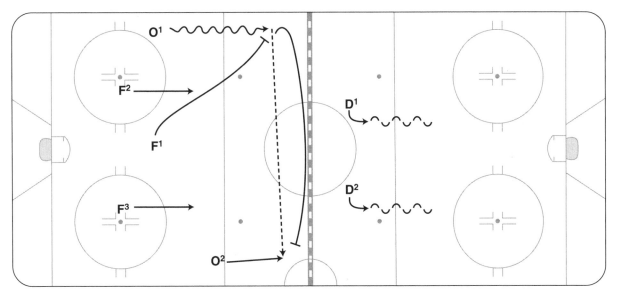

Figure 8.12   Hounding the puck in the neutral zone backcheck.

The advantage of this system is that the opposition is always under pressure through the neutral zone. The puck carrier will have trouble making plays if the backchecking forwards are quick and work hard. In addition, the inside positioning of the defense prevents mid-ice passes. The disadvantage is that at times the backchecking forwards and the defense become confused about what to do if the forwards cannot catch the opposition by the blue line or confront the pass quickly enough. A team must develop rules for these two scenarios to eliminate confusion when they occur. One rule involves having the forward hound the puck until the red line; if the forward is not then even with the puck carrier, the defense takes over and the forward picks up a lane or wide player.

Chapter 9
Defensive Zone Entries

The most critical aspect of defensive zone entries is that the defensive players accepting the attack must correctly read the play. For the purposes of this book, defensive zone entries are defined as the moment the attacking team hits the offensive blue line with the puck. When this happens, the defensive players, who are usually the defensemen and possibly one forward, must scan the rush quickly and identify the number of attackers and defenders. Because of the dynamic nature of hockey, players must make this read in seconds, and rarely is any situation exactly like another. After the defenders see the rush clearly, they should call out whether it is a two on one, two on two, or three on two and communicate to any forwards coming back which player to pick up. The forwards coming back must read the rush quickly from the back side and pick up the right players.

If reads are so important, how do coaches improve the players' ability to identify the rush? Well, they can try a couple of methods. First, they can do read-the-rush drills in practice, in which players face various situations; after they play it out, they get feedback from a coach who is off to the side. A simple read-the-rush drill may include a neutral zone regroup in which the defenseman must step up, read the rush, close the gap, and make it difficult for the offensive team to gain entry with possession. Another drill starts as a two on two with a backchecker and turns into a three on three, set up by the coach sending the backchecking and offensive forwards at different intervals.

The second way to help players identify the rush is to review video and ask what they see and how they would play each situation. Many times while watching video, players comment that during the game they read that they had less time and space than what the video shows. Hearing their perspective is helpful. In addition, during games one coach on the bench can provide feedback and discuss reads with players while the game is going on. The best approach is to ask the players, "What did you see on that rush?" and then tell them what you saw. Finally, to clear up any confusion about reads, set a rule for what players should do if they are unsure. The rule should be this: *Hold mid-ice position, take a few more seconds to sort it out, and then when you are sure, move to outside areas to challenge the puck carrier.*

Handling Defensive Zone Entries

After the puck carrier crosses the line, a number of options are available to the offensive team, as outlined in chapter 3. To develop your team in the area of handling defensive zone entries, you need to review each of the attack options and outline to your team how to cover them. Whether your team is faced with an attacker who delays, a two on one, two on two, or any variation of a three on two or three on three, they will know how to play it.

Note here that for all entries described, we focus primarily on the two defensemen and the first backchecking forward (figure 9.1). As mentioned in the backchecking chapter, the last two forwards coming back into the defensive zone must come back hard through mid-ice (inside the dots) and stop at the top of the circles. They should keep their sticks on the ice to discourage passing options.

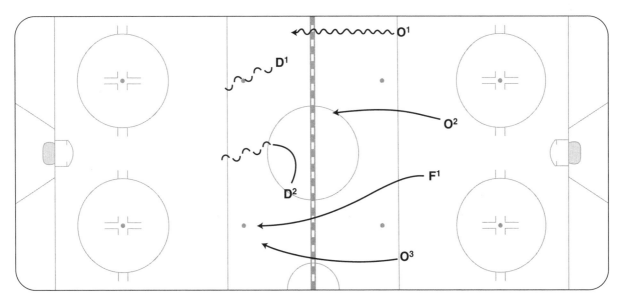

Figure 9.1   Handling the rush with two defensemen and a backchecking forward.

Delays

If the opposing forward delays when entering the offensive zone, the defense first reads whether the rush is even. If the offensive team outnumbers the defensive team, then the defense should hold inside position and wait for help. There are two ways to play an even rush where the puck carrier delays. In the first method, D1 steps up and plays the puck carrier, while F1 locks mid-ice and protects the space behind D1 (figure 9.2a). F1 looks for late players coming into the zone, and D2 plays the middle to wide side area. D2 automatically takes any midlane net drives. The second way to play an even-rush delay is to have the backchecking forward go after the puck carrier while both defensemen drop back inside with their sticks on the ice, ready to take away any plays inside and cover players going to the net (figure 9.2b). Either way is effective, but teams should pick one of the two strategies and stick to it so that both the defense and forwards always know who is going to take the delay player and who is going to stay inside.

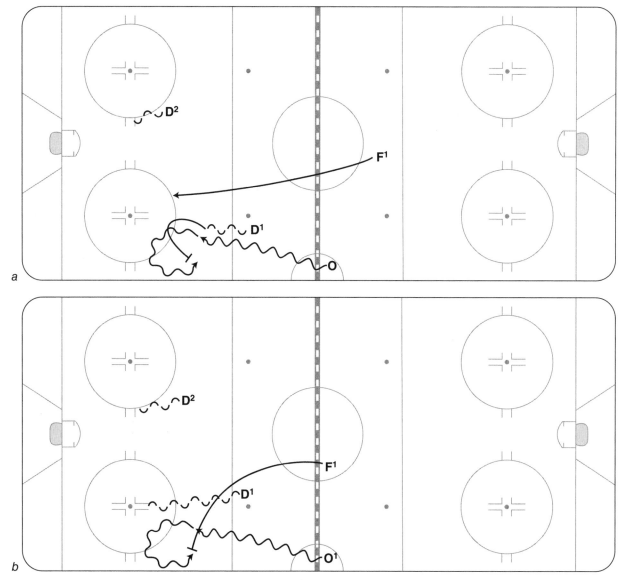

Figure 9.2   (a) D1 playing the delay; (b) F1 playing the delay.

Gap and Strike

A new tactic being employed in the neutral zone over the last couple of years is an early gap and strike. Many teams start with their wingers low on the breakout, so if you have a mobile defense you may want to use this strategy. The gap and strike starts at the offensive blue line or between that line and center ice. When the opposition breaks out, the wide D (D1) moves across and strikes the forward as he starts to gain speed and attack through the neutral zone. His partner (D2) stays back and shifts slightly to mid-ice (see figure 9.3). Note that D1 skates forward with a good angle so that the opposition winger cannot skate or pass inside. Eventually, D1 will run the winger out of room and finish his check along the boards.

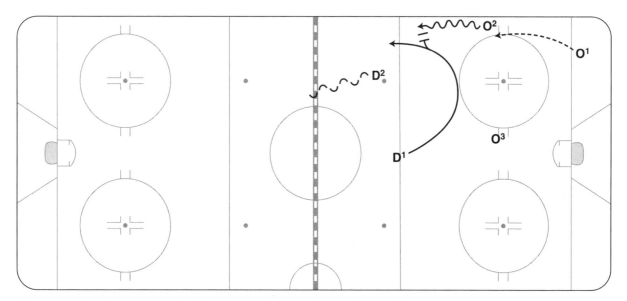

Figure 9.3   On gap and strike, D1 pressures from the inside ice.

Two on One

Coaches have several theories about how to play a two on one, but no factual evidence can tell us which is best. First, the defenseman should stay in mid-ice regardless of whether the two on one is down the middle or wide. Early, he should try to push the puck carrier wide. After the attack moves into the circles, the defenseman has two options:

1. He can be responsible for the player without the puck and leave the player with the puck to the goaltender. To execute this tactic, the defenseman either blocks the passing lane by going down on one knee or turns to take the wide player at the last moment to minimize the risk that the opposition puck carrier will cut to a better shooting position. Ideally, the defenseman should back up in line with the strong-side post or goaltender's pads and not give away too much ice to the puck carrier. When the defenseman turns to take his check, he should still keep an eye on the puck carrier so that he knows what is happening. The primary responsibility of the defenseman in this tactic is to make sure that no pass can be made to the backdoor for an empty-net tap-in (figure 9.4a).

2. The second way to play a two on one is for the defenseman to slide flat on the ice with feet facing the net to take away the passing option and force the puck carrier to shoot (figure 9.4*b*). This slide must be executed with proper timing. The problem with the slide is that until they perfect it, many defensemen slide too far or leave their feet too early, allowing the puck carrier to cut in. In addition, after the defenseman slides he is in no position to defend a rebound. The sliding technique is effective in surprising the puck carrier and often making him panic, thereby forcing a bad pass into the sliding D or a hurried shot. In addition, the sliding technique usually eliminates the pass to the wide side.

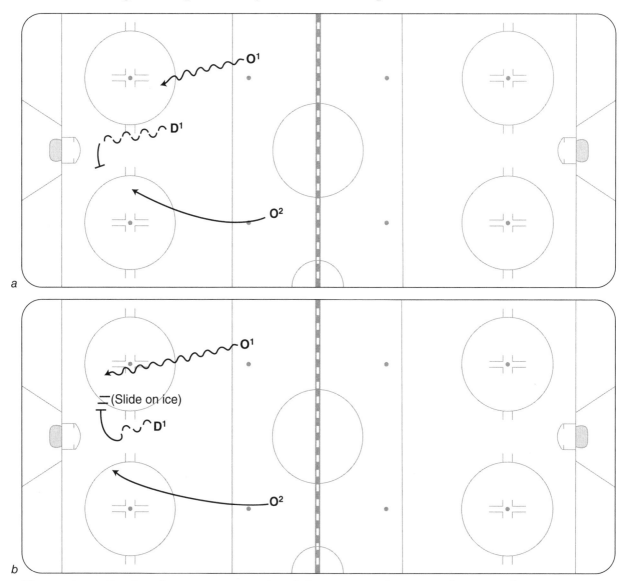

Figure 9.4   During the two on one, the defenseman either (*a*) makes sure that no pass can be made backdoor or (*b*) slides flat on the ice with feet facing the net to take away the passing option.

Two on Two

In all two-on-two situations, the defensemen should make sure they have a tight gap. Without a tight gap, playing the two on two properly is difficult. To maintain a tight gap, defensemen should constantly be reminded to "gap up," which means to move up with the play and tighten up on the rush. As a reference point, they should keep two stick lengths between each other; any farther back and they will lose the ability to move back at the same speed as the rush. Each of the two ways to play a two on two has its strengths and weaknesses.

The first method is for D1 to stay with the puck carrier regardless of what he does. If the puck carrier drives, delays, or cuts to the middle, D1 stays with him and D2 keeps position on the other player. The strength in playing it this way is that the players are not confused about who has whom. The weakness is that sometimes the defensive team can lose coverage, especially when the puck carrier crosses with the second offensive player (figure 9.5a).

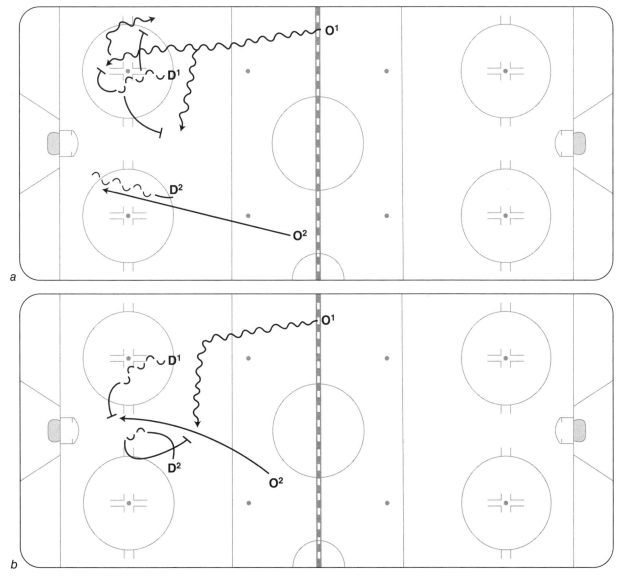

Figure 9.5 (a) In a two on two, one option is for D1 to stay with the puck carrier no matter what. (b) A second option is for D1 to leave the puck carrier for D2 to play when the puck carrier crosses the ice.

The other way to play a two on two is for D1 to take the puck carrier on the drive or delay but to leave him for D2 to play when the puck carrier crosses the ice. D1 then picks up the other player (figure 9.5b). The disadvantage here is that D2 might not be in a strong position to pick up F1, and D2 might miss coverage on F2 in the exchange. The advantage is that both Ds stay in their lanes with good mid-ice position, thus reducing confusion.

Three on Two

When reading a three on two, both defensemen stay in mid-ice and try to delay the attack. Don't confuse what looks like a three on three for what is really a three on two. What we mean here is that at times the defense will say, "I thought the backchecker had the third player," but in reality the backchecker was a step away and couldn't catch the player. If the offensive team sends a back-side drive, the strong-side D1 plays the two on one and the back-side D2 goes with the drive (figure 9.6). For a midlane drive, the back-side D2 plays the two on one, trying to shade (commit to one player while being ready to take the other player) the drive player but ready to come out on the wide pass. D1 plays the puck carrier.

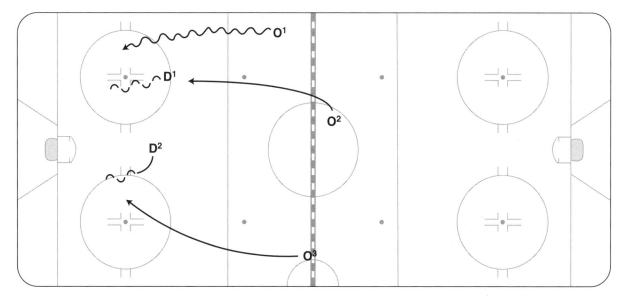

Figure 9.6   Defending a three-on-two back-side drive.

Three on Two With a Close Backchecker

In this situation the backchecker is close to catching the rush but doesn't have position on any of the offensive players (figure 9.7). D1 and D2 should play it as a three on two until the backchecker has caught the opposition's highest player. With the new obstruction rules not allowing the backchecker to hook the offensive player, the defense should not play it like a three on three until the offensive player is clearly caught by the backchecker. The Ds must make sure that the backchecker has body position on his player before they adjust and play it as a three on three. The best choice is to play it safe until they are sure because as soon as one of the defensemen overplays the outside, a two on one could open up inside if the backchecker is not in position.

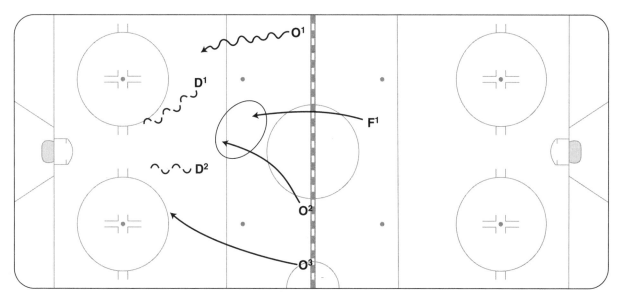

Figure 9.7   A three on two with a close backchecker.

Three on Three

The backchecker must identify the player he is covering. As outlined in chapter 8, some teams like their backchecker in the wide lane and some like him in the mid-ice lane, so the defensemen adjust according to the team's system. The backchecker usually takes the highest player unless he is already in position to take the wide player. He should keep his stick off the body of the free player so that he doesn't take a penalty and should get good body position—close enough to the player to take his stick and at the same time keep an eye on where the puck is (figure 9.8).

If the backchecker is coming back through mid-ice, he should leave any drive players to the defense and pick up the higher areas. Therefore, if the middle offensive player drives the net looking for a pass or deflection, then this player would be covered by D2. F1 must look around for the third

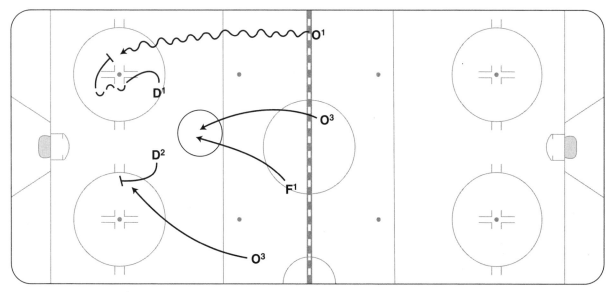

Figure 9.8   The backchecker taking the highest player.

forward and move to check him. Sometimes F1 will have to overplay the outside area if this forward is wider. As the play gets below the circles, he should lock onto his check (figure 9.9).

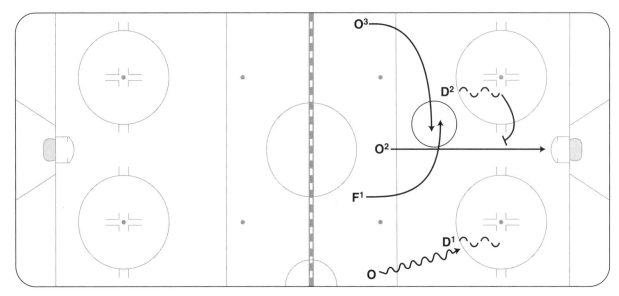

Figure 9.9   The backchecker leaving the drive and taking the highest player.

If the team's neutral zone system has the first forward back locking the wide lane (figure 9.10), then on three-on-three rushes the forward should stay with the player in this lane and the defensemen will adjust to cover the middle and strong side. This setup becomes more of a man-on-man coverage when the play enters the defensive zone.

Finally, if the backcheckers are instructed to hound the puck, then the backchecker attacks the puck carrier all the way into the zone. D1 shifts to the middle, and D2 takes the wide or back-side lane (figure 9.11).

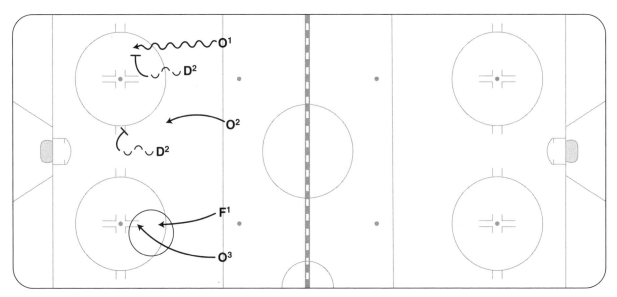

Figure 9.10   The three on three if the team's neutral zone has the first forward back locking the wide lane.

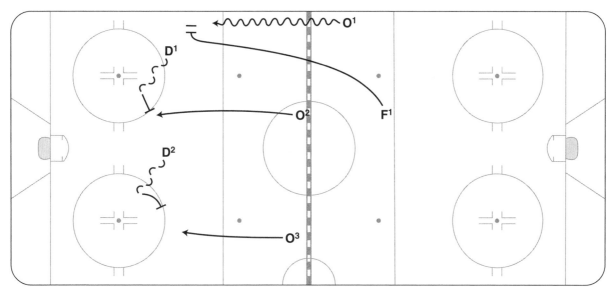

Figure 9.11   Backchecker forces puck, D1 and D2 shift.

Aggressive Stand

Depending on your philosophy as a coach, you might want to take this approach on defensive zone entries. In this situation whenever your team is faced with a three on two, two on two, or even two on one, they have the option of challenging the puck carrier just before he gets to the blue line. If the rush is a three on two, then D2 must take the middle lane at the same time as D1 forces the outside, leaving the wide side open. This pass will be difficult to make.

This tactic is used when the puck carrier might have his head down or has juggled a pass. In these situations D1 would strike right away. Although you are leaving mid-ice protection, the puck carrier is often in a position where he gets surprised and loses control of the puck or his support player goes offside. We don't recommend using it often, but this aggressive play can be effective (figure 9.12).

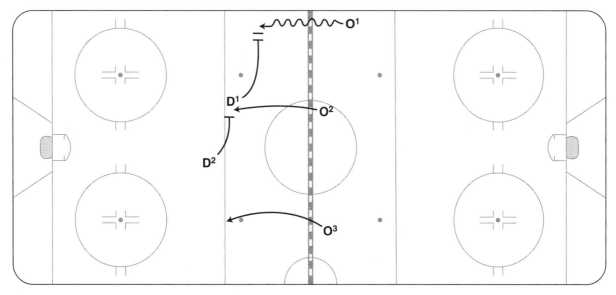

Figure 9.12   Aggressive D1 stand.

Handling the Kick-Out Play

The kick-out play or the kick and run play is one of the offensive tactics described in chapter 3. Defensively, there are two ways to handle the kick-out play if the rush is even. If the offensive team has the advantage, then the defensive team should hold mid-ice and wait for help, but if the rush is even, then either D1 or the backchecking forward (F1) can take the kick-out play while the other holds mid-ice. Because this play happens quickly, the best choice is usually to have the backchecking forward take the kick-out play while D1 stays in his lane (see figure 9.13).

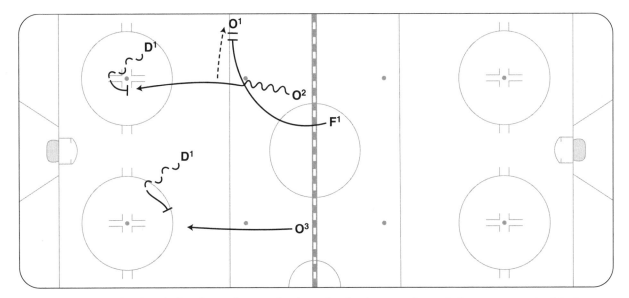

Figure 9.13   The backchecking forward takes the kick-out play while D1 stays in his lane.

This is how to play the kick-out play from a defensive perspective (figure 9.14).

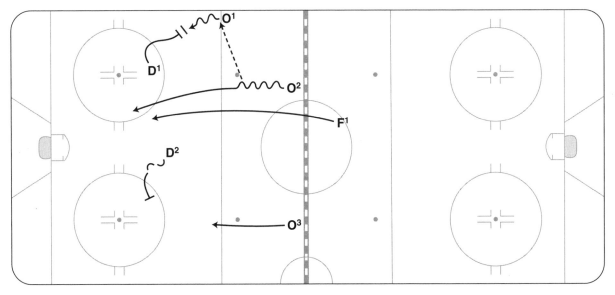

Figure 9.14   D1 takes the puck carrier, while F1 covers middle ice.

Covering the Late Attackers

Backchecking requires commitment and work, as indicated in chapter 8. Not allowing the opposition to get a free fourth player into the attack is a characteristic of strong defensive teams. If a fourth player is in the attack, then the four on three should be played like a three on three. The first three attacking players will be covered, and if a pass is made to the late player, D1, D2, and F1 should hold their checks and let the fourth attacker shoot but not pass. The goaltender will have to be ready for the high shot. If D1, D2, or F1 can get into a shooting lane, he should try to do that but not let the fourth attacker pass because the goaltender must be committed to the shot. Ideally, F2 or F3 on the backcheck will eventually get some pressure on the fourth attacker (figure 9.15).

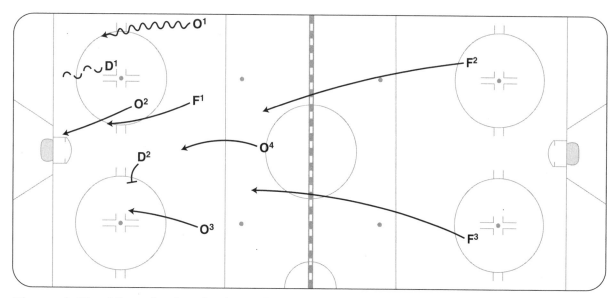

Figure 9.15   Allow the fourth player shot.

Transitioning Into Defensive Zone Coverage

Coaches must remind their teams that at some point the team shifts from defensive zone entry coverage to defensive zone coverage. Our thoughts are that you cannot rush this transition. First, make sure that your entry coverage is set and that the final two backcheckers are in the zone and stopped in mid-ice. When the puck moves to the outside, you can then transition into defensive zone coverage alignment, the subject of the next chapter.

Chapter 10
Defensive Zone Coverage

Defensive zone coverage refers to coverage after the offensive team has set up in the zone and all five defensive players are in the zone. This may happen off a face-off in the defensive zone, when the opponent dumps or chips the puck in, after the opposition enters the zone and takes a shot on net, or when the opposition enters the zone and maintains puck possession for several seconds. Following are some key principles to remember in defensive zone coverage:

○ **Maintain mid-ice positioning.** Players are often in such a hurry to get to the outside to apply pressure to the puck carrier that they overcommit and leave space in the most dangerous scoring area—the low slot. Few goals are scored from outside this area, but in defensive play many teams will be caught with too many players covering the outside space. At younger levels two players often go at the puck carrier, not seeing that the other has already committed. When players understand the value of mid-ice positioning, they will be less anxious to jump. Pressuring the puck carrier to deny time and space is important, but only one person at a time should do it.

○ **Stay between the puck and the net.** When checking opponents, players need to make sure they always have great defensive side positioning by staying in a direct line between the puck and the net (figure 10.1). Support players defensively down low below the dots should always be on this line from the puck to the net.

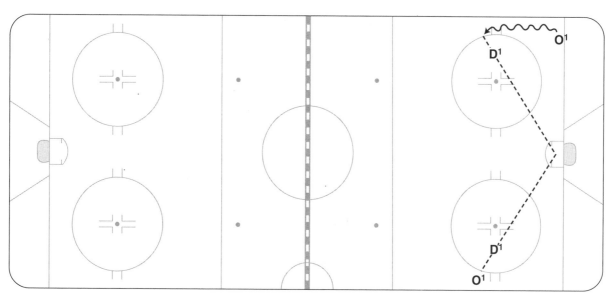

Figure 10.1   Great defensive side positioning requires staying in a direct line between the puck and the net.

○ **Be ready to block shots.** In today's game, defenders often get into shooting lanes and block shots (primarily with the legs) or discourage opposing players from taking a shot. Although blocking a shot hurts, it takes away good scoring chances. Players who sacrifice their bodies to block shots are respected by teammates and coaches. A player may occasionally sprawl to block a shot, which requires timing, but players who make themselves big in shooting lanes block most of the shots.

○ **Keep your stick on the ice.** In offensive situations, coaches often remind players, "Keep your stick on the ice and be ready for the pass." We believe that keeping the stick on the ice is even more important in the defensive zone. By having a stick on the ice, players take away passing lanes and often intercept pucks. When you look at a video clip of all five defensive players with their sticks on the ice, it is amazing how much space is covered. But you often see players in defensive zone coverage with their sticks at the waist. This bad habit should be avoided.

○ **See the puck; see your man.** In all sports, defenders need to be able to see where the offensive player is and where their coverage responsibility is. The defender must keep his head on a swivel and look back and forth between the two, because the position of the puck is changing and his check is moving at the same time.

○ **Find the opponent's stick on rebounds.** When the puck is shot on goal and a rebound occurs, defensive players often try to find the puck, but the free offensive player finds it first and scores. The defender should take the opponent's stick first and then look to respond to the loose puck. The goaltender should tell the defensive players where the puck is (in the corner, in your feet). This call will help defenders respond after they have covered the stick and taken away any immediate rebound chances. Some defensemen also make the mistake of trying to knock the player down in front. When the puck is in the net area, the priority is stick and body position.

Defensive Zone Systems

Teams can use several systems in their defensive zone: the 2-3 system, low zone shrink, half-ice overload, or man-on-man coverage. The 2-3 system should be used against teams that have a balanced attack in the offensive zone, whereas the low zone shrink works well against teams who have trouble generating chances from their defense but generate many chances from below the circles. The half-ice overload smothers the offensive team on one side of the ice, but it is not as effective with teams who are good at changing the point of attack. The man-on-man system is based on pressure and players sticking to their checks. If one player loses his check, excellent scoring opportunities result. We recommend that coaches not change from system to system depending on the opponent. They should pick one that is suitable for their level of play and teach it well.

2-3 System

In this system, the two defensemen work with one forward (usually the center) to cover down low, while the wingers cover the slot and higher areas (figure 10.2). Listed here are the key areas of defensive zone coverage, including teaching points for coaches. This should form a basis for teaching your players how to play in your own zone without the puck. You can also use it as a framework for developing your defensive zone drills. While in the defensive zone, all players should have an active stick, meaning that the stick is on the ice and is moving. This tactic takes away shooting lanes and leads to turnovers and transition opportunities.

Playing Low Three on Three

D1, F1, and D2 work together in layers and play the three low zones (hit zone, support zone, and net zone). The first forward back assumes the

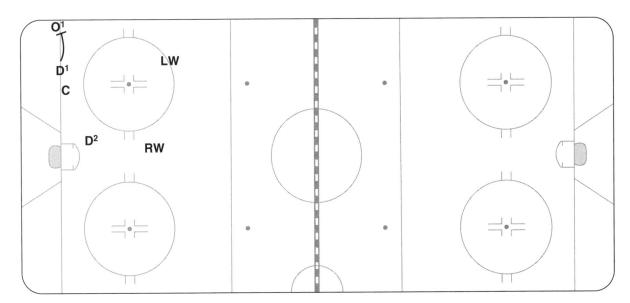

Figure 10.2   In the 2-3 system, the two defensemen work with one forward to cover down low, while the wingers cover the slot and higher areas.

position of F1 (figure 10.3). Most of the time you want your center in this position (assuming he is the better of the three forwards in defensive play), so an exchange may be made when appropriate.

With the new interpretation of the rules at the NHL and amateur levels, body position means everything. Players are less able to create interference, hook, or hold up players, so early defensive positioning is critical.

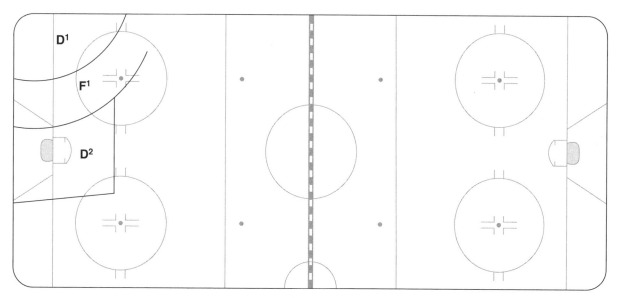

Figure 10.3   Low zone positioning for D1, F1, and D2.

Hit Zone

In this area, the first defensive player quickly closes on the puck carrier and makes contact with the opponent's body (figure 10.4). He must show patience if the puck carrier has clear possession before he can get there. If the defensive player sees the opposing player's number, he closes quickly but must be careful of hitting from behind; if the defensive player sees the opposing player's logo, he contains. By containing, the defensive player holds his position briefly and then cautiously goes at the puck carrier. Containing means keeping the puck carrier in a set space by holding inside position and not letting him get to the net. After the puck is moved or the puck carrier loses possession, the defensive player stays with his check (does not hook) until that player is no longer a passing option. The defensive player then releases that player and moves into one of the other zones. The desired goal is for all defending players to keep their positioning between the opposing players and the goal they are defending.

Support Zone

In this zone (figure 10.4), the defensive player is aware of both the puck carrier and the closest passing option. He makes sure that the puck carrier cannot walk to the net if the first player gets beaten or falls down, and he is ready to take away the opponent's closest passing option. He must give himself some space to react to the movement of players and the puck. At all times, he tries to stay above the goal line in support coverage. Because teams rarely score from behind the goal line, the team's defensive positioning should not have players rushing into this area.

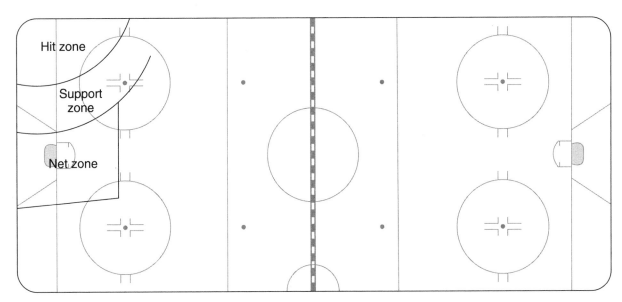

Figure 10.4 The hit zone, support zone, and net zone.

Net Zone

One player, usually a D, must always be in this zone (figure 10.4). He must be aware of the third offensive player and play halfway to any overload shooters (the offensive player on the half of the ice where the puck is). If breakdowns occur, he must be patient and not leave this area unless replaced by a teammate. He keeps his stick on the ice and stays out of the blue crease area, allowing the goaltender to have free movement.

Strong-Side Top Zone

F2 holds inside position at the top of the slot (figure 10.5). F2 must be ready to slide out tighter to his point if the puck carrier has the ability to pass there or cover him tight if he comes into the slot. When players cycle up high out of the corner, F2 must hold the top of the circle and deny inside access. After a pass is made out to the point, F2 must approach the defenseman in the shooting lane to take away a direct shot on net.

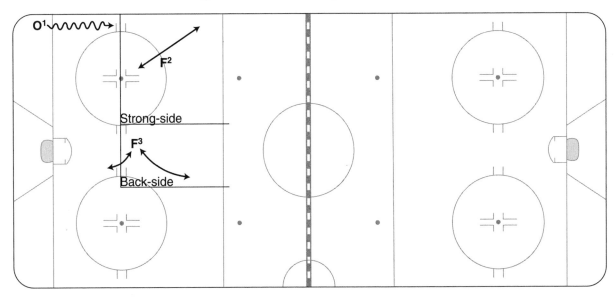

Figure 10.5 F2 covers the strong-side top zone, while F3 covers the back-side slot.

Back-Side Slot Coverage

F3 slides down lower on the back side (figure 10.5). If the net D is caught out of position, F3 will protect the low slot. He needs to be aware of the back-side point sliding in. If F3 loses sight of where the back-side defenseman is, then he will have an opportunity to move into a dangerous scoring area for a wide pass outside the vision of the goaltender. F3 must always have his head on a swivel.

Low Zone Shrink

In this system, all five defensive players collapse in tight and basically play the opponent five on three low (figure 10.6). The theory is to take away all plays to the slot by outnumbering the opponent and clogging up the scoring area. Most NHL teams use this collapse around the net style of play when the puck is below the goal line or after a point shot. After the puck is passed back to the defenseman, the wingers who have collapsed in tight move out to block the shooting lane.

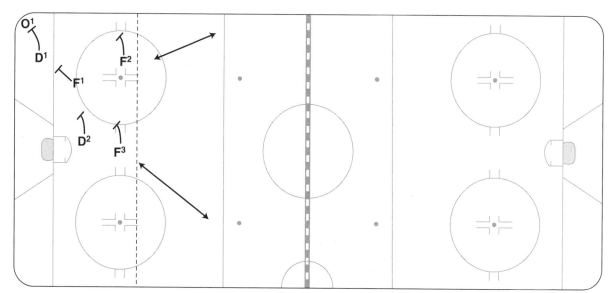

Figure 10.6   The low zone collapse coverage areas.

Playing Low Five on Three

D1, F1, and D2 work together and play the three low zones (hit zone, support zone, and net zone; figure 10.7). The first forward back assumes the position of F1. Most of the time you want your center in this position, so an exchange may be made when appropriate. The other two forwards sink in tight as well. The adjustment from the 2-3 system is that all three low players move tighter to the corner. The cue for the shrink to happen is when the puck carrier is contained in the corner. D2 can now move to the strong-side post and then right into the pile if D1 and F1 have contained the puck in the corner. F3 plays close to the net, covering the low slot, while F2 (who is also collapsed below the dots) tries to deny passes back to the point.

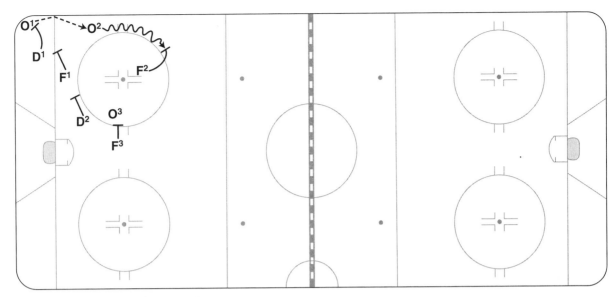

Figure 10.7 Low five-on-three coverage.

High Zone Coverage

When the offensive team moves the puck back to the point, F2 expands out in the shooting lane (figure 10.8). F2 should move quickly but be under control when the defenseman is ready to shoot. F2 should get into the shooting lane when he anticipates a shot. At times he will have to slide and block the shot. F3 holds the slot by moving out slightly. When the opponent passes the puck D to D, F3 moves out in the shooting lane and F2 rebounds back to the low slot.

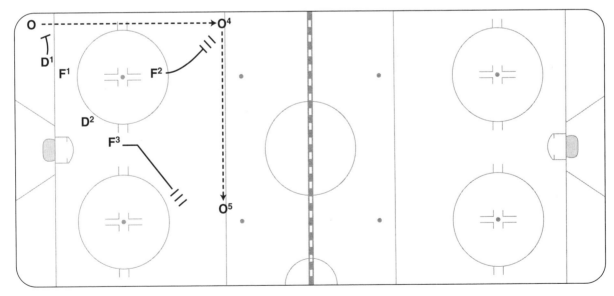

Figure 10.8 High zone coverage.

Half-Ice Overload

This system is a blend of the 2-3 and low zone shrink. In this system, the defensive group splits the rink in half, trying to squeeze the offensive team to one-half of the ice (figure 10.9). Plays to the back side are given up but made difficult because of the number of bodies in the way and the difficulty of making the long cross-ice pass. D1, F1, and D2 take care of the strong-side corner and at times will be playing the opponent three on two in that area. These three defensive players squeeze the offensive space that the opponents have to work in, and after the puck is recovered, they either quickly move it up the strong side or escape out the wide side.

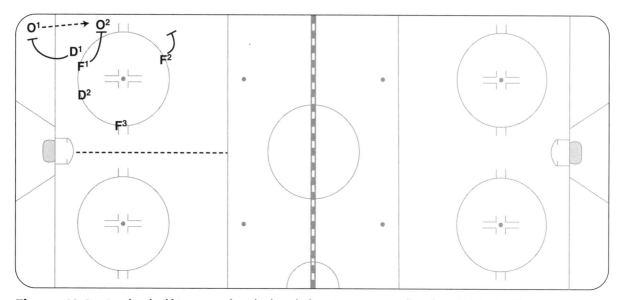

Figure 10.9   In the half-ice overload, the defensive team splits the rink in half.

If the defensive team has three players down in the corner, then the most important player off the puck is F3, who covers the slot but also shades to the strong side. F3 must be aware of the opponent's third forward and cover anyone who comes to the front of the net while at the same time be looking to see whether the opposing back-side defenseman is moving into the scoring area. The opposition will try to sneak a defenseman down the back side, so F3 has to be aware and alert. F2 takes away the strong-side defenseman by playing much closer to the boards, therefore denying a pass out to the strong-side point. F2 needs to start inside the circle, move out to cut off players cycling up the boards, and have an active stick to cut off passes to the point.

The advantage of this system is that it lessens the ability of the offensive team to find room to move and make plays on the strong side. Many teams like to cycle and then attack the net, but with this system, space to cycle is all but eliminated. When offensive players play against teams that use the half-ice overload, they often complain that they have no time! The one disadvantage is that quick plays to the net may result in a two on one on F3 if the opposing defensemen drive to the front of the net, but this pass is difficult to make.

Man-on-Man Coverage

This system relies on constant puck pressure and denying time and space to the opponent. D1 starts by pressuring the puck carrier and then, after a pass is made, sticks with that player as he tries to get open. The only place D1 won't follow the player when he doesn't have the puck is out to the blue line; D2 has tight coverage on any players in the slot. F1 now pressures the pass, and if the puck is moved he sticks to his man (figure 10.10). This continues with D2 in the low zone area, while F2 and F3 have responsibility for the opposing defensemen. F2 and F3 cover the defensemen whether they move in through the slot or slide down the boards. The man-on-man system eliminates confusion with regard to whom a player is covering, but if the opposition is creative and incorporates lots of motion, staying with your check becomes harder. The new rules preventing clutching and grabbing have made it harder to play a true man-on-man system, but it can be effective if the defenders are good skaters. The offensive team has minimal time with the puck before being pressured, and players away from the puck have trouble finding space to get open for a return pass. This system is also simple to learn because of the strict stay-with-your-guy coverage.

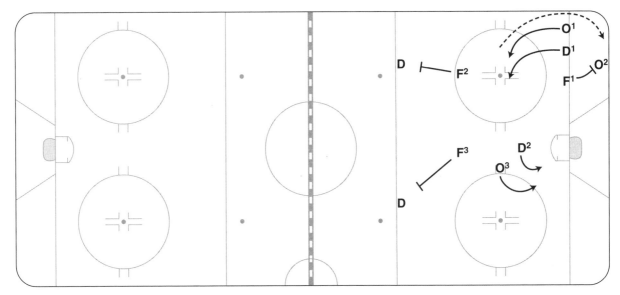

Figure 10.10   Man-on-man coverage.

Situational Guidelines for Defensive Zone Coverage

No matter which system you choose to use defensively, unique situations will always come up that give players trouble in coverage. Listed here are several of them.

Covering Active Ds

When covering active Ds, both F2 and F3 have a responsibility to cover their points if the opposing Ds move into scoring position. More teams are encouraging their defense to be active. If the defenseman whom F2 or F3 is covering moves into the slot, he must be covered tight. If the defense-man slides down the boards, two options are available. F2 or F3 can either cover tight and move down the boards and into the corner with the D or let the D go and hold the inside position (figure 10.11). After the opposing D is down low in the corner, he can be covered by the defending Ds or low forward. F2 or F3 can sink down and play inside but should not get dragged into covering a D in a nonscoring area.

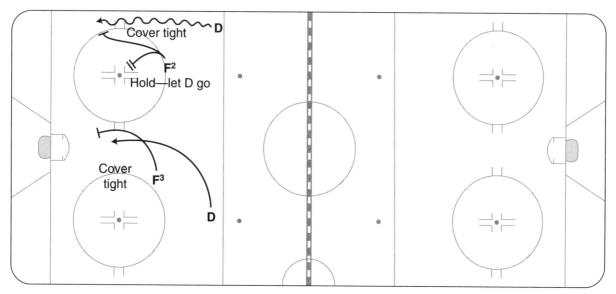

Figure 10.11   Covering active Ds.

If they are worried about the offensive ability of the opposition D, some teams put their wingers higher in defensive zone coverage. They may play as tight as 10 feet (3 m) away when the puck is down low and right on the Ds when the puck is moved high.

Handling a Low Two on One Off a Breakdown

When a breakdown occurs in the corner after a defender falls down or misses his check, the opponent may attack two on one versus the net defender (figure 10.12). The net defender must be patient and hold the net area. As the puck carrier advances, the defender allows the goaltender to take one offensive player while holding the midnet position and defending the pass across. The D at the net must block the passing lane while at the same time forcing the puck carrier to shoot from a wide position.

Defending a Player Behind the Net

First, the defender should recognize that a player is behind the net and intercept the pass. If the situation is even, the defender should pressure the puck carrier right away. When pressuring, he should try to force the puck carrier away from where he got the pass and away from support. If the player is unsure or the opponent has the advantage, he should wait to pressure until all defending players get back to position. RD flushes (for right-shot opponent); C holds mid-ice, aware of the back door; LD holds

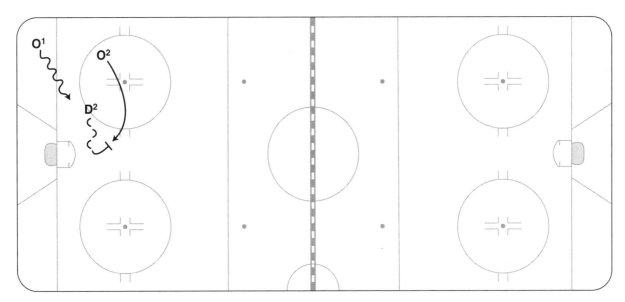

Figure 10.12 Handling a two on one out of the corner.

the back post; and the high wingers sink in tight (figure 10.13). After the flush has started, LW (the side you are forcing them to) will start to slide back out toward his point, while RW stays tight in the slot. In all situations when the opposing team has the puck below the goal line, only one defender should be below the goal line so that the defenders outnumber the opponents in the house (or scoring area) (see 10.13).

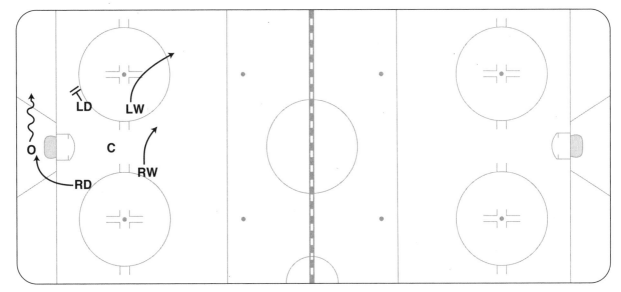

Figure 10.13 Defending a player behind the net.

Defending the East–West Cycle

One strategy that offensive teams utilize to break tight defensive zone coverage is to move the puck quickly from side to side behind the net. When this happens, D2 at the net should quickly pressure the puck carrier to take away their time and space (unless a player is open in front). The D pressuring the puck carrier should keep his stick on the puck to take away passes out to the slot. F3 moves to the wide side, and F2 moves into the low slot. D1 and F1 now move across into their layers or shrink coverage (see figure 10.14).

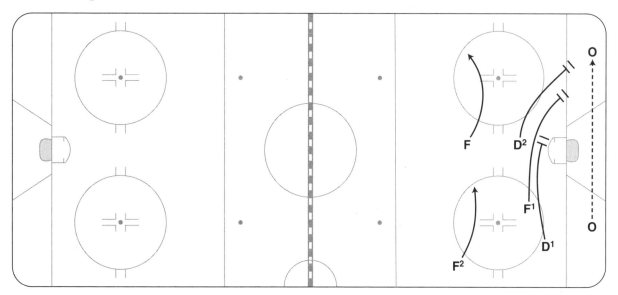

Figure 10.14 Defending the east–west cycle.

Covering the Board Scissor Exchange

When the opposition D slides down the boards and receives an exchange pass from a forward cycling up the boards, coverage can be accomplished in basically two ways. The first is for F2 to move with the D down the boards and cover him tight all the way into the corner (see figure 10.15a). D1, who is moving up with the opposition forward, covers him after the exchange is made.

Because this exchange often happens quickly, we believe that F2 should go after the D only if he can get on him early. If he cannot, he leaves him to the down low coverage F1 to pick up. D1 would still shade the opposition forward on the exchange (see figure 10.15b).

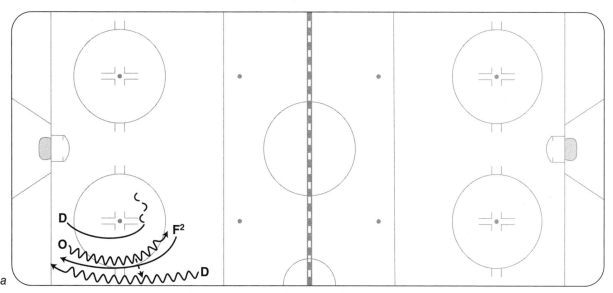

Figure 10.15a F2 stays with D on the scissor cycle.

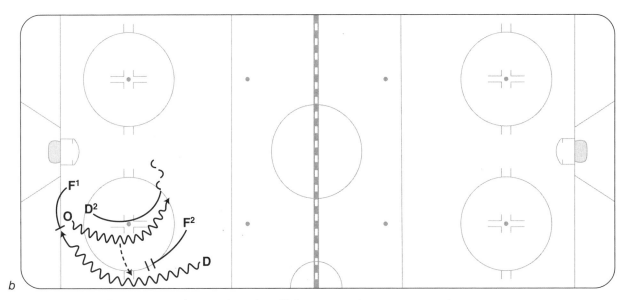

Figure 10.15b   F2 switches or hands-off the D on the scissor cycle.

Covering the Overload Shooter

Teams can cover the overload shooter in two ways. Every team in the offensive zone wants to have a player with the puck in the corner, one forward at the net, and one in a shooting overload position. This player is often set up somewhere in the strong-side offensive circle. One option is to have D2, who is responsible for the net area, slide out into the circle and be ready to take away passes to the overload shooter. If this is your coverage choice, then F3 must be aware of any plays to the low net area (see figure 10.16a).

The second option is to have F3 slide over and cover the overload shooter while D2 holds the net front or strong-side post. F2 may also help with the coverage, but he is usually tighter to the boards and the overload shooter is often set up more inside (see figure 10.16b).

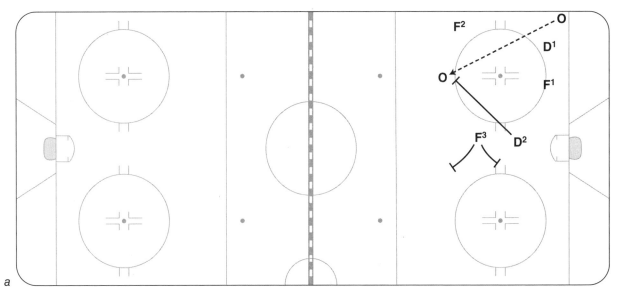

Figure 10.16a   D2 covers the overload shooter.

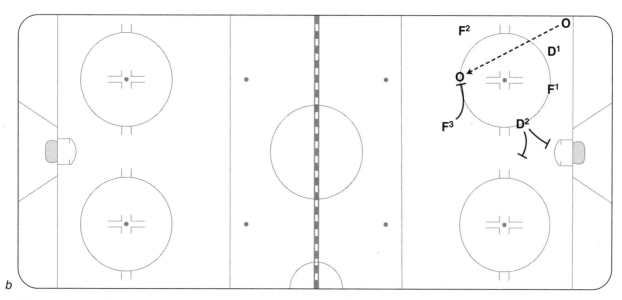

Figure 10.16*b* F3 collapses to cover the overload shot.

Chapter 11
Penalty Kills

Today's game of hockey can be characterized by two focuses and two words: *special teams*. Over the past few seasons, much has changed at all levels of hockey. Most of this change stems from increased attention by officials on the obstruction that had snuck into our game. Players and coaches had become adept at running interference and slowing down not only the game but also its most skilled players. A by-product of this change is a gigantic increase in the volume of penalties and an obvious effect that power plays and penalty kills have on the outcome of each game.

The penalty kill has in many ways turned into an art. Players who in years past may have played a lesser role because of their lack of offensive gifts are now playing a major role in making sure that the opposing power play does not affect their team's chances of winning. Here are the keys to successful penalty killing:

- Outwork the power play. Most PP units relax to a degree because of the extra man, so be prepared to outwork them.
- Win face-offs. Possession of the puck and a quick clear will not only force the PP unit to go back 200 feet (61 m) for the puck but also frustrate the PP unit, which is what you want.
- Talk. Communication improves positioning and awareness.
- No big hits. Never hit on the penalty kill, as tempting as it is; you should only bump and run. Keep your feet moving and pressure the opponent. Making a big hit takes players out of the play, which you can't afford when already down one player.
- Have an active stick. Keep it on the ice at all times and in the right passing lane.
- Get body position in shooting lanes and know when to go down to block shots. Blocking shots can be a big boost to the penalty kill.

○ When in the zone, pressure the puck in straight lines—rebound back into position quickly after you pressure and lead with your stick as you return.

○ Compete hard for loose pucks.

○ When clearing the puck, make sure it goes 200 feet (61 m). Try to score only when you have a lane to take the puck into the offensive zone.

○ Never get tied up with the player at the net. Most leagues prevent you from moving that player legally, so after he is there, do not create a double screen in front of your goaltender; play around him and have an active stick.

○ Players coming out of the penalty box must know where to go. Coaches should set rules for all players coming out of the box when the puck is in your end.

Face-Offs and Penalty Kills

All penalty kills have one thing in common: They start with a face-off. Many pundits of our game see the neutral zone face-off as a throwaway item, especially while killing penalties. We disagree. Every face-off is an opportunity to gain puck possession, and every detail of winning these face-offs must be attended to. For example, lazy positioning can seep into our game. In the neutral zone both defensemen sometimes pull off the line and hang back toward their own end at face-offs.

In this simple example of attention to details, abandoning the left or right side of the face-off increases the opponent's ability to gain puck possession. Always place players on the penalty kill, including defensemen, tight to the face-off (figure 11.1), so that they can contest for the loose puck and thereby increase your ability to gain possession. Possession of the puck

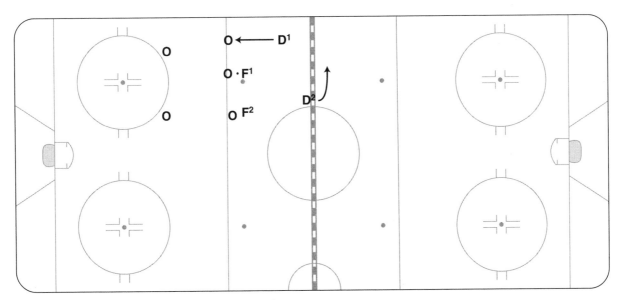

Figure 11.1   Always place players tight to the face-off on the penalty kill.

on the penalty kill may last only seconds, but every second decreases your opponent's ability to score with the player advantage.

For obvious reasons, the defensive zone face-off becomes a crucial component of a successful penalty kill. Proper possession of the puck in the defensive zone often allows your team to relieve pressure and advance the puck 180 feet (55 m) away from your goal.

A key component of aligning or positioning your players (especially who takes the face-off) has much to do with the center's strong side. During Ryan Walter's nine seasons with the Montreal Canadiens, he played a number of those seasons with Guy Carbonneau. Carbo was a right shot, Walter was a left shot, and both were good at winning face-offs on the strong side. What an advantage! On face-offs to the left of the goalie, Walter could easily draw the puck on the backhand; face-offs to the right of the goalie put Guy on his backhand strong side.

The defensive zone penalty-killing face-off alignment has many options. Let's discuss a few.

Most NHL teams try to have the center draw the puck back toward the corner, hoping that the boards-side defenseman can jump quickly off the line to gain possession of the puck or bump the puck to his partner behind the net (figure 11.2). Ideally, this boards-side defenseman is on his forehand when he approaches the puck. If this is the case, the best option is to lay the puck to the inside winger, who moves quickly toward either the opposite half boards or the opposite side of the net.

On seeing the puck won cleanly, the inside winger races to the corner or the half boards to retrieve a bank pass or slow rim by the boards-side defenseman.

We have found over the years that minor details are important, such as making sure that a right-handed defenseman is on the ice to maximize a won face-off opportunity. (In this case, because the face-off is left of the net, having a defenseman with a right-hand shot on the boards to handle the puck is an advantage if the draw is won cleanly.)

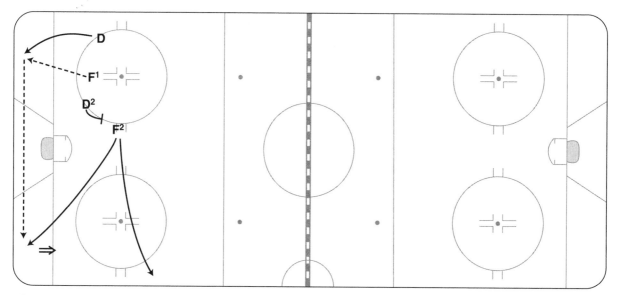

Figure 11.2 A common penalty-kill face-off strategy is to have the center draw the puck back toward the corner.

Never give your opponent soft possession of the puck off the draw. Always make sure that all opposing players are contested for possession of the puck (figure 11.3). If the puck is drawn to the boards, your team should not easily give up possession. Make sure that the boards-side D contests any tied draws hard. You may say that these are small details, but details are important when dealing with the penalty kill.

There are some other important points to consider about defensive zone PK face-off alignments. We prefer the winger to be inside the pocket of your team's inside defenseman (figure 11.4), and here's why. Hundreds of times we have seen this winger jump through toward the center, win a loose puck, and clear it down the ice.

We also prefer this alignment because the inside winger has a better chance to jump off the lost face-off and force pressure than the center

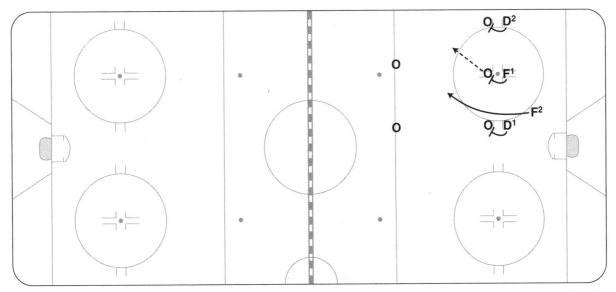

Figure 11.3   Always contest all opposing players off the draw.

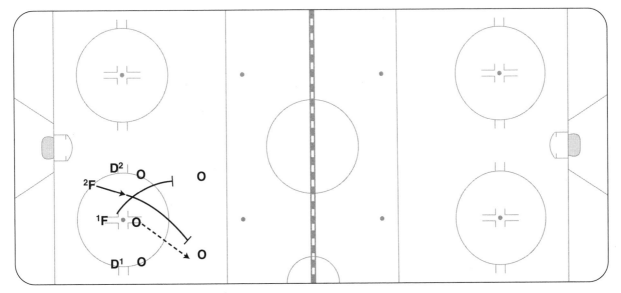

Figure 11.4   The winger should be inside the pocket of your team's inside defenseman.

does. In Montreal off a lost face-off, that inside winger would press the puck hard, and the center would then respond to the secondary positioning (figure 11.5). This alignment works especially well now because face-off interference is called much more tightly. The opposition cannot obstruct this inside winger as much as they could in previous eras of our game.

With the game tightening up, the obstruction rule has changed how teams set up their players for face-offs. In this alignment in the past, when the center cleanly won the face-off, the boards-side defenseman would hold up the opposing player a bit, the inside winger would hold up the opposing winger a bit, and the inside defenseman would retreat and slap the puck down the ice (figure 11.6). Obviously, this alignment is still excellent, but both the winger and the boards-side D must be careful on the holdups.

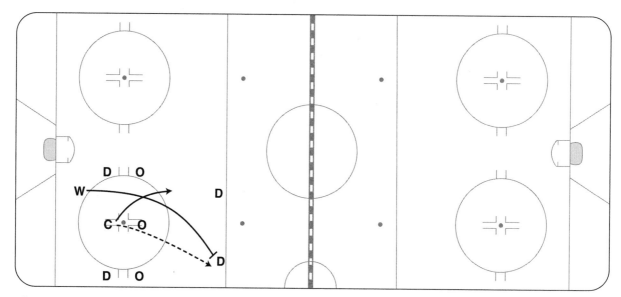

Figure 11.5   Off a lost face-off, the inside winger can press the puck hard and the center responds to the secondary positioning.

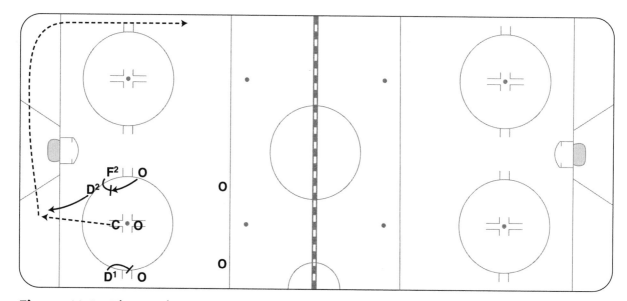

Figure 11.6   The inside D retreats and slaps the puck down the ice.

Another effective way to clear the defensive zone when the face-off is won cleanly is the winger press. In this alignment, the boards-side D rims the puck hard around the boards, and the winger now staying outside presses or runs the opposing D to make sure that the puck departs the zone (figure 11.7).

Whatever face-off alignment is used, coaches can see how important it is to have every player on the ice in sync and understanding his role. Remember, the face-off is the only time that hockey players get to play football. Face-offs are a great opportunity for you or your center to call the play and then celebrate when the players on the ice perfectly execute it.

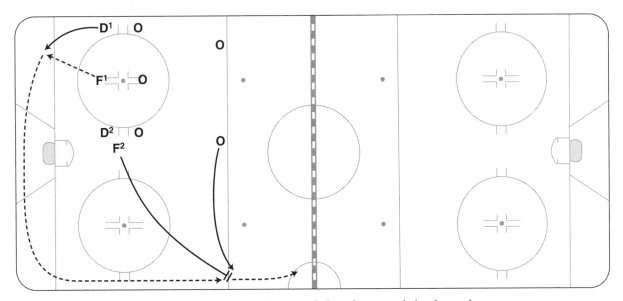

Figure 11.7   The boards-side D rims the puck hard around the boards.

Forechecking and Penalty Kills

Now that you have cleared the puck 200 feet (61 m) from your net (initiating the forecheck) with the help of your expert face-off alignment, let's look at ways to respond to your opponent's breakout. Coaches use different styles of up-ice positioning, and it all depends on the objective of their attack. For example, do you want to angle your opponent toward the red line? Do you want to take away speed and a primary passing option? Do you want to pressure deep up ice or meet the attack at the far blue line? Do you want to prevent a long pass and possible breakaway? Your team's objective determines how your players, especially the two forwards, align themselves on the forecheck.

After clearing the puck or carrying it out of the defensive zone, penalty killers have three options:

1. Change to get fresh players on the ice. A change is the priority at any time close to 30 seconds into the shift.

2. Pressure the puck when it is dumped down and try to disrupt the breakout.

3. Challenge the PP and try to score. Many PP units have a forward on defense and are made up of the team's best offensive players. On most teams these players lack defensive skills, so the PP unit's ability to defend is below average. If attempting to score, don't get fancy—take the puck straight to the net. If you try to make too many plays, the chance of a turnover increases and most likely you will be caught and too tired to react appropriately. If you simplify the attack and go hard to the net, more than likely you will draw a penalty or get a decent scoring chance.

This section describes five forechecking options. In reality, the PK unit rarely disrupts the PP breakout deep in the opposition's own end; therefore, on the forecheck you should position yourself through the neutral zone so that you are able to pressure the entry.

Tandem pressure is a more aggressive style of forecheck pressure, allowing the forwards freedom to angle and press the puck carrier. This style puts more pressure on the opponent in the neutral zone but can spread out the four penalty killers over two zones.

The forwards-wide approach offers token pressure up ice and creates a four-player alignment across the defending blue line. This setup forces the opposition to chip or dump the puck into the zone and accomplishes its goal of taking the puck out of the power play's hands so that the PK has an equal chance of retrieving the puck. The forwards-wide approach works well against power plays who prefer to carry the puck into the zone on entries because pressure can be applied on that puck carrier to turn over the puck.

The retreating box (or the backing-up box) keeps all puck possession to the outside and allows angled pressure and no cross-ice passing. The retreating box works well against power plays that dump the puck into the zone because it keeps the PK D farther back into the zone and therefore gives them a better chance at puck retrieval. The retreating box does allow the power play more possession entries but never through the middle. In other words, opponents can skate with speed on the outside of the box and maintain possession of the puck until challenged deeper in the zone.

The same-side press forecheck forces the opponent's entry toward one side of the ice where all the defending pressure can be applied. This system allows both forwards to angle the direction of the play and allows that strong-side defenseman to step up and make the blue line hard to enter. Teams who move the puck well laterally in the neutral zone may have a chance to break this forecheck, but the same-side press makes it difficult to enter on the strong side.

The passive 1-3 backs up in unison and tries to hold a close gap in the neutral zone. This formation is more passive but has the same goal of getting the power play to dump the puck into the zone (taking the puck out of their hands) and giving the four penalty killers an opportunity to retrieve and ice the puck. This alignment is primarily set up to confront the PP unit at the blue line and force a turnover or dump-in.

TANDEM PRESSURE

F1 angles and pressures the opposition, trying to get there as soon as the opposing player picks up the puck (figure 11.8). F1 recovers after forcing a pass or stays in the battle if he creates a scramble. F2 angles in on the first pass, making sure he is in position to get back while trying to force the player to unload the puck. D1 and D2 maintain a tight gap, making sure they are aware of any stretch players. F1 fills in the mid-ice lane, while F2 stays up in the middle, skating backward or angling forward and trying to force the entry to one side.

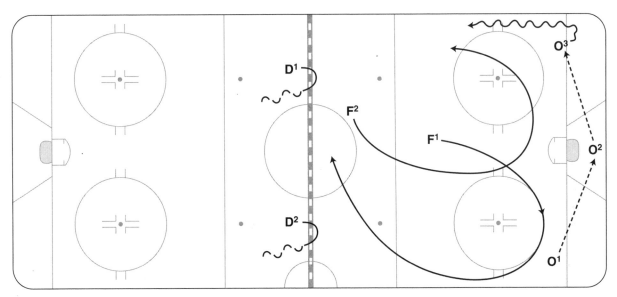

Figure 11.8   Tandem pressure forecheck.

FORWARDS WIDE

F1 angles and pressures the opposition, trying to get there as soon as the opposing player picks up the puck (figure 11.9). F1 then moves back and takes the wide lane while skating forward. F2 swings and takes the opposite wide lane, also skating forward. D1 and D2 stay up in the middle; they need to have a tight gap and confidence to be tight in the neutral zone.

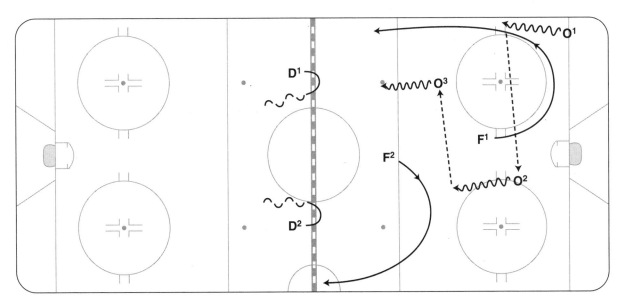

Figure 11.9   Forwards wide penalty kill forecheck.

■ RETREATING BOX

F1 forces the opposition if he can and then skates backward up one side of the ice in line with the dots (figure 11.10). F2 skates backward up the other side. D1 and D2 tighten up in mid-ice. All four players skate backward together. When the opposing puck carrier crosses the blue line, F1 or F2 forces that player to his backhand. Therefore, if the player is a left shot, F2 forces him toward F1. F1 tries to deny the pass back to where he came from.

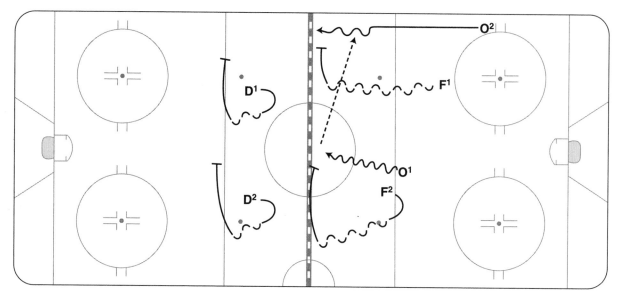

Figure 11.10   Retreating box forecheck.

■ SAME-SIDE PRESS

F1 and F2 wait in the neutral zone for the opposition to break out (figure 11.11). F1 angles the puck carrier to one side with a good stick, preventing passes back. F2 angles across to the same side and goes after the pass or the puck carrier. D1 and D2 tighten up in mid-ice. D2 is ready to challenge passes to the far side, and D1 is ready to retrieve pucks dumped in.

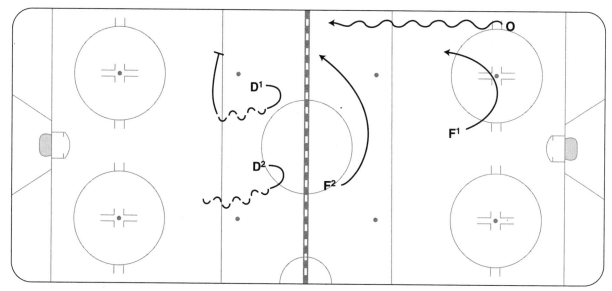

Figure 11.11   Same side press forecheck.

■ PASSIVE 1-3

F1 applies pressure only when he is sure he can get the puck and clear it, or he can force the other player as he picks up the puck (figure 11.12). F1 now retreats with a tight gap, initially skating backward, and he then forces the puck carrier to one side. F2 stays in mid-ice behind F1, also skating backward with a tight gap. D1 and D2 stay up; they need to have a tight gap and confidence to be tight in the neutral zone. They also must be aware of any stretch players getting behind them. D1 or D2 must attempt to confront the entry at the blue line by standing up the puck carrier and forcing a dump-in.

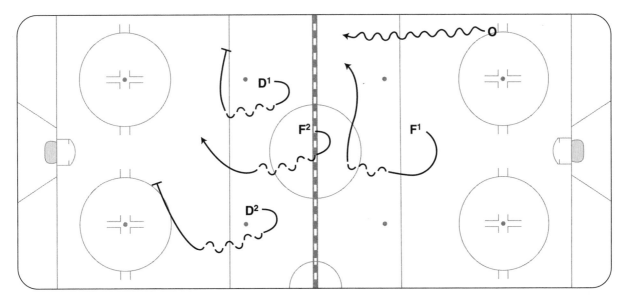

Figure 11.12   Passive 1-3 forecheck.

Pressuring the Entry

The entry is one area of the penalty kill where you should focus your time as you develop the special teams unit. If you stall the PP—at your blue line or as soon as they enter your zone—and clear the puck, you have effectively killed about 20 seconds off the clock and have a chance to change, while the PP unit will generally stay out and try to enter again. Teams may challenge the entry by making an immediate stand at the blue line, forcing the puck carrier at the half boards or pressuring the dump-in. Described here are ways to confront the setup of the PP unit, depending on the forecheck used.

■ TANDEM PRESSURE

D1 confronts the puck carrier, at the blue line if possible, while F1 goes after any pucks chipped in (figure 11.13). F2 holds the slot. D2 retreats to the net as an option for F1 to bump the puck to. If the PP unit carries the puck deeper, then D1 confronts the puck carrier at the half boards, and F1 seals up top. F2 holds the slot area, and D2 holds the net area. If the puck is dumped in, then D2 goes hard to the dump-in. F1 and D1 also go to the puck. F2 holds the slot area.

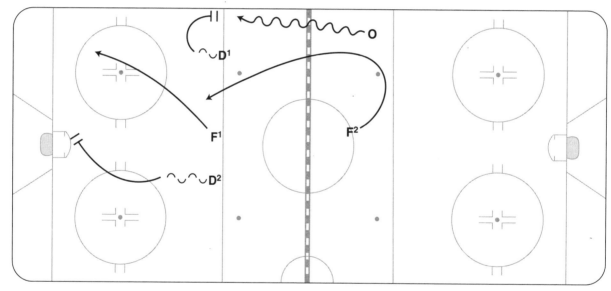

Figure 11.13   D1 confronts the entry at the blue line.

FORWARDS WIDE

D1 and D2 stay up in the middle where the PP unit will try to bring the puck (figure 11.14). If the pass is made to the wide lane, then F1 and F2 challenge the outside lanes. On the dump-in, F2 and D2 go to the corner along with D1. F1 supports the net.

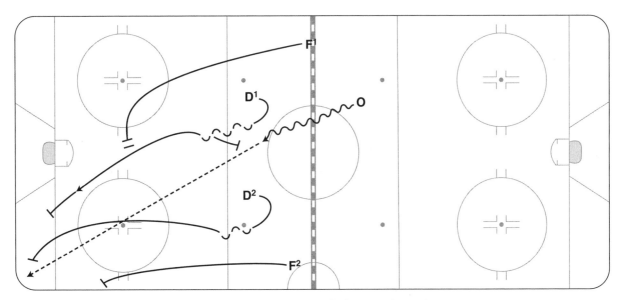

Figure 11.14   D1 and D2 stay in the middle with forwards wide.

RETREATING BOX

F2 or D1 tries to confront the entry at the blue line (figure 11.15). D2 goes after pucks chipped in, and F1 holds mid-ice. If the PP unit skates the puck in, then D1 or D2 confronts the entry at the half boards. F1 and F2 hold the top positions. If the PP unit dumps the puck in, then D1 and D2 both go to the puck. The closest forward tightens up, and the other forward holds the slot.

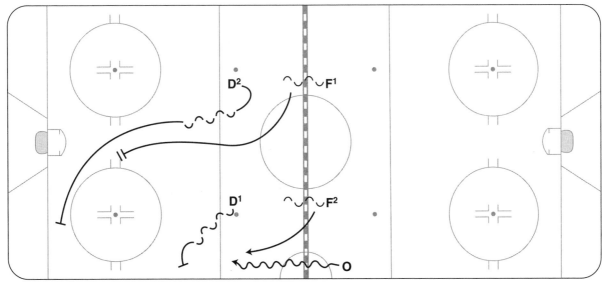

Figure 11.15   Pressuring the entry with a retreating box.

■ SAME-SIDE PRESS

F1 angles the puck carrier to the outside (figure 11.16). F2 tries to force the entry at the blue line or force the puck carrier to dump the puck. D2 goes after any pucks chipped in. With pressure from F1, F2, and D2, the PP usually cannot skate the puck in unless a pass is made to the wide side. On dump-ins, D1 goes to the corner with support from F1 and D2. F2 holds the slot.

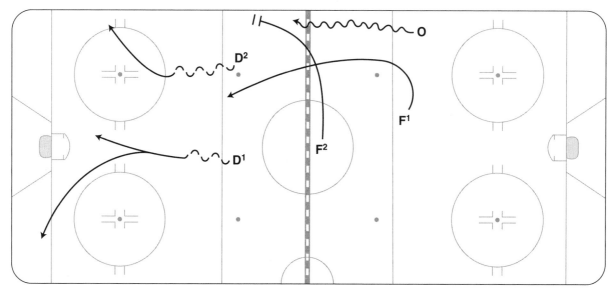

Figure 11.16   Using the same side press.

■ PASSIVE 1-3

This setup is similar to the setup of the tandem press. D1 confronts the puck carrier at the blue line if possible, while F2 goes after any pucks chipped in (figure 11.17). F1 holds the slot. D2 retreats to the net or is an option for F2 to bump the puck to. If the PP unit carries the puck deeper, then D1 confronts the puck carrier at the half boards and F1 seals up top. F2 holds the slot area, and D2 holds the net area. If the puck is dumped in, then D2 goes hard to the dump-in. F2 and D1 also go to the puck. F1 holds the slot area.

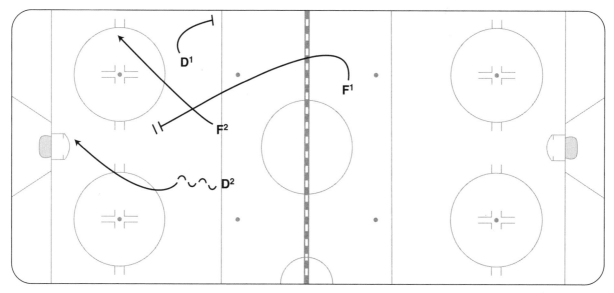

Figure 11.17   Passive 1-3.

■ BACKING-UP DIAMOND

Many teams at all levels incorporate the diamond in the way they forecheck and as they back off into the neutral zone. The goal of the diamond formation is to eliminate a direct middle pass to a speed forward and to angle the puck carrier toward the boards with the intent to get the puck out of their hands. Most penalty killers want to press puck carriers into short ice on or before the red line, but accomplishing this task is often a tall order. The secondary goal of the diamond is to force the offensive team to dump the puck in. All power-play units prefer to enter the zone with strong puck possession, so disrupting this puck possession is the primary goal of your PK forecheck alignment (figure 11.18).

The backing-up moving diamond formation is obviously preferable to a standing-still diamond (we see many PKs get into deep trouble here). The forecheck timing and depth of all four players is critical to sustaining movement and backward reactive speed.

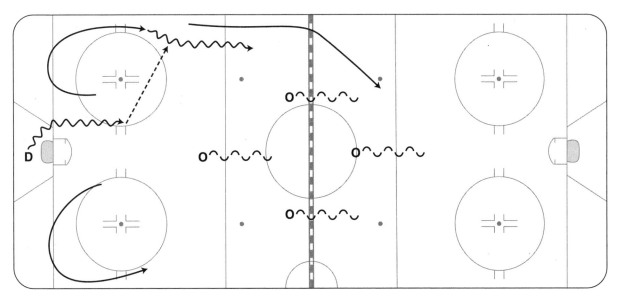

Figure 11.18 Penalty killers use a backing-up diamond look.

Defensive Zone Play

While in the defensive zone, the penalty-killing unit moves from active contain to contain pressure to all-out pressure, based on the reads of when to pressure. Every coach will be comfortable with a different degree of pressure. Some coaches make a simple rule for their players to read when to press and when not to press. The rule is called "eyes and backsides." If your player sees that the opposing player with the puck is looking directly at him, he moves into a more passive containing mode. If the player sees an opponent's backside or number, he applies maximum pressure. Obviously, when a player is turned to get the puck and is not facing mid-ice (backside and numbers), he is not ready to make a play and therefore can be pressured harder. Remember, when one player moves to pressure, each subsequent pass must be pressured.

Scoring Shorthanded

Because many defending teams are using the flip pass or the off-the-wall and out play to ice the puck, PK forwards are getting good at sending the far-side winger to press the puck down ice and potentially get a good offensive bounce. Scoring goals while on the PK used to be rare, but as up-ice and neutral-ice pressure is increasing, turnovers ending in scoring chances are becoming more of the norm (figure 11.19).

The penalty killers should assert more pressure when they know that the puck carrier will have a difficult time controlling the puck and making a good play. Here are some examples:

O The PP has poor control, or a player juggles a pass.

O The player with the puck has no immediate support.

O The player with the puck has his back turned to the net.

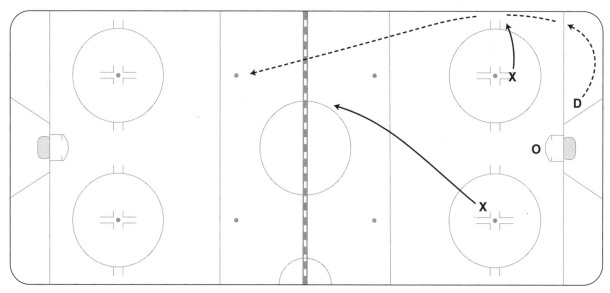

Figure 11.19   Far-side winger contests the puck.

○ The puck is being rimmed from one player to another along the boards.

○ A puck is loose from a rebound or missed shot.

○ The ice conditions are poor late in the period.

Following are some situations PK units may face and ways to play them. We describe various power-play options and the way in which the penalty killers should react.

■ LOW–HIGH PRESS

When O2 receives a pass from O4 or O1, D1 pressures him up the boards (figure 11.20). D2 is ready to take away any return passes to O1. F1 takes away the passing lane to O4. F2 stays in the slot, aware of passing options to the back side. Players should keep their sticks in the most dangerous passing lane, which could be to the slot player or back-side D.

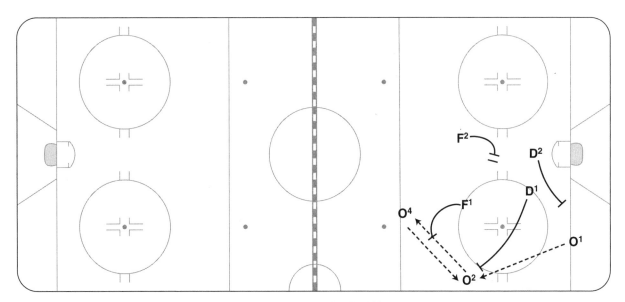

Figure 11.20   D1 and F1 combine to pressure the half boards.

■ CZECH PRESS

F1 forces O4 at the point (figure 11.21). O4 passes back to O2 on the side boards but too high for D1 to pressure. F1 now pressures back on the pass and forces O2 down the boards. D1 is ready to pressure the pass to O1. D2 holds the slot and prevents any cross-ice passes. If the puck is passed back to O4, two options are available: (1) F1 can return up high to pressure, or (2) F2 can pressure, and F1 returns to the slot. F2 would pressure only if he can get there at the same time as the pass.

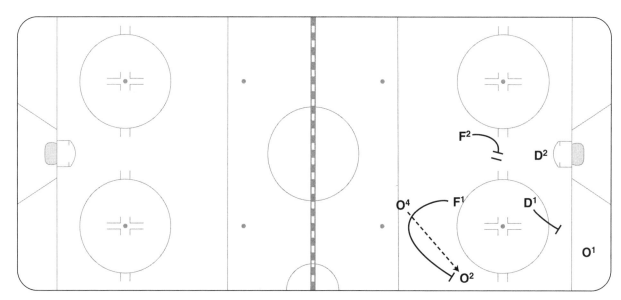

Figure 11.21　F1 executes the Czech press.

■ DIAMOND FORCE

F1 pressures or stays in O4's shooting lane as he slides with the puck across the blue line (figure 11.22). D1 moves up slightly, ready to go after O2 if the pass goes there. F2 sinks back into the diamond and is ready to get in the shooting lane of passes to O5. D2 plays the net. Players stay in this formation as long as O4 continues to stay in the middle of the blue line.

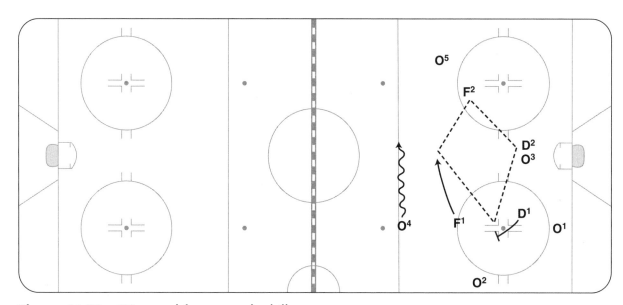

Figure 11.22　Diamond force penalty kill pressure.

■ FORCING THE BACK OF THE NET

Many teams like to set up behind the net on the PP or take the puck behind. D1 recognizes a chance to pressure and forces O1. D2 holds normal position, avoiding screens or picks, and is ready to challenge the walkout (figure 11.23). F1 slides down to replace D1. F2 moves to the middle of the triangle in front of the net, aware of any opposing Ds coming in from the point. Trying to deny passes to players behind the net is important—players should anticipate that play and cut it off as the pass is made.

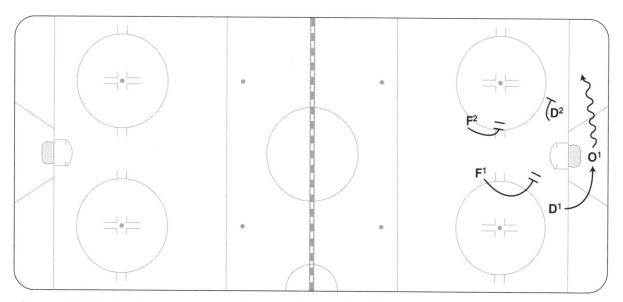

Figure 11.23   Forcing the power play out from behind the net.

■ TIGHT COLLAPSE

If the puck does end up behind your net, then all players should sink in tight (figure 11.24). They need to be aware of players moving in and have an active stick to take away passing lanes as the puck carrier moves out. D1 or D2 may hold his position or force the puck carrier to one side.

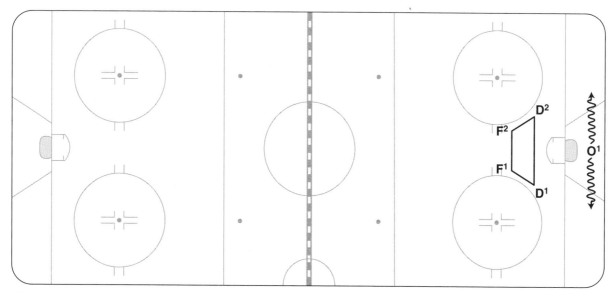

Figure 11.24   Four players execute the tight collapse.

■ HIGH BOX PRESS

Many power plays desire to move the puck back to their defensemen to get the puck on net through traffic. Penalty kills are often more passive when this happens because the forwards are working to block the shot by getting in the lane. The high box press allows the forwards to be more aggressive by forcing the power-play defensemen to make quick decisions. This high pressure activates the penalty-kill defensemen to press the play on the half wall and reduces the time and space available to the puck carrier. This high box press increases the chance of both turning the puck over near the half wall and relieving pressure by icing the puck (see figure 11.25).

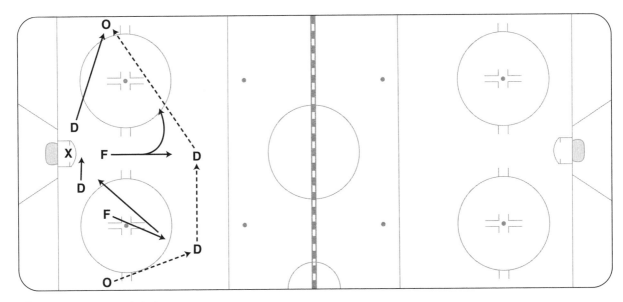

Figure 11.25   High box press.

Three-on-Five Penalty Kill

The three-on-five penalty kill is a difficult challenge, but at its best, it can be a work of art. The three on five is one area of the team game that, when successful, can create excitement and positive bench momentum for your team. The key to defending the three on five is to have all three players in sync with each other's movements and the system you implement. Coaches have to decide how tight they want to play it or how aggressive they are going to be. Following are three approaches that coaches like to use.

■ INVERTED TRIANGLE

This setup is suited to kill a five on three where the opponent has two Ds up top (figure 11.26). F1 and D1 (D1 could be a defenseman, although some teams like to use another forward) move up and down on their sides as the puck is moved from high to low. F1 and D1 should not go too wide or too high. D2 plays the net area and moves from post to post. D2 must deny the side-to-side pass from O1 to O2. F1 and D1 must be ready to block shots. During five on threes, the key goal is to stay tight and compact and be strong on rebounds.

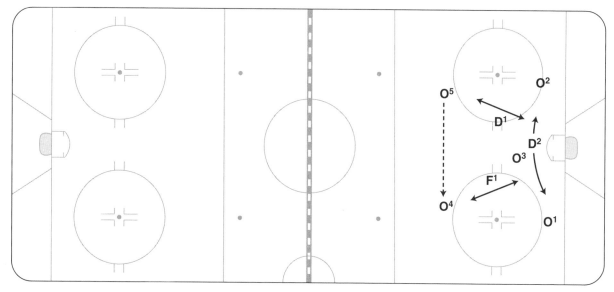

Figure 11.26   Using the inverted triangle when killing a five on three.

■ SPLIT THE DS

This setup is another option to kill a five-on-three penalty when the opponent has two Ds up top (figure 11.27). F1 stays in the middle of the ice, denying any high passes through the middle and any passes between the two Ds. D1 and D2 play the base of the triangle. When the puck is at the bottom with O1, then D1 forces him out wide and D2 covers the net. F1 stays in the low slot. This penalty-kill setup does not give up much down low, and it takes away any D-to-D up-high passes with the stick of F1.

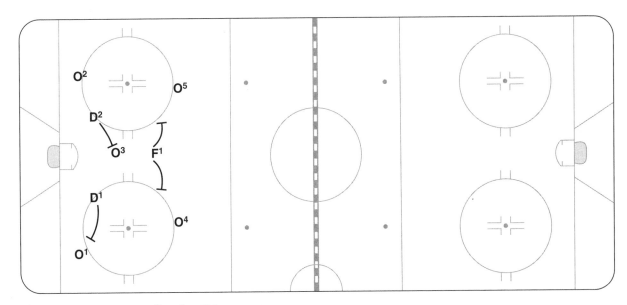

Figure 11.27   F1 splits the D's.

TRIANGLE, ONE HIGH

This setup is primarily suited to kill a five on three where the opponent has one D up top. F1 stays in the middle of the ice (figure 11.28). When the puck is up top, he stays head to head with the one opposing D. D1 and D2 form the base of the triangle. When the puck is at the bottom with O1, then D1 forces him out wide and D2 covers the net. D1 and D2 must also get in the shooting lanes of O3 and O4 when they have the puck. F1 stays in the low slot. Players should recognize where one-timer shots could come from and have active sticks.

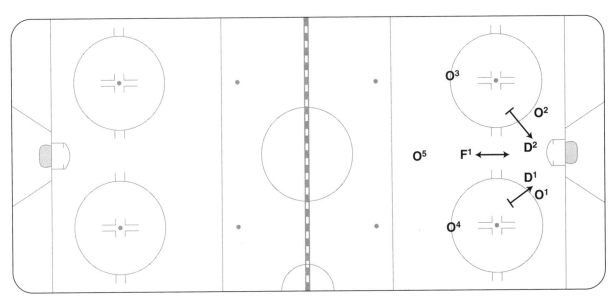

Figure 11.28   One high penalty kill versus five on three.

Three-on-Four Penalty Kill

The three-on-four penalty kill adds its own complexity and is similar to yet different from killing the three on five. The difference is that the defending three must decide whether they are going to take away the top two shooters or stay near the front of the net. Usually the four on three is much easier to kill than the five on three. The PK unit focuses on playing around the man at the net, leaving them three on three against the shooters.

■ TRIANGLE, ONE HIGH

Most teams on a four-on-three power play set up in a diamond with one player at the net, so the triangle penalty kill with one high is the most effective system to use. F1 stays in the middle of the ice (figure 11.29). When the puck is up top, he stays head to head with the one opposing D. When the puck is passed, F1 stays in the middle and uses his stick to deny the pass from O2 to O3. D1 and D2 are ready to move out and take the shooting lane away from O2 and O3. D1 and D2 do not tie up with O1 at the net but are ready to defend his stick and get body position if the puck is shot through.

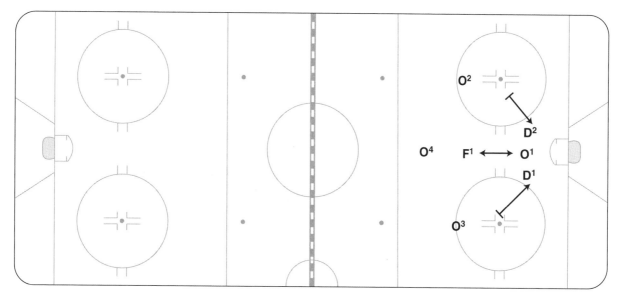

Figure 11.29   Three-on-four diamond with F1 in the middle.

Remember the old adage "Defense wins championships." Working on your team's PK structure, getting all players on the same page, and having your goaltender be your best penalty killer are all ways to give your team a better chance to win.

Part III

Building Your Competitive Edge

Chapter 12
Face-Offs

The offensive face-off gives coaching staffs and players their only opportunity to implement static set plays, like those that occur in football. Teams should prepare their plays off ice first and then work to integrate these face-off plans into their practices. Once a month, take time in practice to run through what you want the players to do at each face-off dot. Doing this takes time and tends to slow the pace of practice, but roughly 60 face-offs occur in a game, which means 60 times to win or lose possession of the puck, so the effort is worth the time. In addition to all players going through the face-offs, the centers must work on the skill of taking the draw. Not much time is needed for a coach to do 50 reps with a center before or after practice, focusing on his technique. Centers should work on winning draws on the forehand, on the backhand, by tying up, and at times by touching the puck through to catch the opposition by surprise. Make sure that one of your coaches becomes an expert at teaching these face-offs skills. High-level hockey has changed in this area of the game. When Ryan Walter began to play in the NHL as a center man, both centers tried to cheat laterally by adjusting the position of their skates to their advantage. Today, the requirement that skates face north–south has changed the way that center men try to generate an advantage. The center should get his skates as close to the center dot as possible, forcing him to hold the stick in a lateral position instead of straight out in front of him. This lateral stick positioning maximizes the center man's leverage and positioning to win the face-off.

In the past many coaches taught their players to never turn the bottom hand on the stick because doing so was telling their opponent which way they would be drawing the puck. Turning the bottom hand is another way to increase the power and leverage needed to win face-offs. Most face-offs are won by powering under the opponent's stick or obstructing the opponent's stick with your own and kicking the puck back to your players. Few face-offs are won by chopping at the puck or picking the puck out of the air.

Face-off strategies in the defensive zone tend to be a little more conservative. The goal is still to win possession of the puck, but not losing the draw directly to the opponent is primary. To accomplish this strategy, the face-off tactics change as well. During his playing career, Ryan took many face-offs against Mark Messier. We like the face-off move that Mark used, so we will call this one the Messier. Instead of going directly after the puck, Mark's first move was directly toward his opponent's stick, interfering with his ability to win the face-off. Mark would then draw the puck directly back to secure puck possession for his team. Many players use this tactic but did not have Mark's level of success, and here is why. Mark had a trick. He would elevate his bottom hand, thereby extending the amount of stick that he could reach toward his opponent's stick. This maneuver allowed Mark to generate maximum interference against his opponent's ability to win the face-off.

Understanding the strategy of face-offs and teaching the skill of winning face-offs will create more control for your team and help elevate the confidence of your players. Increased confidence comes from increased preparation. Continuously practicing the tactics and skill of your team's face-offs will pay off in a big way.

If your team is playing at an advanced level, start to rotate each winger through face-off technique practice as well. Preparing your wingers to be better than average on winning face-offs allows your center men to be much more aggressive on their draws. This type of extra preparation pays off when your center is kicked out of the face-off circle on the penalty kill and the winger replaces him.

Consider having a face-off play book that includes responsibilities as well as diagrams illustrating the execution patterns. Some teams have developed a DVD or USB sticks to give to the centers, who much like a quarterback in football need to know the formation and how to set up. This video should have dialogue and a clear illustration of the plays. Because of the clarity and camera angle, a good method is to collect plays from NHL, college, and junior games and edit the material down for your players.

Finally, depending on the age of your group, you may want to have the centers pick the option for their line for that night or come to you with a play they think will work. This type of player ownership can be effective; the players will definitely focus if they choose the play because they want it to work.

Have face-off plays for all face-off dots and for specific game situations. The way that a team lines up five on five is much different from how they line up for four-on-four and three-on-three situations. Don't forget power-play five on four, four on three, and five on three; penalty-kill four on five, three on four, and three on five; and late-game pulled-goaltender plays defensively and offensively. Over the course of my NHL career across three teams and seven head coaches, we implemented many face-off set plays, but they tended to be drawn from the following categories.

Offensive Zone Face-Offs

Offensive zone face-offs are an opportunity to create a scoring chance off a set play. Even if teams lose the draw, they can still recover possession and get a shot or chance. Many sophisticated offensive face-off alignments have been developed over the years, but the alignments discussed here cover the basics of offensive zone strategy and provide enough options for teams at every level. You may want to challenge your staff to come up with a set play of their own, but don't overwhelm your team with too many choices.

Offensive Zone: Won Draws

In the offensive zone, winning the draw and maintaining possession are critical. This section describes various set plays off won draws. A team cannot run all of them every night. Having some variance is important, but as with all systems of play, execution is the key to success. Give the team one play to run for every game; that way they will become used to all the setups so that later in the year they can adjust on the spur of the moment. In addition, having variety in plays from game to game keeps the opposition off balance and forces them to have to react in coverage. Make the opposition coaches work to figure out what you are running and how to cover that setup.

■ DEEP POSSESSION

For a number of reasons, an offensive center might call a face-off play in which he actually helps his opponent win the face-off back toward the corner of the offensive zone (see figure 12.1). The tactic behind this deceived loss is to have both wingers positioned and ready to press the defender when he wins the draw back to the corner. This quick and unexpected

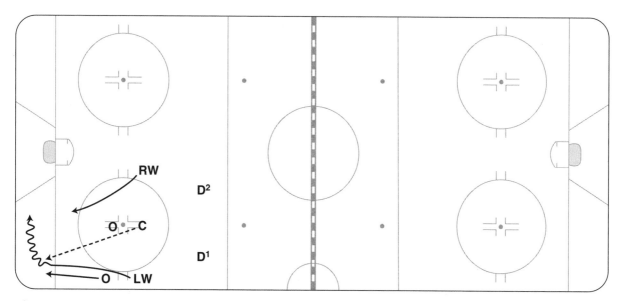

Figure 12.1   Deep possession face-off.

pressure often turns over the puck and therefore creates its desired effect, which is puck possession and a possible scoring chance or play on the net. Off the turnover, the player with the puck may decide to make a quick play to the net or take the puck behind the net and come out the other side. This strategy should be used only once or twice a game or if the center is struggling to win draws against a particular opponent (giving that player a strategy to gain possession while losing the draw).

■ INSIDE WINGER DRAW

This face-off starts with the direct intent to win the face-off back to the offensive defenseman. As defending players scramble to front or block the shooting lane of the offensive defenseman, the inside winger (RW) skates above the circle and out to the side boards (see figure 12.2). The center and LW must go hard to the net. The offensive defenseman's goal is to pull the puck toward the middle of the ice and fake a slapshot. As defenders react to this deception, the defenseman passes the puck laterally to the inside winger, who ends up with a clear shot toward the net through traffic. One variation is for C to drive the net and then push back to get open in the higher slot area. RW can now pass to C.

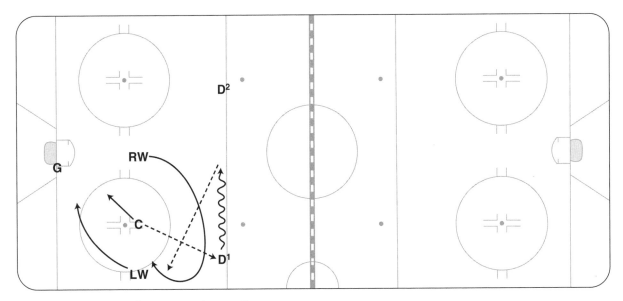

Figure 12.2   Inside winger face-off.

■ ROLL OUT

This offensive face-off alignment works well against teams who press hard toward both defensemen off the face-off. As the two wingers press the D, the roll-out alignment gives a great pass and shot option. Off a won draw to D1, the two wingers (RW and LW) change positions (see figure 12.3). The center drives to the front of the net. D2 drives wide; D1 backs across the blue line, fakes a shot, and passes to LW, who has found the soft ice (high and lateral from D1). LW now has the option of shooting through traffic or passing to RW or D2.

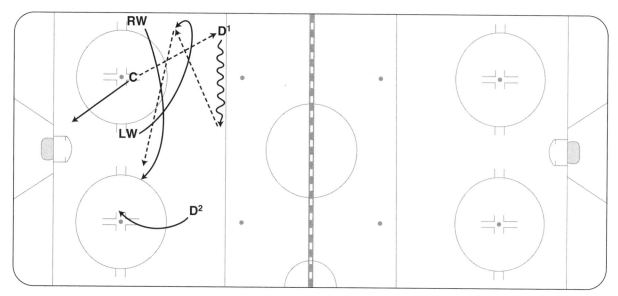

Figure 12.3   Roll out face-off.

■ END AROUND

Much like the inside-out draw, this alignment uses the inside winger moving to the boards (see figure 12.4). Instead of a high option, it creates an opportunity to take the puck to the net low. This face-off also starts with the direct intent to win the face-off back to the offensive defenseman, but the puck doesn't make it back and lies in the space right behind the center. The inside winger (RW) pulls or draws back toward the boards and in doing so grabs the puck and goes around the pile. As RW moves toward the back of the net, he may either take the puck to the net or pass to C or LW, who attempts to get open.

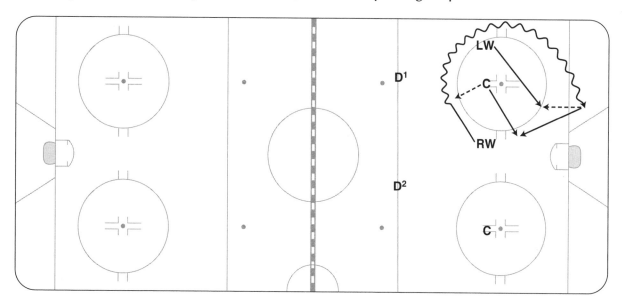

Figure 12.4   End around face-off.

■ OFF-SIDE SHOT

Some face-offs are not always won directly or completely back to the point. When the center senses that he is going to tie up the opponent's stick and win puck possession with his feet, then this simple alignment is effective. In this face-off alignment, the two wingers typically switch positions, unless the boards-side winger is already shooting off his strong side. The center looks to win possession of the puck in the space just slightly behind him (see figure 12.5). This allows the boards-side winger to step laterally toward the net and place a quick shot on net through traffic. Sometimes in this situation the center only has to tie up his opponent and leave the puck in the space behind him, which allows the winger to step into the shot.

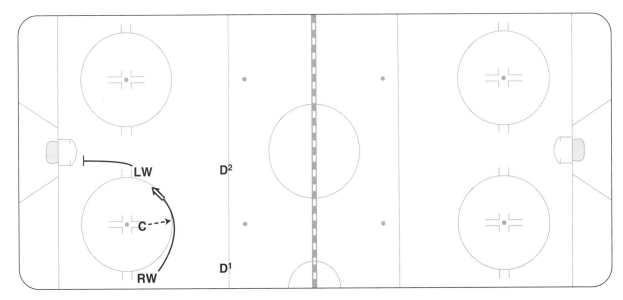

Figure 12.5   Off-side shot face-off.

■ SAN JOSE SLIDE

This offensive face-off alignment works well when your team is trying to change things up. It is another play that creates a lot of confusion for the defensive team. The center draws the puck back to D1, who moves quickly down the boards as he receives it (see figure 12.6). RW, who is on the boards, rolls over the top of the circle and sets up on the far post (the back door), taking the defender with him. LW also goes to the net, giving the defenseman an option to pass to the net at any time. As D1 moves down the boards, C makes it look as if he is going to the net and then moves back a couple of steps into a soft area in the high slot, where he is open for a one-timer pass from D1. The reason that C will be open is that the opposing center will probably go after D1. This movement off the face-off creates confusion in coverage for the defensive team.

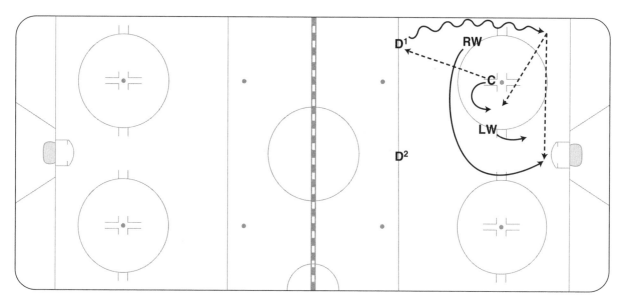

Figure 12.6 San Jose slide face-off.

▪ FOUR UP

Like a football team that is behind in a game with little time left on the clock, at times the team may be looking for a simple Hail Mary type play. With a four-up face-off alignment, both wingers are on the inside and one D is down on the boards-side hash marks (see figure 12.7). This alignment gives the center many options, making it hard for the defending team to cover. Some defending teams try to shoot the puck out past the one defenseman on the blue line; guard against that happening by having the inside winger slightly back and in the lane. The four-up face-off allows the center to tap the draw ahead and then pass to one of the two wingers in front, draw the puck back to D1 for a screen shot, or steer the puck to the boards for D2 to shoot or to pass to D1. This alignment is often used when seconds are left on the clock at the end of periods or the end of games because it results in a quick play on net with numbers in front.

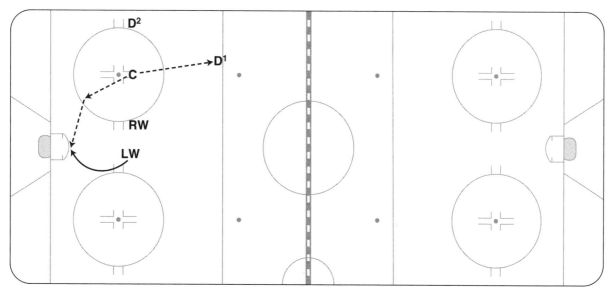

Figure 12.7 Four up face-off.

■ TIE-UP FOR POSSESSION

At times, centers just look to create possession of the puck for their team. Possession is often best obtained not by trying to win the puck but by blocking or tying up the stick of the opposing center (see figure 12.8). If the offensive center can obstruct the stick of the defending center long enough, both offensive wingers can attack the face-off circle to try to win puck possession. This strategy is often referred to as scrambling the puck. When one center is dominating the other, the player who is constantly losing the draw can try to tie up the other center to increase the odds of his team getting the puck.

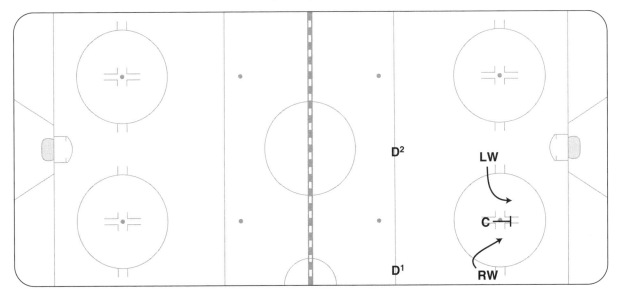

Figure 12.8   Sometimes centers tie up and look for help from their wingers.

■ OVER UNDER

This simple face-off alignment works equally well at all levels of the game. On either side of the offensive zone, the inside or middle winger skates behind the center man (over the puck) as the boards-side winger skates hard toward the net (under the puck.) This action gives the center maximum support in retaining possession of the puck (see figure 12.9).

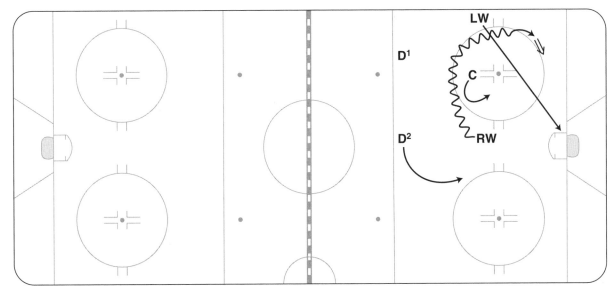

Figure 12.9   Over under face-off option one.

Although the over under is a simple process after the inside (over) winger gains possession of the puck, he can generate many scoring options. By drawing the defenseman lined up on the board with him toward the net, the boards-side winger creates separation and more space for the (over) winger to make plays. The first goal of this winger with the puck is to shoot it on net (see figure 12.9). Another simple option for the winger with the puck is to fake the shot and pass back to the center man, who slides into an open slot position (see figure 12.10).

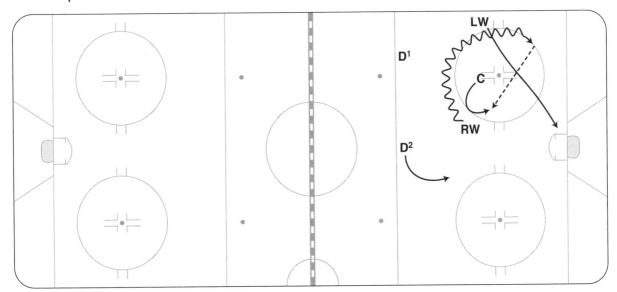

Figure 12.10   Over under face-off option two.

A simple third scoring option off the over under face-off alignment has the boards-side winger not drive the net, but instead skate behind the net to receive the puck and open up many other behind-the-net options, which include jamming the puck on net, passing to the center man sliding into the slot, and passing back to the defensemen to activate a shot through maximum traffic (see figure 12.11).

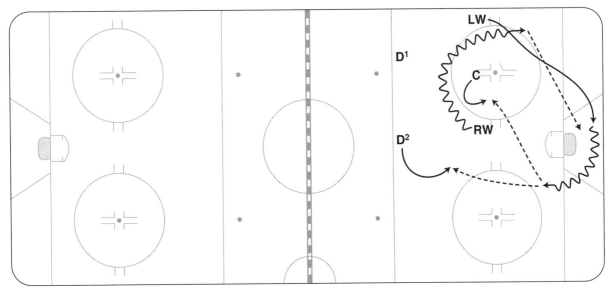

Figure 12.11   Over under face-off option three.

Offensive Zone: Lost Draws

Players should be prepared to win the draw and set up offensive plays as described, but they should also know what to do when the center loses the draw. If players are ready to react and they understand how they are going to pressure the opposition to recover the puck, they will be much more successful in doing so. Listed here are strategies to regain possession and essentially initiate a forecheck.

■ DOUBLE PRESS

When the C loses the draw, he moves to a high position in the slot (see figure 12.12). RW shoots through on the inside of the circle and pressures the defenseman getting the puck. RW must make sure that the D doesn't turn quickly up the strong side. He forces the defenseman to go into pressure by pushing him out the wide side. LW also jumps quickly to take away the wide side of the net and any D-to-D passes. D1 is ready to pinch on any pass to the opposing winger on the far boards. D2 stays in mid-ice as the safety.

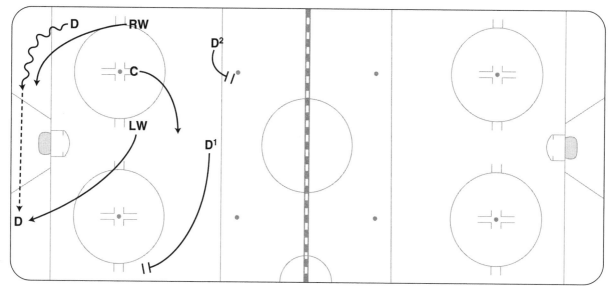

Figure 12.12   Double press off lost draw.

■ 1-2-2 FORCE

On the lost draw, RW pressures hard into the corner, forcing the defenseman around the net or to pass to his partner (see figure 12.13). On any D-to-D passes, RW moves across either behind or in front of the net and forces. C is ready to take away plays up the right boards and takes away the mid-ice seam as the puck moves to the wide side. LW takes away the far boards. D1 and D2 stay in mid-ice and react to any passes up the middle.

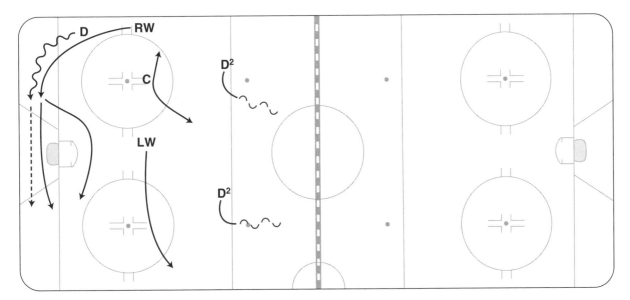

Figure 12.13   Forcing with one player off a lost draw.

Neutral Zone Face-Offs

At one time, many coaches, especially European coaches, gave little thought to draws in the neutral zone. Their feeling was that they were not important and didn't lead to anything. Most times their players would line up and halfheartedly take the draw. Now almost all coaches realize the importance of winning the face-off and gaining puck possession. Because of the change in emphasis on neutral zone draws, many new strategies have evolved to create a quick attack off this face-off or to apply forechecking pressure when the draw is lost.

Neutral Zone: Won Draws

Only a few face-off plays create an offensive advantage in the neutral zone. Opponents will press with one or two players off a lost face-off in the neutral zone, taking away passing lanes or closing ice, so having a plan with the puck is crucial. These actions tend to emulate neutral zone regroup options for moving the puck up ice. Described here are seven face-off plays from the center-ice and blue-line face-off dots.

■ CENTER ICE, THREE OPTIONS

C draws the puck back to D1, who passes to D2 (see figure 12.14). C swings away and builds up speed. RW stretches to the far blue line. LW slants in to the middle of the blue line. D2 has the option to pass up to RW on the stretch, to LW in the mid-ice seam, or to C wide. D2 may also skate the puck to the red line and dump it in for C on the wide side.

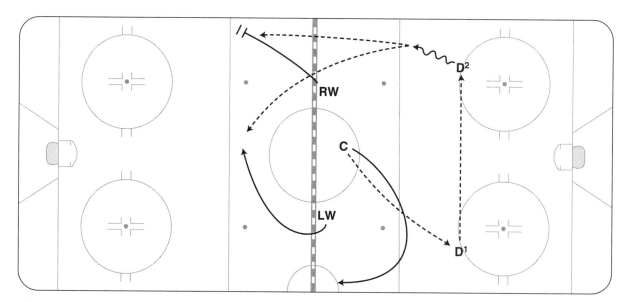

Figure 12.14   Center ice three-option draw.

HIGH DEFLECTION

This face-off play also takes place at the center circle. After C wins the draw, he moves above the red line (see figure 12.15). Both wingers go out to the top corner of the blue line. D1 passes to D2, who looks to pass to C for a quick chip into the corner for RW. D1 may also pass to RW, who chips the puck behind the defense for C to pick up. This play is a good one to start the game and apply quick forechecking pressure against the opponent.

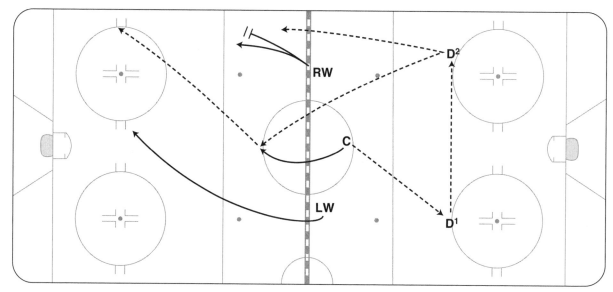

Figure 12.15   High deflection face-off.

FORWARD BACK

LW drops back for the draw and LD is up (see figure 12.16). C pushes the puck to the left side. Anticipating the draw, LW shoots through the hole and looks to skate or chip the puck by the opposing defenseman. RW also jumps quickly with LW.

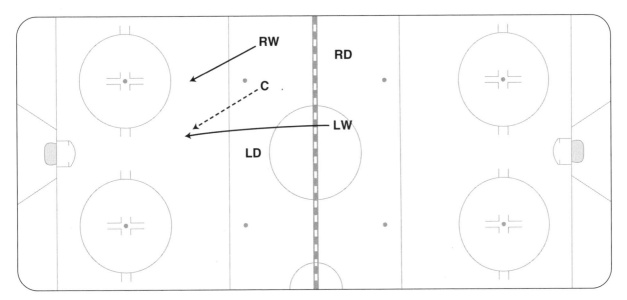

Figure 12.16   Neutral zone forward back face-off.

■ WEAK-SIDE SLANT

This face-off takes place at the defensive blue line. C draws the puck back to D1, who passes to D2 (see figure 12.17). D2 skates to mid-ice. LW picks or screens the player inside so that D2 has more time with the puck. RW goes hard to the corner of the far blue line. D2 banks the puck to the high blue-line area for RW to skate to. C jumps up through the middle to create a potential two on one on the opposing defenseman.

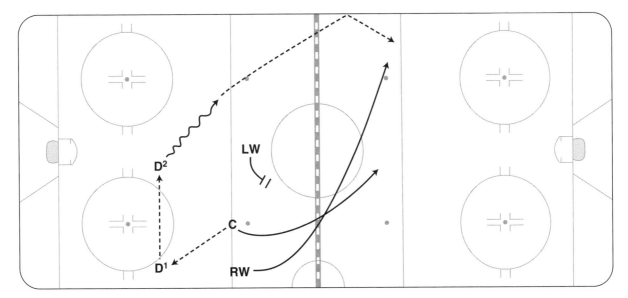

Figure 12.17   Weak-side slant face-off.

■ CENTER SLASH

C wins the puck back, and D2 passes to D1 (see figure 12.18). RW reads clear possession and sprints to the far blue line. C blocks the opposing C and then sprints through the middle lane. LW stays wide and low for a cross-ice support pass. D2 drops to support D1. D1 has pass options to C or RW sprinting to the far blue line and, if neither is open, has the wide pass back to LW.

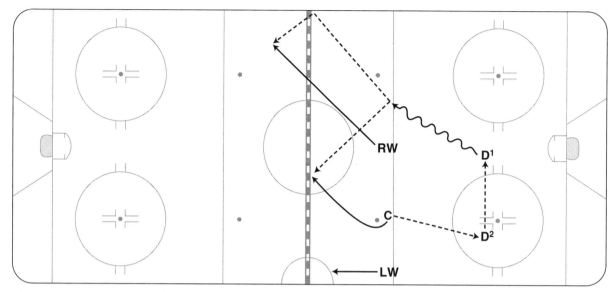

Figure 12.18   Center slash face-off.

■ CENTER SWING-AWAY

Off a won draw, C swings away from the D-to-D pass (see figure 12.19). LW sprints toward the boards and RW fills the middle lane. D2 may pass to LW or RW, but the main option is to get the puck wide to C, who has built up a lot of speed.

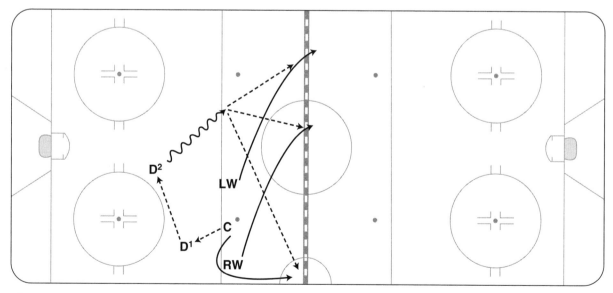

Figure 12.19   Center swing-away face-off.

■ HARD RIM

This face-off is used in leagues with touch icing when the team desperately needs to get possession in the offensive zone and create a quick scoring chance. There is a risk of icing the puck. C draws the puck back to D1, who quickly shoots it hard along the boards into the far end (see figure 12.20). LW races to the puck, trying to beat the opposing D. After LW gets the puck, he bumps it behind the net to RW, who then looks to bring it to the net.

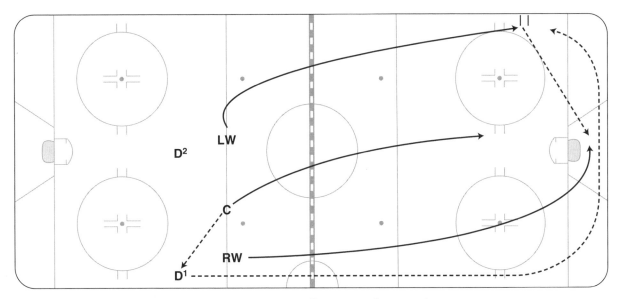

Figure 12.20   Hard rim to gain possession off a neutral zone draw.

Neutral Zone: Lost Draws

To regain possession of the puck off a lost draw, these strategies may be used on any of the five neutral zone face-off circles. In most situations, this sets up a team's neutral zone forecheck.

■ DOUBLE PRESS

When the draw is lost, both wingers move quickly to pressure the opposing defense (see figure 12.21). C locks the mid-ice area, preventing any passes to the other team's center. D1 and D2 are ready to take away passes up the boards and to move up quickly to pinch on the pass.

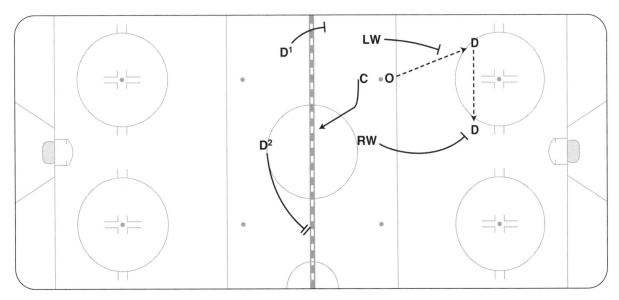

Figure 12.21   Double press on lost draw.

■ BOARDS-SIDE PRESS

On the lost draw, the boards-side winger (LW) forces the defense to pass the puck across the ice, into traffic (see figure 12.22). C locks the middle. RW takes away the far boards. D1 and D2 keep a tight gap in mid-ice.

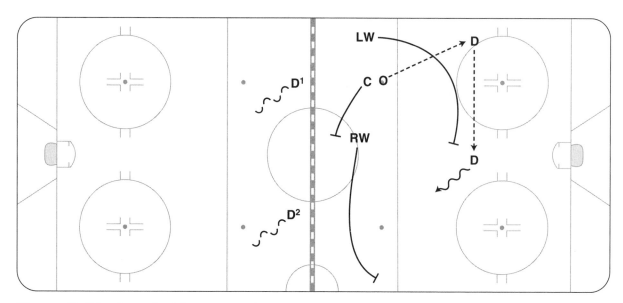

Figure 12.22   Boards-side press on loss.

■ INSIDE-OUT PRESS

When the draw is lost, C quickly moves up between the two opposing defensemen and angles the puck carrier to the outside (see figure 12.23). As C forces the play to the right, RW takes away the boards and any passes to that winger. LW locks the middle. D1 is ready to get any chip plays in behind RW. D2 plays mid-ice while being aware of passes to the wide side.

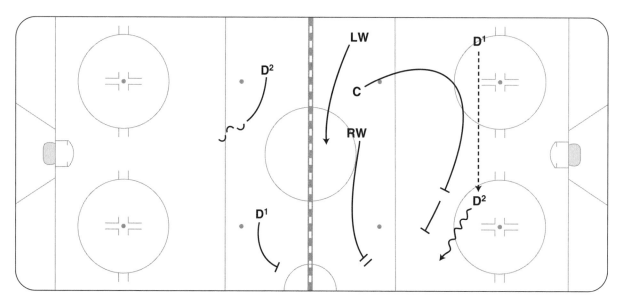

Figure 12.23   Inside-out press on lost face-off.

Defensive Zone Face-Offs

Winning a face-off in the defensive zone results in an opportunity to break out and go on the attack. Losing the face-off in the defensive zone forces a team to defend and essentially go into defensive zone coverage until a turnover happens. We discuss both situations and provide strategies for each.

Defensive Zone: Won Draws

Described here are seven plays that teams can use when they win the draw in the defensive zone. Teams should practice breaking out on a won draw from both sides of the ice. The option used will depend to a degree on how the opposition forechecks and what you believe your team can execute. The final two options in this section, the breakaway and quick-change plays, are trick plays that might be used only a couple times a year. They can be used at any time of the game but generally are saved for moments when you are down by a goal, because each of them includes a degree of risk. The rate of successfully completing these plays is much lower than for the others provided, but if your opponents are not ready, you may catch them by surprise

■ SPIN AND UP STRONG SIDE

If the opposition forechecks with their boards-side winger hard and takes away the pass to D2, then D1 goes back for the puck and spins off pressure, moving the puck up to LW on the strong-side boards. Before reversing the puck or spinning off, D1 must first carry the pressure to make the opposition think he is going behind the net. C supports low, and RW moves across to support (see figure 12.24). D1 may also bank the puck off the boards or glass into the neutral zone, and both wingers can race to that area. This play will surprise teams who pinch their defense and may result in a two on one.

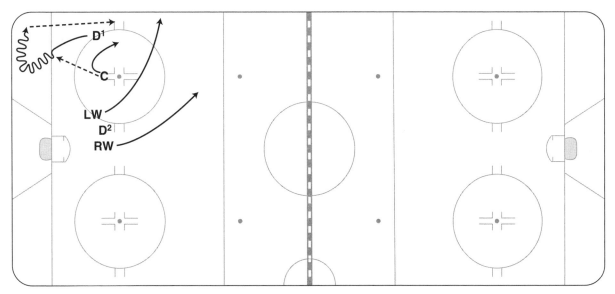

Figure 12.24   Spin and up strong side defensive zone draw.

■ REVERSE TO CENTER

Again, the opposition team pressures hard with the boards-side winger. D1 goes back for the puck and carries the pressure, trying to gain the back of the net. Knowing that he will not make it, he reverses the puck to C. Depending on pressure, D2 supports the front of the net or moves to the wide side, ready for a D-to-D pass. D2 should stay in front whenever D1 is under heavy pressure. LW moves back to support the boards, and RW moves across the ice in support (see figure 12.25).

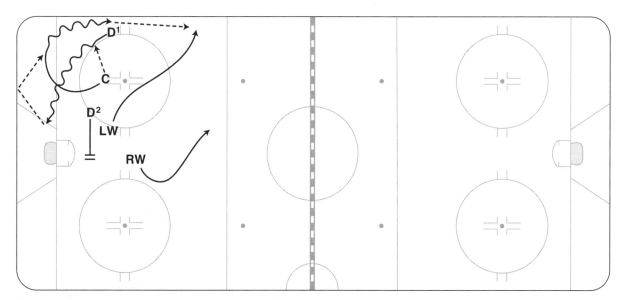

Figure 12.25   Reverse to center face-off in the defensive zone.

■ D-TO-D SHORT POST

Off a won draw, D1 gets the puck and makes a short pass to D2 at the near post (see figure 12.26). From the near post, D2 skates behind the net and reads options to rim the puck, make a direct pass to the winger or center in mid-ice, or possibly execute a return pass to his partner.

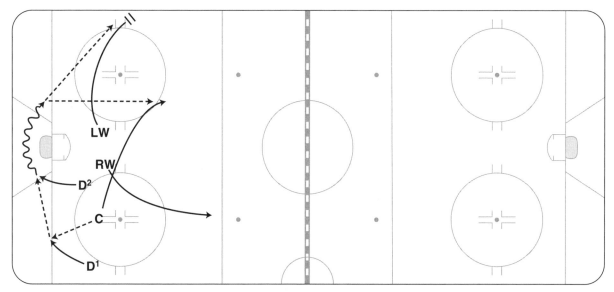

Figure 12.26   D-to-D short post face-off.

■ BUMP TO PARTNER

If the opposition forechecks with only one player, D1 quickly bumps the puck to D2, who releases to the wide side of the net in anticipation of the D-to-D pass. When D2 moves out to the wide side, he should try to be turned around facing up ice and ready for the pass when it arrives. RW moves out to the boards, and LW comes across through the high slot. C supports low (see figure 12.27).

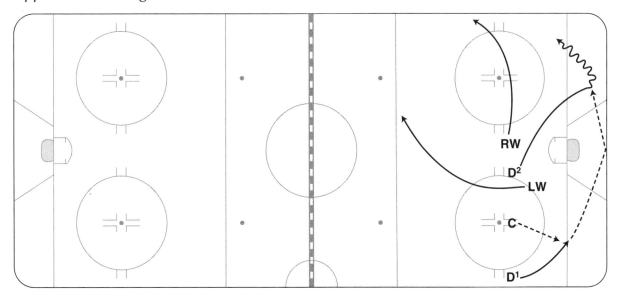

Figure 12.27   Bump to partner face-off.

■ WIDE RIM

This play can be used to catch the opposition off guard or late in a game when you are up or down by a goal. C wins the draw back to D1, who rims the puck (the Ds may switch sides before the draw to make the rim play easier). RW goes out to the point and then slants across to support LW (see figure 12.28). LW must get to the corner of the blue line before the opposing D. LW has the option to skate with the puck and go through the neutral zone or chip to RW if the opposing defenseman stays in the zone and pinches.

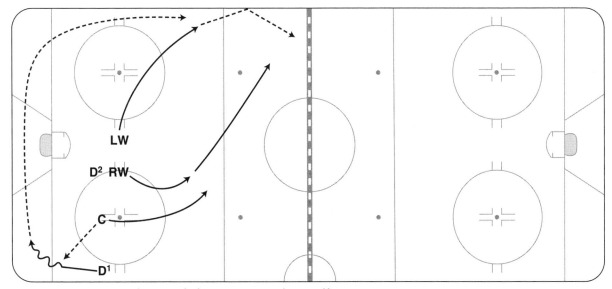

Figure 12.28   Wide rim defensive zone face-off.

■ BREAKAWAY PLAY

C draws the puck back to D1, who quickly skates around the net (figure 12.29). D2 screens to give D1 time to make a play. RW goes hard to the opposing defenseman as if he were going to cover the D. LW slides out to the boards, calling for the pass. RW slants to the center-ice circle. D1 lays or lofts the puck out to RW for a breakaway. RW should have a breakaway because the opposing defense will not have time to react. In leagues that have touch icing, the worst-case scenario is that RW gets the puck in the offensive zone. For automatic icing, the worst-case scenario is that the face-off will come back into your zone.

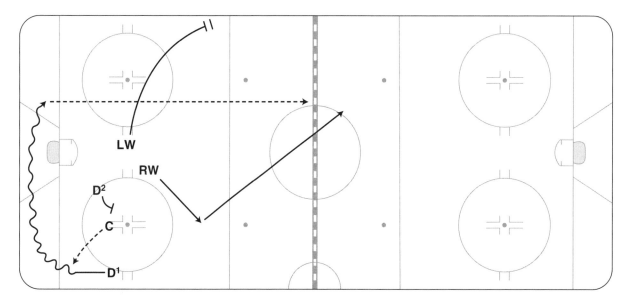

Figure 12.29   Breakaway play face-off.

■ QUICK-CHANGE PLAY

This surprise play should be practiced and used at key moments of the game or season. After opposing teams know you use it, they may watch for it and be able to react quicker. This play might be used once or twice a year as a trick play when a team is down by a goal with the face-off in their own zone. C draws the puck back to D1 (see figure 12.30). RW goes hard to the opposing defenseman as if he were going to cover the D. RW then goes by the D and onto the bench. One forward is waiting at the opposite end of the bench and quickly heads out to the far blue line. LW goes to the boards for a pass. D1 fakes a pass to LW and passes to the new forward at the far blue line.

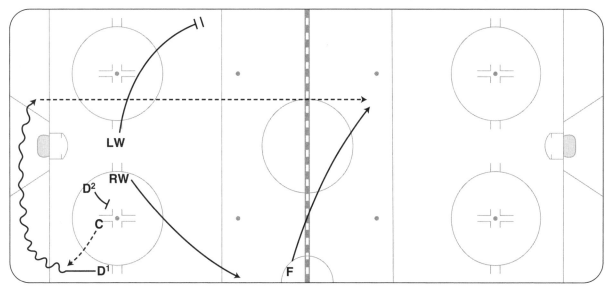

Figure 12.30 Quick change face-off.

Defensive Zone: Lost Draws

Teams may use two variations of alignments in their defensive zone. Outlined here are the responsibilities for each player when the face-off is lost. Five across is the most common alignment, in which all players are set to defend; D back gives you an offensive advantage if you win the draw, but it requires some quick adjustments if you lose.

■ FIVE ACROSS

This common setup is generally used for 80 percent of all defensive zone draws. When C loses the draw, he stays with the other team's center (see figure 12.31). RW shoots through on the inside of the circle and pressures the point. LW moves out to the high slot and is ready to go after the other D if a pass is made. D1 and D2 stay with their forwards. Five across has become the NHL standard defensive zone face-off alignment. The only variation is that D2 will be a few steps back with some teams so that he can break out quicker when the draw is won. All five players have clear assignments and can adjust off this positioning.

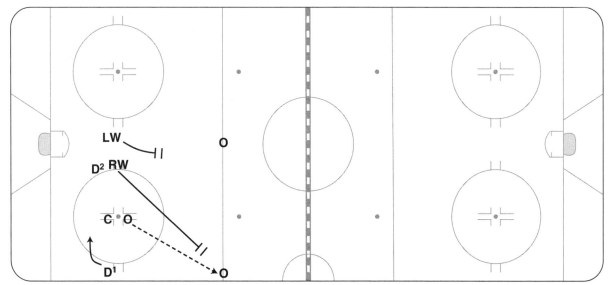

Figure 12.31 Five across is an effective way to pressure off lost draws in the defensive zone.

■ D BACK

Some teams like to have a D directly behind the center on the draw for an easy breakout (see figure 12.32). If you lose the face-off in this setup, C stays with the other center. RW pressures the boards point, and D1 takes the forward he was lined up against. LW moves into the high slot, ready to pressure the other defenseman if a pass is made. D2 steps up quickly and takes the inside forward.

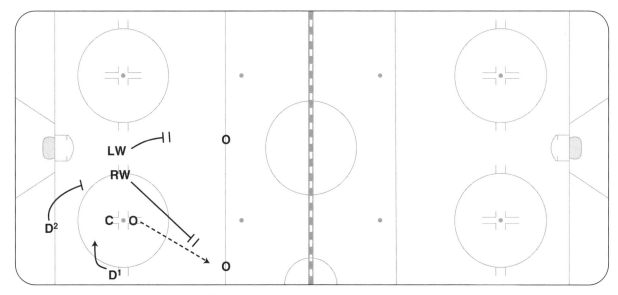

Figure 12.32   D back face-off.

Power-Play Face-Offs

Winning or tying up and getting possession on power-play draws are crucial. If the other team clears the puck, the power-play unit generally needs 20 seconds to get set up again, which is both frustrating and tiring. Described here are three ways to get possession and set up. Players and coaches should also try to recognize what the penalty-killing unit is trying to do if they win the draw; by doing so, you may be able to regain possession even though you lost the draw.

■ TRADITIONAL ALIGNMENT

When C wins or ties up on the draw, both wingers move in to push the puck back to the Ds. On lost draws, RW shoots through to the corner and puts pressure on the opposing D. LW takes away the D-to-D penalty-kill clear or assists RW in the corner. C reacts to apply pressure and support RW and LW (see figure 12.33). Although you would like to win all draws because gaining possession on the power play is so important, you may want to tell the center to tie up his opponent and allow the wingers to help. The odds of getting possession are better.

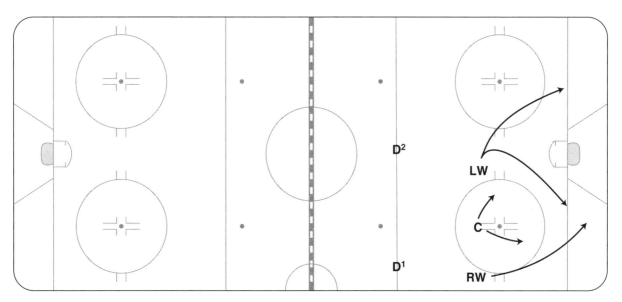

Figure 12.33   Traditional alignment on power play face-off.

■ DOUBLE UP OUTSIDE

In this setup, two forwards are on one side to provide an extra player to try to get puck possession. RW and LW line up along the boards. On a draw when the puck is loose, RW screens and LW pulls the puck back to D1. D2 always lines up in a position that blocks the lane for the opposing center to shoot the puck down the ice immediately off the draw. In this example, if the opposing center is a left shot, then D2 would need to play back a step (see figure 12.34). On lost draws, LW shoots through to the corner and ties up the opposing defenseman. RW comes in to get the loose puck.

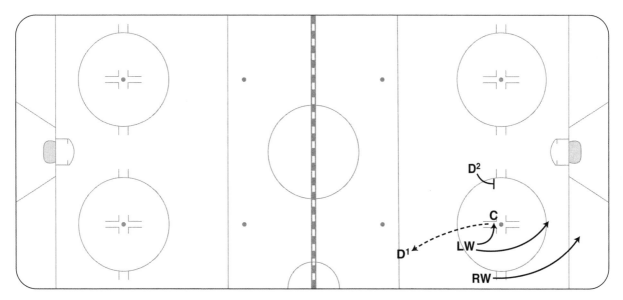

Figure 12.34   Double up outside look on power play face-off.

■ DOUBLE UP INSIDE

In this setup, two forwards are now on the inside, D1 is on the boards, and D2 is back on the blue line (see figure 12.35). On a draw when the puck is loose, RW and LW move in to get the puck back to D2. RW initially lines up in a position that blocks the lane for the opposing center to shoot the puck down the ice immediately off the draw. In this example, if the opposing center is a left shot, then RW would need to play back a step. On lost draws, RW shoots through to the corner and ties up the opposing defenseman. LW comes in to get the loose puck. At times off this draw, LW will be open at the net when the puck is loose in the face-off circle. If RW gets the puck when it is loose in the circle, he can make a quick play to LW.

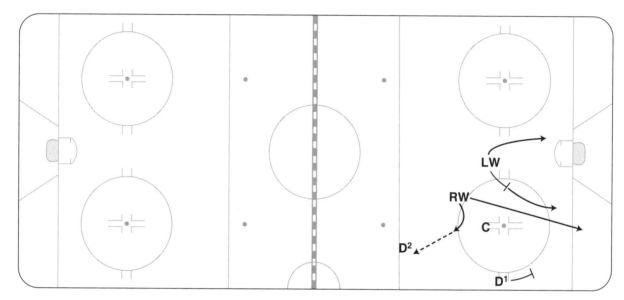

Figure 12.35   Double up inside look on power play face-off.

Penalty-Kill Face-Offs

Because the face-off is such an important part of the penalty kill, it was covered in depth in chapter 10 on penalty kills. As mentioned in that chapter, gaining possession on special teams is important. Penalty-killing units want to frustrate the power play by making them go back down the ice 200 feet (61 m) to get the puck and start a breakout. More face-off options are presented in the Face-Offs and Penalty Kills section in chapter 10, but here are two common strategies to use after winning draws in the defensive zone.

■ CORNER BUMP

In this situation, when C wins the draw, LW drops down to the wide corner (figure 12.36). D1 bumps the puck over to LW, who clears the puck. D2 should screen the opponent's inside winger to provide time for LW to get the puck and shoot it down the ice.

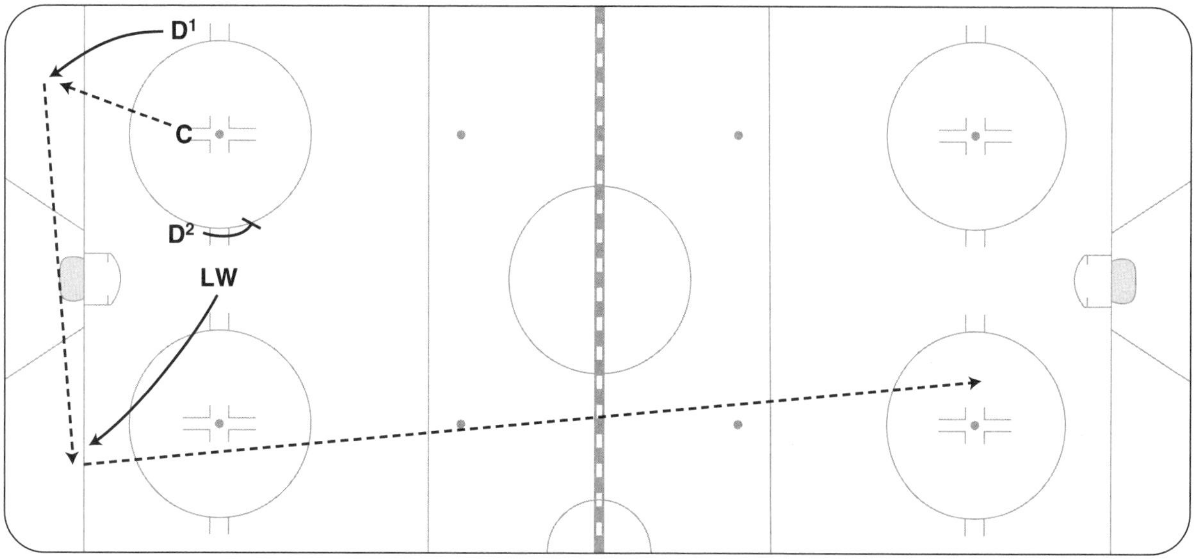

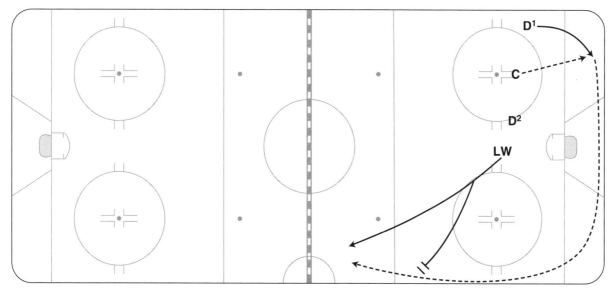

Figure 12.36 Corner bump penalty kill face-off.

■ RIM CLEAR

It is best if the Ds switch sides to give the boards-side defenseman the ability to shoot the puck around the boards hard (see figure 12.37). C tries to win the draw back to the corner or tie up his opponent and allow the puck to sit in behind. D1 (who is now a left shot) moves in quickly and rims the puck hard on the boards or the glass.

Figure 12.37 Rim clear penalty kill face-off.

Special Face-Off Situations

In this section, we cover face-off strategies for four-on-four play and late-game pulled-goaltender situations. Although four-on-four face-offs aren't common in a game, the team needs to be prepared, especially because overtime at most levels uses four-on-four play to decide the game. Pulled-goaltender situations also don't happen often, but good execution of face-offs can be critical in getting that tying goal.

Four-on-Four Face-Offs

We outline one offensive and two defensive alignments for four-on-four situations. On lost draws, coverage is much more difficult when teams are four on four because the center is often tied up taking the face-off and can't get out to the opposing defenseman. Having the D take the draw is a strategy that should be considered.

■ FOUR ACROSS

The center tries to win the draw back to D1 or D2. If the draw is lost, F2 must resist the temptation to go out to the boards-side defenseman and stay in the slot (see figure 12.38). The center battles to get out to pressure the strong-side defense. If the puck is passed D to D, then F2 moves out in the shooting lane. D1 picks up the opposing center. D2 takes the inside forward. This alignment is the more traditional one used in a team's defensive zone, but it does result in problems for the center getting out quickly.

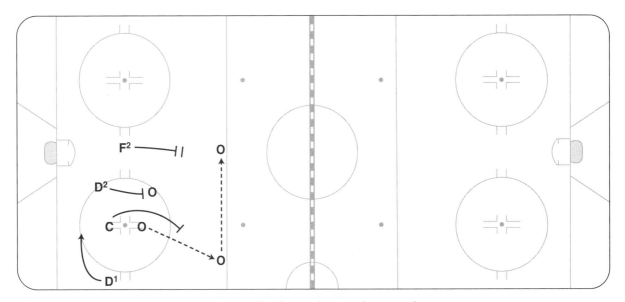

Figure 12.38   Four across on face-off when playing four on four.

■ D TAKES THE DRAW

This sound defensive alignment is not commonly used because the defense has to practice taking face-offs. Have D1 take the draw and D2 line up beside the other team's remaining forward (see figure 12.39). On a lost draw, D1 and D2 take the other team's forwards, and F1 and F2 go to the opposing defensemen. If the opposition lines up with three up on the draw, then D1 should look at shooting the puck through for F1 and F2 to go two on one.

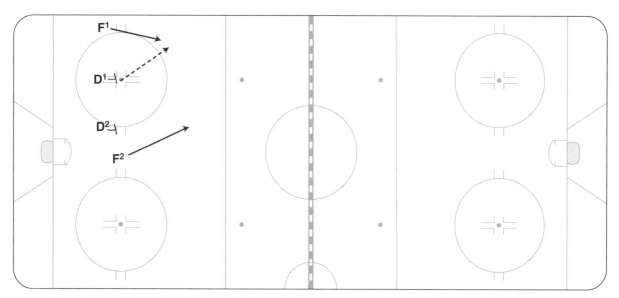

Figure 12.39   Using the defense to take the four on four face-off.

■ BOARDS-SIDE ROLL

After winning the face-off in four-on-four situations, teams should make it difficult for the opposition by having a wide option. C takes the draw and wins it back to D1 on the boards (see figure 12.40). D1 lines up a few steps back from the hash marks on the boards side. D1 has the option to shoot with F2 at the net or pass to D2 for a one-timer shot. D1 and D2 should switch sides, making it easier for them to shoot.

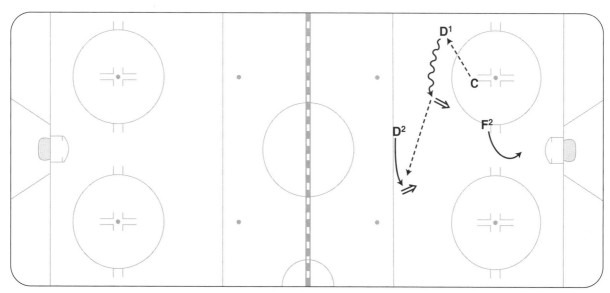

Figure 12.40   Boards-side roll offensive face-off play.

Pulled Goaltender

The excitement ratchets upward when a team pulls the goaltender for an extra attacker. Usually, this occurs in the last minute of the game, and the strategy should be to create a chance right off the draw. The play doesn't have to be complicated, but all players need to know what option is being executed. Here are a few strategies.

■ INSIDE-OUT PLAY

C wins the draw or leaves the puck in behind him. LW, C, and EX (extra forward) drive the net (see figure 12.41). RW swings to the outside and takes the puck or receives it from D1. C pops out into the slot. RW looks to make a play to C, back to D1, to the front of the net, or to D2 on the back side.

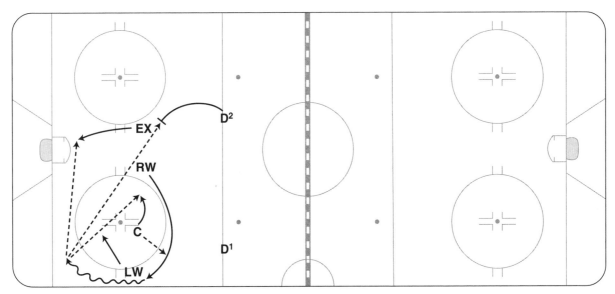

Figure 12.41   Pulled goaltender inside-out face-off play.

■ D SLIDE PLAY

RW is back for the draw, and D2 is up on the inside of the circle (see figure 12.42). C draws the puck back to D1. RW goes to the net. EX (extra forward) goes to the net. D2 slides out and is ready for a one-timer shot (in this example, D2 is a left shot). D1 may shoot at the net or pass to D2 for a quick shot.

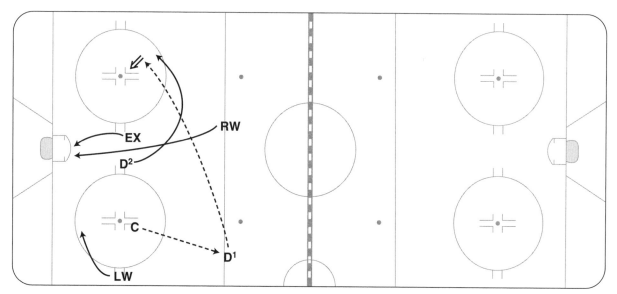

Figure 12.42   Pulled goaltender D slide face-off.

■ DOUBLE OPTION

Two forwards line up on the inside (see figure 12.43), and one is on the boards (this player must be a left shot). C can draw the puck to the boards so that EX (extra forward) can take a quick shot, or the center can tap the puck ahead and make a quick play to the net for LW and RW.

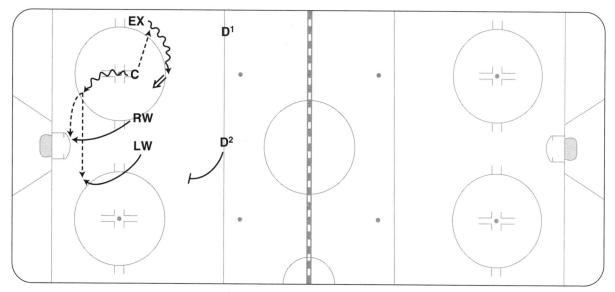

Figure 12.43   Double option face-off play with bulled goaltender.

Chapter 13
Pre-Scouting
Your Opponent

Every NHL team pre-scouts every opponent to prepare for games. At the highest levels of our game, coaches are able to glean huge amounts of information by watching video of their current opponent's previous games. Players want to know how to win each game. They want to know that the coaching staff knows how to give their team the edge. Players need to be focused on the specific process that gives them the best chance to win. This information delivery process starts with pre-scouting your team's opponent, and the information is delivered during your pregame team meetings.

What Your Players Need to Know

The game of hockey often uses the word *tendencies* to describe what teams do and how they do it. Pre-scouting your team's opponent is about understanding their tendencies and planning your team's response to give your players their best chance to win. Different coaches like to focus on different parts of their opponent's game, including offensive and defensive strategies, and most coaches focus on the special-team-play strategies that have been used during recent games.

Pre-Scouting the Opponent's Offensive Strategies

Often teams break down opposition tendencies around when their opponent has the puck and when they do not have the puck. If this is how your coaching staff organizes your game strategy, then your opponent's offensive strategy could start with their breakout patterns. Pre-scouting your opponent's offensive strategies can be exhaustive, so it should highlight the specific strengths and processes that your opponent has used to be successful recently. The key question that coaches need to ask themselves in this area is "What specific offensive tendencies has my opponent showed recently (what is giving their team success), and how should our team be aware of these tendencies and counter them to increase our game success?"

Offensive tendencies range from won face-offs in all zones, to turnovers, to defensive zone and neutral zone breakouts, to offensive zone entries, to how they react with the puck in the offensive zone. A large portion of what your opponent does with the puck may be on the power play, and at the higher levels of our game, the coaching staff's pregame meeting will spend a specific amount of time on how to counter the opposition's power-play breakout, entry, and setup.

Pre-Scouting the Opponent's Defensive Strategies

The key questions to ask while pre-scouting the opponent's defensive strategies are "How do they play without the puck? What are their responses to certain tendencies? Are they aggressive in certain situations, or does our team have more time in certain parts of the ice?" Players want insights into how to beat their opponent, and showing (or telling) your team how your opponent may react during specific defensive situations really increases player confidence.

Defensive strategies are often the exact opposite of the offensive pre-scout focus. In all zones, how your opponent reacts off lost face-offs is important information. Special attention is placed on how your opponent reacts in their defensive zone and how they forecheck. Again, extra focus will be placed on what strategy your opponent uses for the penalty kill and how your power play can take advantage of this.

Let's look at a real game example of how this works best. During recent games, your coaching staff notices that your upcoming opponent often stands their defenseman behind the net and swings their center man deep into the corner as a way to generate breakout speed. Obviously, this tactic is a tendency, so players want to understand how to counter it. One of the best ways to take away this advantage would be to have F1 forecheck aggressively up toward the side of the net that the center man is swinging to and place his stick in that passing lane. This defensive response to your opponent's breakout tendency reduces their ability to pass the puck to the speed player. Developing the solution to your opponent's tactic allows your players to feel prepared not only to play the game but to win it (see figure 13.1).

Just as a quick aside, both of us have found during our coaching and playing career that as your team matures so can your pre-scout meeting process. Especially if you have the luxury of showing video of your opponent's tendencies, instead of telling your players how to respond, ask them (or a specific player) what their suggestion would be to counter a specific opponent strategy. We have found that this leadership approach increases player engagement and begins to create the type of learning culture found on winning teams.

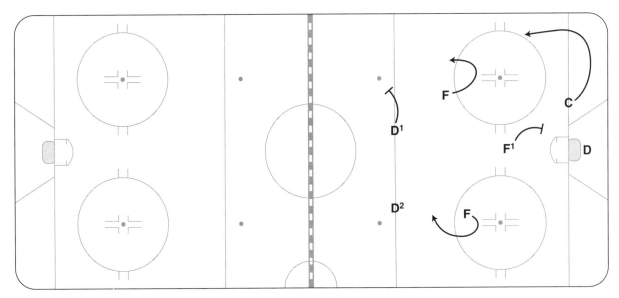

Figure 13.1   Forecheck response to opponent's control breakout.

Pre-Scouting Power-Play and Penalty-Kill Tendencies

One key focus of the pre-scout should be how to counter your opponents' power-play and penalty-kill tactics. Most power plays prefer to execute breakouts that they are comfortable with, but great power plays also have breakout options to counter penalty-kill forecheck tendencies. Let's say that you identify that your opponent's penalty kill forecheck tends to swing their two forwards deep and then use a box formation as they back up into the neutral zone. Power plays have many breakout options that work against this tactic. The double swing breakout works well against the box PK forecheck, especially if your power play slashes one winger on an angle from the boards into the middle of the box as a passing option (see figure

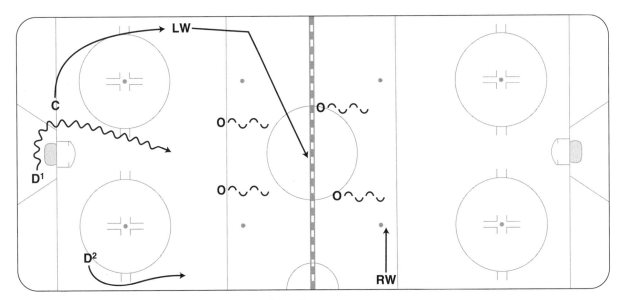

Figure 13.2   Breakout response to PK box formation.

13.2). Slashing that winger off the boards toward the middle ice often opens space for the center man who was swinging into the corner and now has great speed with the puck up the boards. Your pre-scout information has delivered not only a sense of what your opponent will do in this situation but also delivers a complete solution for your players to execute.

Pre-Scout Sheets

The following pre-scout sheet allows you to record individual tendencies, strengths, and weaknesses of each opponent player along with your opponent's team tendencies.

Mike Johnston has used the following simple but powerful outline with the Portland Winterhawks in the Western Hockey League; see figure 13.3. (We have copied a blank template for you to personalize; see figure 13.4.)

Figure 13.3 Sample scouting form.

Team Name vs. Team Name: GP-54 W-32 L-18 OTL-3 SOL-1

#___ **Forward L**—Feet are always moving. Very slippery in traffic. Can make plays all over the ice—Barzal like. Don't let him in behind Ds. **5 SHG** **GP-54 G-38 A-47 Pims-24**	#___ **Forward L**—Smart. Quick release and finds scoring areas quietly. Does force plays under pressure, looks almost timid. Loses centers on draws. **GP-49 G-24 A-41 Pims-34**	#___ **Forward R**—Small guy but strong and boxy on his skates. Strong stick. Always looking for each other on the rush. Flies the zone quick, keep in front of you. **GP-49 G-21 A-37 Pims-26**
#___ **Forward L**—Fast, skilled. Worker, shows quickness in wide lane. One hand on his stick with the puck, can get bumped off it. **GP-42 G-18 A-29 Pims-35**	#___ **Forward R**—Plays hard and with edge. Good skater, always on the puck. Scoring abilities and gets to the hard areas. Hot head, undisciplined. **GP-50 G-12 A-17 Pims-79**	#___ **Forward L**—Picked up during the season. Plays hard, stirs the pot. Gets to the net for chances. Worker along the boards. **GP-49 G-4 A-8 Pims-77**
#___ **Forward L**—Wants to play a skilled game, but stays on the outside. Decent speed. Looks to 26 for plays. Lacks drive and compete. **GP-45 G-15 A-17 Pims-24**	#___ **Forward R**—Playing with confidence since picked up in trade. Two goals last game. Attacks on PK. Lumbering skater, keep away from net. **GP-37 G-10 A-8 Pims-14**	#___ **Forward R**—Offensive player. Good hands. Dishes the puck, sees the ice. Shields the puck well, protects and then shoots. Limited compete. **GP- 51 G-16 A-18 Pims-32**
#___ **Forward R**—Worker. Energy style of player. Stirs the pot. Gets involved physically. Not a lot of skill in his game. **GP-51 G-9 A-6 Pims-42**	#___ **Forward L**—Scrappy, high compete, bigger body. Looks to fight. Goes to the net hard. Having a good year offensively. **GP-49 G-5 A-18 Pims-53**	#___ **Forward R**—First-year player, smart and skilled. Shifty with the puck in tight spaces. Can outmuscle him along the boards. **GP-32 G-0 A-5 Pims-6**
#___ **Defense L**—Veteran player. 20 years old. Heavy player, looks for physical play and will go over the edge. Runs out of position. Simple with the puck—first pass guy. **GP-41 G-4 A-5 Pims-69**	#___ **Defense R**—Most offensive D. Active in the rush. Not big and can overpower him. PP QB. Need to counter quickly against him when he is on the ice. Minus player. **GP-53 G-11 A-18 Pims-35**	

(continued)

(continued)

#___ Defense L—Smart, makes a good first pass. Must play behind him on the rush and coming out of zone. Good size and stays up in the NZ. Struggles to recover after stepping up. **GP-52 G-0 A-26 Pims-44**	**#___ Defense R**—Good mobility, gets involved in the rush. Good puck skills to get the puck out. Weak at the net front and in the corners. Can get to him with pressure on FC. **GP-53 G-1 A-14 Pims-39**
#___ Defense L—Competes, moves the puck well. First-year player. Strength is an issue. Two-way player. Good stick and skating is smooth. **GP-47 G-3 A-5 Pims-6**	**#___ Defense L**—Steady two-way role player. Leader. Simple with the puck and making a first pass. Skating is OK but struggles against wide lane drives. **GP-44 G-2 A-10 Pims-55**
#___ Goalie—Quick. Battles hard and competes on pucks. Small and has a hard time seeing thru screens. Can beat him upstairs. **GP-46 W-28 L-12 OTL-3 SOL-1 GAA-3.19 SV%-.911**	**#___ Goalie**—Makes himself look small. Can get beat upstairs. Weaker version of their starting goaltender. Battles hard on pucks. Angles are off. **GP-21 W-4 L-6 OTL-0 SOL-0 GAA-4.01 SV%-.882**

TEAM TENDENCIES

1. Stretch to offense quick—use a lot of quick stretch passes in breakouts and regroups
2. Like plays around the net in the offensive zone—low jams, stuffs, and walks
3. 1-2-2 F/C—fairly passive
4. High cycle offensive zone—like to use cycle plays in the offensive zone and have active Ds
5. Top line production—top line is dangerous and creates most of the offense

DEFENSIVE ZONE COVERAGE

D1/C—Work together down low

D2—Will drift away from the net, corner support

RW/LW—Play our points high in the zone

Can walk off the boards under winger

Ds be active off the point

OFFENSIVE ZONE PLAY

Collapse tight in coverage

- They use the back of the net for jams, stuffs, and wraps
- Need wingers to collapse in tight
- Ds hold the post—don't double up

	KEYS TO SUCCESS
1.	**Keep their top line in check**—Be aware when they're on the ice. They like to stretch the zone quick, so don't let them get behind our Ds. Make them defend in coverage.
2.	**Don't feed their transition game**—We need to be strong managing the puck in all three zones. Blue to blue, be direct, and keep the puck moving ahead. In the OZ, we can't make blind plays to the slot area.
3.	**Make the right decision on the corner of the blue**—Their Ds will challenge the blue line on entry. We need a middle-lane drive in a close support position. Make an inside play, play to the dot, or chip off the boards. We will create two on ones.
4.	**Heavy, strong, possession game in OZ**—Hang onto the puck in offensive zone. Shield it, protect it, and work to keep it. Ds can activate off the blue line because they play man to man.
5.	**Five-on-five play and gain PP advantage**—We don't need to play them four on four; we want five-on-five hockey. Stay away from net front pushing and shoving. Work to draw penalties and allow our PP to take over.

Figure 13.4 Scouting form.

_____ vs _____ : GP-___ W-___ L-___ OTL-___ SOL-___

#___ Forward L—	#___ Forward L—	#___ Forward R—
GP- G- A- Pims-	GP- G- A- Pims-	GP- G- A- Pims-
#___ Forward L—	#___ Forward R—	#___ Forward L—
GP- G- A- Pims-	GP- G- A- Pims-	GP- G- A- Pims-
#___ Forward L—	#___ Forward R—	#___ Forward R—
GP- G- A- Pims-	GP- G- A- Pims-	GP- G- A- Pims-
#___ Forward R—	#___ Forward L—	#___ Forward R—
GP- G- A- Pims-	GP- G- A- Pims-	GP- G- A- Pims-

#___ Defense L—	#___ Defense R—
GP- G- A- Pims-	GP- G- A- Pims-
#___ Defense L—	#___ Defense R—
GP- G- A- Pims-	GP- G- A- Pims-
#___ Defense L—	#___ Defense L—
GP- G- A- Pims-	GP- G- A- Pims-
#___ Goalie—	#___ Goalie—
GP- W- L- OTL- SOL- GAA- SV%-	GP- W- L- OTL- SOL- GAA- SV%-

TEAM TENDENCIES

1.

2.

3.

4.

5.

DEFENSIVE STRATEGY

OFFENSIVE STRATEGY

KEYS TO SUCCESS	
1.	
2.	
3.	
4.	
5.	

From M. Johnston and R. Walter, *Hockey Plays and Strategies,* 2nd ed. (Champaign, IL: Human Kinetics, 2019).

Index

Note: Page references followed by an italicized *f* indicate information contained in figures.

About the Authors

Mike Johnston is the Vice President, Head Coach, and General Manager of the Portland Winterhawks hockey team (Western Hockey League), where he was recently named the Western Conference Coach of the Year.

Johnston's coaching career began at the age of 23 at Augustana College in Alberta. In 1989, he took over as head coach of the UNB Varsity Reds of the AUS. During a five-year span as coach of the UNB squad, Johnston's teams won three conference championships. He was an associate coach in the NHL for the Los Angeles Kings and the Vancouver Canucks over an eight-year span. As the coach and general manager of the Winterhawks from 2008 to 2014, he amassed a record of 231-114-10-10, winning four conference championships and landing him second on the Winterhawks' all-time wins list. Johnston returned to the National Hockey League (NHL) in 2014 as head coach for the Pittsburgh Penguins. Johnston ended up coaching 110 games in Pittsburgh and finished with a record of 58-37-15.

Over his coaching career, Johnston has had extensive experience in international play. In 1994, Johnston became General Manager and Associate Coach of the Canadian national men's hockey team, followed by a one-season stint as Head Coach in 1998. He won gold medals at the 1997 and the 2007 World Hockey Championships, along with a silver medal in 1996 and a bronze medal in 1995. In 1994 and 1995, Johnston's teams won gold at the World Junior Ice Hockey Championships. He was also on the coaching staff as an assistant coach with the first-ever NHL entry at the Olympic Games in Nagano, Japan.

In addition to his education and kinesiology degrees, Johnston completed his master's degree in coaching science at the University of Calgary.

Ryan Walter played and coached 17 seasons and more than 1,100 games in the National Hockey League. Drafted second overall by the Washington Capitals in 1978, Walter was named the youngest NHL captain in his second of four seasons. He went on to play nine seasons with the Montreal Canadiens, winning a Stanley Cup in 1986. He returned to his hometown to play his last two years for the Vancouver Canucks.

Walter was named captain of Team Canada in the World Junior Tournament, was selected to play in the NHL All-Star game in 1983, and played for Team Canada in three world championships. He became a vice president of the National Hockey League Players' Association and was honored as NHL Man of the Year in 1992. Ryan has also served as a minor hockey coach, an assistant coach with the Vancouver Canucks, and the head coach of the Canadian national women's team.

Walter has a master of arts degree in leadership/business, is the author of five books, and is a regular contributor to online and print magazines, newspapers, radio, and television. He is the cofounder and president of two start-up companies, and he has served as an NHL and IIHF coach, a TV hockey broadcaster, a hockey adviser and actor for both television and movies, and president of a professional hockey team. Currently, Ryan's passion for training leaders, coaches, and high performers gets activated every day as he works with companies, corporations, and sports teams to increase their performance energy and synergize their cultural teams (www.ryanwalter.com).